THE COMPREHENSIVE GUIDE TO ACT® PREP

MARKS PREP

The Comprehensive Guide to ACT® Prep

Copyright © 2018 Marks Education, Tutoring and Test Preparation, LLC.

ACT® is a registered trademark of ACT, Inc, which neither sponsors nor endorses this product.

Senior Editors: Anthony Celino and Dan Hertz

Preface

Dear Student and Parent,

Thank you for purchasing this book, which provides proprietary content and highly effective strategies for each part of the ACT. Please take a few minutes to read this Preface. It contains helpful background information and practical advice on how to best use this book in conjunction with the free resources provided by ACT.

Nitin Sawhney
Managing Director, Marks Prep
nitin@markseducation.com

What Makes This Book Different?

The ACT contains very challenging Math questions including some advanced topics not taught in most high schools, some tricky grammar, and challenging Reading and Science sections which are difficult to finish. Recent ACTs (those published since 2016) include more advanced math topics, such as Matrices, Complex Numbers, Conic Sections, Vectors, and Expected Value and some tricky variations of comma rules not typically seen in prior years.

With carefully constructed strategies for each question type on the ACT, including all recently added questions, Marks Prep tutors have simplified preparation for the ACT. Using these strategies, our students (classes of 2011–2018) have achieved, on average, 7.2 points worth of improvement on the ACT test. In this book, written after months of careful preparation, we lay out our methods with clear and accessible language so others who cannot access our tutoring services may benefit similarly.

We have created highly-effective, easily-learned strategies for each section of this book (English, Math, Reading, Science), which are followed by problem sets that reinforce those strategies. These materials have helped our students in the high school class of 2018 improve, on average, 8 points from baseline 10th grade PSAT test to final ACT test (equivalent to about 290 SAT points). On average, our students use approximately half the number of tutoring sessions recommended by other firms to achieve these gains.

Who Should Take the ACT?

Many students can do better on the ACT than on the SAT, especially those who are good at reading quickly but not necessarily at reading passages written before the 20th century. The SAT often includes one passage written in the 1800s, which can be challenging for those not accustomed to reading older material. The ACT is also the better test for those who did well on Geometry and not Algebra and those who would prefer to not have to wade through the difficult reading on the SAT Math section.

Can Students Who Don't Like Science Do Well on the ACT?

Many students are afraid of the notorious ACT Science section. However, some of our highest score improvements are achieved with students who don't particularly like science. With our strategies and practice on 4–6 actual ACT Science sections, these students are able to make tremendous progress on that section.

Do Students Need Any Other Resources to Do Their Best on the ACT?

Every student should supplement this book with past ACT practice tests available for free on the web. Tests administered during and after 2016 include the advanced Math topics shown in this book.

What Is Marks Prep?

Marks Prep is the test preparation and tutoring division of Marks Education, which provides tutoring, test preparation, and admissions counseling to students all over the world.

Each Marks Prep tutor is an experienced full-time educator and a top 1% test taker who sits for the ACT and other tests every year. We use the knowledge gained from taking these tests and working with our students to write efficient strategies and materials for all the tests we tutor—from the SSAT and ISEE to the SAT, ACT, GRE, GMAT, MCAT, and LSAT.

The full-time tutors at Marks Prep have, for the past ten years, tutored hundreds of students each year across the United States and the world, via Skype and other platforms. From the class of 2011 onwards, students who have worked with us for at least six sessions have, on average, improved more than 7 points on the ACT. In contrast to many other firms, we use only actual College Board PSATs and real past ACTs for baseline tests. More specific score improvement data for all tests (including graduate school tests) are available on our website, marksprep.com.

We also work with several schools and non-profits to help them improve their students' standardized test scores and change college admissions outcomes and to thus markedly enhance their School Profile.

Table of Contents

ACT Score Tracker

Date	English	Math	Reading	Science

Tips for Peak Performance

The Week Before the Test

- **Get eight hours of sleep each night.** Remember, sleep makes you smart. Studies have shown strong links between inadequate sleep and many aspects of test taking including attention span, emotional intelligence, attention to detail and oral recall.
- **Eat lots of complex carbohydrates and healthy protein.** Breads, pastas and other complex carbs give you energy you will need for the five-hour marathon ahead of you.
- **Visualize carefully the test you are about to take.** Top performers (including athletes, actors and dancers) often use visualization to create a mental image of success. In your mind, create a detailed picture of the test—from section to section. Visualize yourself achieving your targets in each part of the test. As you do this, try to anticipate potential distractions (stress, a loud classmate, an overly watchful proctor, etc.) and then visualize yourself proceeding calmly and confidently through all such distractions.

The Night Before the Test

- **No studying past 9:00 PM.** Last-minute cramming leads to last-minute jitters, and it can keep your brain whirring long past the time you stop studying—which will keep you from falling asleep. Read a book for school, go for a run, or watch a movie. Do something fun that doesn't keep you up late. The idea is to be completely relaxed on test day.
- **Lay out your pencils, appropriate calculator, ID, Admission ticket, watch (with no beeps!), and a snack.** Check the batteries on your calculator. Granola bars are a good snack. So are PB&J sandwiches. Starbucks bottled beverages can help give some people a nice mid-test boost.
- **Go to bed!** If you can't fall asleep, don't worry. Just lying in bed can be very restful. Read a boring book, if you like. That might help put you to sleep.

Test Day

- **Wake up early!** Studies show that it takes the average person about three hours (after waking up) to function at peak capacity. The ACT begin around 8:00 in the morning. Try to wake up at least 2 or 2.5 hours before the test.
- **Get some aerobic exercise.** Because of the length of the test (including filling out forms and breaks, the ACT can last up to 4.5–5 hours), you can end up feeling quite brain-dead toward the end. Aerobic exercise oxygenates your blood and can help you to focus for longer amounts of time.
- **Get a big, healthy breakfast with some protein.** Try not to eat heavy foods that can be difficult to digest. Eggs and toast, cereal, bagels with cheese, and such foods generally work well. Remember, standardized testing is a stressful, draining process.
- **Dress in Layers.** Test centers can be very warm (A/C not working) or very cool (A/C cranked up!). If you wear several layers, you can adjust your clothing according to the temperature of the room.
- **Breathe.** Deep breathing is a great relaxation technique. It also helps in blood circulation. During the test, remember to stretch and breathe deeply often.
- **Fifteen minutes of Reading or Math in the morning.** Often students find that they are not completely awake for the first section of the test. Doing a reading passage on the morning of the test can help wake you up.
- **Test-day checklist**: Snack, Pencils, Photo ID, Watch (no beeps), Admission ticket, Appropriate Calculator (e.g. a TI–84).
- Go CRUSH the test!

ACT Mathematics Formula Sheet

Geometry

Vertical angles are congruent: $\angle A \cong \angle C$ and $\angle B \cong \angle D$.

Adjacent angles are supplementary: $\angle A$ and $\angle B$ are supplementary, $\angle A$ and $\angle D$ are supplementary.

For parallel lines m and n:

$\angle A \cong \angle D \cong \angle E \cong \angle H$ and

$\angle B \cong \angle C \cong \angle F \cong \angle G$.

$\angle A$ is supplementary to $\angle B$, $\angle C$, $\angle F$, and $\angle G$.

Polygons

Sum of interior angles of a polygon with n sides is $(n-2)\cdot180°$

Measure of each interior angle of a regular polygon with n sides is $\dfrac{(n-2)\cdot180°}{n}$

Triangle Area: $A = \frac{1}{2}hb$	Rectangle Area: $A = \ell w$ Perimeter: $P = 2\ell + 2w$
Square Area: $A = s^2$ Perimeter: $P = 4s$	Parallelogram Area of a $A = bh$
Trapezoid Area $A = \dfrac{b_1 + b_2}{2}h$	Right Circular Cylinder Volume $V = \pi r^2 h$

Rectangular Solid

Volume: $V = abc$

Surface area $A = 2ab + 2ac + 2bc$

Longest diagonal: $d = \sqrt{a^2 + b^2 + c^2}$

Right Triangles

Pythagorean Theorem: $a^2 + b^2 = c^2$

Pythagorean Triples: $\{3, 4, 5\}$, $\{5, 12, 13\}$, $\{8, 15, 17\}$, ...

30-60-90 triangle	45-45-90 triangle

General Triangles

Third side of a triangle rule: $a + b > c$ where c is the longest side.

A triangle is obtuse if $a^2 + b^2 < c^2$ where c is the longest side.

A triangle is acute if $a^2 + b^2 > c^2$ where c is the longest side.

Circles

Circumference $C = 2\pi r$

Area $A = \pi r^2$

Inscribed and Central Angles

$m\angle APB = \frac{1}{2}m\angle AOB$

If AB is a diameter, then $\triangle APB$ is a right triangle.

$\dfrac{\text{length of arc}}{2\pi r} = \dfrac{\text{angle}}{360°}$

$\dfrac{\text{area of sector}}{\pi r^2} = \dfrac{\text{angle}}{360°}$

Coordinate Geometry

Slope–intercept form of line:	$y = mx + b$
To find the y–intercept of a line:	Set $x = 0$, solve for y.
To find the x–intercept of a line:	Set $y = 0$, solve for x.
Slope formula: $m = \dfrac{y_2 - y_1}{x_2 - x_1}$	Slope of a **horizontal** line = 0 Slope of a **vertical** line is *undefined*. **Parallel** lines have the *same* slope. **Perpendicular** lines have negative reciprocal slopes, e.g. 2 and –½
Midpoint Formula: $x_m = \dfrac{x_1 + x_2}{2}$, $\quad y_m = \dfrac{y_1 + y_2}{2}$	
Distance Formula: $d = \sqrt{(x_2 - x_1)^2 + (y_2 - y_1)^2}$	
Equation of a circle in the coordinate system:	$(x-h)^2 + (y-k)^2 = r^2$ Center (h, k) Radius r
Given the point (x, y), reflecting it across:	
the x-axis yields:	$(x, -y)$
the y-axis yields:	$(-x, y)$
the origin yields:	$(-x, -y)$

Quadratics

$\left.\begin{array}{l}(x+y)^2 = x^2 + 2xy + y^2 \\ (x-y)^2 = x^2 - 2xy + y^2\end{array}\right\}$ The perfect square formulas

$x^2 - y^2 = (x+y)(x-y)\}$ The difference of two squares

FOIL = First Outside Inside Last

$(a+b)(c+d) = \underset{\text{First}}{ac} + \underset{\text{Outer}}{ad} + \underset{\text{Inner}}{bc} + \underset{\text{Last}}{bd}$

Quadratic Formula

The roots of the equation $ax^2 + bx + c = 0$ are $x = \dfrac{-b \pm \sqrt{b^2 - 4ac}}{2a}$

Parabolas

Standard form of a parabola: $y = ax^2 + bx + c$

Vertex form of a parabola with vertex (h, k): $y = a(x-h)^2 + k$

Percents

Percent of:	$\dfrac{\text{is}}{\text{of}} = \dfrac{\%}{100}$		
Percent greater than:	$\dfrac{\text{new}}{\text{original}} = \dfrac{100 + \%}{100}$	Percent less than:	$\dfrac{\text{new}}{\text{original}} = \dfrac{100 - \%}{100}$

Exponent Rules

$a^0 = 1$	$a^{-x} = \dfrac{1}{a^x}$	$\left(a^x\right)^y = a^{xy}$	$a^x b^x = (ab)^x$
$a^x a^y = a^{x+y}$	$\dfrac{a^x}{a^y} = a^{x-y}$	$a^{1/x} = \sqrt[x]{a}$	

ACT Mathematics Formula Sheet

Series and Sequences

Arithmetic Sequences

nth term in the sequence: $a_n = a_1 + (n-1)d$

First term a_1 Common difference d

Sum of first n terms $S_n = (a_1 + a_n)\dfrac{n}{2}$

Geometric Sequences

nth term in the sequence: $a_n = a_1 r^{n-1}$

First term a_1 Common ratio r

Statistics

Average	$\text{average} = \dfrac{\text{sum of things}}{\text{number of things}}$
Median	The middle number (or average of the two middles) of an ordered set of numbers
Mode	The number which occurs most often in a set of numbers
Standard Deviation	Measurement of how spread out numbers are from the middle of a set
Expected Value	The weighted average of a set

Probability

$\text{Probability} = \dfrac{\text{successful outcomes}}{\text{total possible outcomes}}$ or $P(A) = \dfrac{s}{n}$

If a problem uses the word **or** between two possible outcomes, you must *add* the probabilities.

EXAMPLE:

The probability of rolling a 1 on a standard die is 1/6.
The probability of rolling a 3 on a standard die is 1/6.
The probability of rolling a 1 *or* a 3 on a standard die is 1/6+1/6=1/3.

If a problem uses the word **and** between two events, you must *multiply* the two probabilities.

EXAMPLE:

The probability of rolling a 1 on a standard die is 1/6.
The probability of getting heads on a fair coin is 1/2.
The probability of rolling a 1 *and* getting heads is (1/6)(1/2)=1/12.

Arrangements, Permutations, and Combinations

Arrangements	Multiply the numbers of choices for independent events (using slots)
Factorial (!)	the product of every integer from n down to 1. e.g. $5! = 5 \times 4 \times 3 \times 2 \times 1$
Permutation	truncated factorial, used when *order matters*: e.g. $_7P_3 = 7 \times 6 \times 5$
Combination	altered permutation, used when *order doesn't matter*: e.g. $_7C_3 = \dfrac{_7P_3}{3!} = \dfrac{7 \times 6 \times 5}{3 \times 2 \times 1}$

Trigonometry

SOH–CAH–TOA	Inverses
$\sin\theta = \dfrac{\text{opposite}}{\text{hypotenuse}}$	$x = \sin\theta \iff \theta = \sin^{-1}(x)$
$\cos\theta = \dfrac{\text{adjacent}}{\text{hypotenuse}}$	$x = \cos\theta \iff \theta = \cos^{-1}(x)$
$\tan\theta = \dfrac{\text{opposite}}{\text{adjacent}}$	$x = \tan\theta \iff \theta = \tan^{-1}(x)$

Important identities $\tan x = \dfrac{\sin x}{\cos x}$ $\sin^2 x + \cos^2 x = 1$

Law of Sines $\dfrac{\sin A}{a} = \dfrac{\sin B}{b} = \dfrac{\sin C}{c}$

Law of Cosines $c^2 = a^2 + b^2 - 2ab\cos C$

Number Terms

Digit	the numbers 0–9
Integer	any whole number, whether positive, negative, or zero
Multiple (of integer n)	an integer that is divisible by the integer n e.g. 4, 8, 12, and 16 are all multiples of 4
Factors (of integer n)	integers by which n is divisible e.g. the positive factors of 6 are 1, 2, 3, and 6
Prime number	a positive integer with precisely two factors: the number itself and 1. NOTE neither 0 nor 1 is prime.
Consecutive numbers	numbers (e.g. integers, or primes) that follow one another in order e.g. 16, 18, and 20 are consecutive even integers
Real number	any number that can be expressed on a number line (whether rational or irrational)
Remainder	the number left over when one integer is divided by another e.g. the remainder when 17 is divided by 3 is 2
Exponent	a number which indicates how many times another number is multiplied by itself
(nth) Root (of p)	a number which is multiplied by itself a number of times n to produce p (e.g. 4 is the third root of 64)
Sequence	an ordered set of quantities e.g. 0, 1, 1, 2, 3, 5, … is the **Fibonacci Sequence**
Set	a collection of distinct elements, often depicted within brackets. e.g. the set $A = \{0, 1, 2, 4\}$ consists of the elements 0, 1, 2, and 4

English Test Manual

The English section is the first of the four multiple-choice sections on the ACT. It consists of 75 questions in five passages with approximately 15 questions each. Students are given 45 minutes—or nine minutes per passage—to complete the section. A passage and its questions appear side-by-side, and the passages are spaced so that questions align with the underlined part of the passage they are addressing. You can answer questions as you read, though it is advisable to at least wait until you have finished reading a sentence before attempting a question that deals with that sentence.

Overview

The ACT English section measures your ability to revise and edit a piece of writing. Broadly speaking, this section has two types of questions: *Grammar and Punctuation* and *Rhetorical Skills*. Because you approach these types of questions in very different ways, it is important to identify each type as you see it and to use the strategy appropriate for that question type.

Grammar and Punctuation

These questions refer to an underlined portion of the essay and ask you to choose the best word, punctuation, or sentence structure. The ACT designates these as *Conventions of Standard English*.

In the next several pages, we will go over rules for topics such as commas, semicolons, colons, subject-verb agreement, and pronouns. When you are going through the grammar and punctuation questions on the ACT, you should recall the rules you've memorized to help you determine which answer choices are wrong and which one is correct. Note that the ACT only tests a subset of grammar and punctuation rules. The rules that are tested regularly are the focus of the first part of this chapter. Review the rules and try the editing exercises for each topic. Once your skills are strengthened, try the multiple-choice problem sets to get a feel for how these topics get tested on the ACT.

Rhetorical Skills (Meaning and Good Writing)

These questions may refer to an underlined portion, a paragraph, or the entire passage. They will ask about structure, organization, and writing strategy as well as overall meaning and tone. A lot of these questions are just like reading comprehension questions, and so you should approach them similarly. The ACT designates Rhetorical Skills questions as *Knowledge of Language* and *Production of Writing* questions.

On these questions, you'll want to focus on the meaning and style. There is usually nothing grammatically wrong with any of the answer choices, so they can all sound somewhat correct. Some of these questions may look exactly like grammar questions. For those, usually the correct answer is the most concise and straightforward answer choice, one that avoids introducing a vague pronoun or tangentially related phrase.

Read and study from the information about Rhetorical Skills question types in the second half of this section. Then try the Rhetorical Skills Practice Passage that closes the section out. Once you've covered this whole section, you will be ready to practice on actual ACT English passages.

Grammar and Punctuation

The ACT focuses on a fairly small set of grammatical concepts, including:

- Punctuation (particularly commas, semicolons, colons, and dashes)
- Pronouns
- Apostrophes (possessives and contractions)
- Verb Usage
- Modifiers
- Parallel Structure
- Word Choice

In the following section you will review the relevant rules for each of these concepts, try some editing exercises, and look at examples of how grammar and punctuation are tested on the ACT.

Parts of Speech Review

The ACT will not ask you a question that requires you to know the specific definition of a part of speech. Rather, having a basic understanding of the parts of speech will help inform the structure behind different grammar and punctuation rules and provide a shared vocabulary to use in discussing such rules.

Noun   a person, place, or thing.

> <u>Stephen</u> took his <u>sister</u> to the <u>library</u> to check out a <u>book</u>.

> **Singular noun**   refers to just one: **book, building, child.**

> **Plural noun**   refers to more than one: **books, buildings, children.**

> **Collective noun**   a singular word that refers to a group made up of multiple people or things: **family, team, group, organization, class, flock, pack.**

Pronoun   a word that replaces another noun (called the antecedent).

> Sally woke up early so <u>she</u> would not be late for <u>her</u> interview.

> **Subject (nominative) pronoun**   replaces the subject of a sentence, the noun doing the action.

>> Susie plays hockey. <u>She</u> is on the varsity team.

>> Jack and Jill went up a hill; <u>they</u> did not have fun.

> **Object (objective) pronoun**   replaces the object of a verb or preposition, the noun receiving the action.

>> Derrick passed the ball to Susie. Then she passed the ball back to <u>him</u>.

> **Possessive determiner**   an adjective that describes ownership of a noun.

>> Lacey is willing to share <u>her</u> fries but not <u>our</u> burger.

> **Possessive pronoun**   a pronoun used to show ownership.

>> Lacey told me that the burger was actually <u>hers</u> and not <u>ours</u>.

Verb   a word describing an action.

> Before Stephen <u>runs</u> outside, he <u>is</u> going <u>to brush</u> his teeth.

Adjective   a word that describes a noun.

> The <u>mangy, scrappy</u> dog likes to run around the <u>tall, stately</u> oak tree.

Adverb   a word that describes a verb, adjective, or other adverb.

> Though he had performed <u>extremely well</u> on the test, Ian <u>sheepishly</u> raised his hand.

Preposition   a word that describes locations and links a noun to the rest of the sentence.

> <u>In</u> the summer, Lisa and Garrett hike <u>along</u> a piece <u>of</u> the Appalachian Trail <u>with</u> their friends, Lou and June.

Conjunction   connecting word that joins two parts of a sentence.

> Since you and I joined, the team has five players, <u>but</u> it is still looking for more people.

> **Coordinating conjunction**   used to join together two independent clauses. These include **for, and, nor, but, or, yet, so** (FANBOYS).

>> I grew up in Denmark, <u>so</u> I still have many friends there.

> **Subordinating conjunction**   used to join an independent and dependent clause or to make a clause dependent. These include **after, although, as, because, before, if, since, unless, until, when,** and **whenever.**

>> I will speak with my friend <u>when</u> I get back from my vacation.

Parts of Sentence Review

Subject   the noun or pronoun that is doing the action of the sentence; the noun the sentence is about.

> <u>Jane</u> recently decided she would spend her junior year studying in Paris.

Verb   the word or group of words that expresses the action of the sentence. Always paired with a subject, the verb indicates what the subject is doing or what is being done to the subject.

> The barking dog <u>runs</u> around the park.

> The scurrying mouse <u>was chased</u> by the cat.

Clause   a group of words that contains a subject and a verb. Every sentence must contain at least one independent clause, but many sentences in the passages that make up the English section have multiple clauses.

> **Independent clause**   a clause that can be a sentence on its own. Independent clauses can be joined to a subordinate clause or another independent clause.

>> <u>Though Nick was running late for his flight, he stopped for breakfast anyway.</u>

>> <u>I often relax after dinner and consider the importance of the proper use of conjunctions.</u>

> **Subordinate/dependent clause**   part of a sentence that contains a subject and verb but is not capable of being a sentence on its own. These can come before or after an independent clause, or they can even be in the middle of another clause, enclosed by paired **commas** or **dashes**.

>> <u>Because it's nice out,</u> my roommate and I are having dinner on the roof.

>> Mondays, <u>which are the days I usually have physics tests,</u> are my least favorite.

Phrase   a group of words without a subject or a verb. There are many different types of phrases, but there are two types that are essential to know for the purpose of the ACT.

Prepositional phrase   a group of words that begins with a preposition and ends with a noun.

> <u>In my opinion,</u> summer vacation is best spent relaxing on the beach or hiking in the mountains.

Appositive phrase   a noun phrase that does not contain a verb and renames or explains another noun. Like some subordinate clauses, a nonessential appositive can be inserted into an independent clause by placing paired commas or dashes around it.

> Henry, <u>my brother's oldest child,</u> is an exceptionally precocious boy.

Punctuation and Sentences

Punctuation questions make up a large portion of the English questions on the ACT. Fortunately, the ACT is concerned with only a relatively small set of rules, focused on commas, semicolons, colons, dashes, and apostrophes. Because apostrophes are usually tested in conjunction with pronouns, they are not covered in this section even though they are technically punctuation marks.

Commas

The **comma** (,) is used in many different ways. The following guidelines help in understanding when to use commas.

Try to punctuate the sentence correctly in each numbered exercise by adding or removing commas as needed. NOTE THAT NOT ALL SENTENCES CONTAIN ERRORS.

DC, IC **1** Use a comma to join together a dependent clause followed by an independent clause.

> Before I moved to the DC area, I lived in Philadelphia.

Dependent clauses often (but not always) start with **subordinating conjunctions** (such as **after, although, as, because, before, if, since, so that, though, unless, until, when,** and **whenever**).

1. As Jonathan walked down the street, he thought about how long it had been since he'd last been to this part of town.

2. Although I hadn't seen him in years, I recognized him instantly.

3. If I had enjoyed the movie, I would have given it a more positive review.

IC DC **2** Do *not* use a comma to join a dependent clause to an independent one if the *dependent clause follows the independent*. Compare the two sentences below:

> Whenever I'm working, I like to drink coffee.

> I like to drink coffee whenever I'm working.

In the first sentence, the independent clause follows the dependent, and a comma is required to join them. In the second sentence, the dependent clause follows the independent, and a comma between the two is therefore *not* correct.

1. I like to sing loudly to myself~~,~~ as I take my shower.

2. I like to eat a good breakfast because it leaves me prepared for the day.

IC, CC IC **3** Use a comma to join two independent clauses by placing a **coordinating conjunction** after the comma. Coordinating conjunctions are easily remembered by the acronym FANBOYS (**for, and, nor, but, or, yet, so**).

> I spoke with him last week, and I haven't seen him since.

1. Garrett wanted to throw Leila a surprise party, but he knew that it would be impossible to keep a secret from her.

2. I need to finish my Common Application by this weekend, so I need to start working on my supplements.

3. He knew he remembered the song, yet he couldn't recall what its name was.

4 Use commas to separate **subordinate clauses** or **appositives** from the main independent clause. You can identify these **nonessential** clauses and phrases by checking whether the phrase or clause can be removed without changing the meaning of the sentence or making the sentence incomplete. If so, the commas are required.

> The White House, official residence of the President of the United States, is located at 1600 Pennsylvania Ave.

> My cats, who have never learned to tell time, always think it's time for dinner.

1. Mary, who loved her little lamb, was sometimes a little careless about his whereabouts.

2. Mary's lamb, a little lamb, had white fleece.

A and B
A, B, and C

5 Use commas to separate three or more items in a *list*.

> My friends had gathered from places as far away as Denmark, England, Singapore, and South Africa.

The comma before **and** is called a serial comma (also known as an Oxford comma). Its necessity is debated, and it is therefore not specifically tested on the ACT, though it is used it in passages.

1. When Brianna was younger, she would tell people her favorite colors were red, orange, yellow, green, blue, and purple.

2. My friends, Tommy, Bob, Chris, and Matt, are meeting me at the party.

6 Do *not* use a comma between **cumulative** adjectives, which build on each other. If you cannot place **and** between two adjectives, you should NOT put a comma between them.

> At the party, we ate a delicious red velvet layer cake.

There are no commas in the list of adjectives above because **layer** describes **cake**, **red velvet** describes the **layer cake**, and **delicious** describes the **red velvet layer cake**. You cannot insert **and** between any of the adjectives and have the phrase make sense, so there should be no commas. Usually cumulative adjectives only make sense in a specific order. For example, one would not bake a **layer red velvet delicious cake**.

1. Though Kevin wanted a red, two-door, sports, car for his 16th birthday, his parents had said that was out of the question.

2. He recuperated from his injuries by resting in a small, English, country village away from the busy, crowded city.

7 Use a comma between **noncumulative** adjectives that each describe the same noun and are not joined by **and** (but could be).

> My friends and I followed the narrow, winding path up to the old, ruined castle.

If you can put **and** between the adjectives, there should be a comma between them because each of the adjectives modifies the noun separately. Usually noncumulative adjectives can be reordered without affecting the meaning. You should *never* place a comma between the **last adjective** and the noun itself!

1. Despite the hot, dry, strong wind, we decided to hike up the mountain anyway.

2. Her employer wrote a reference saying that Lisa is a smart, fun, interesting, girl.

8   Do NOT put a comma between a **title** and the person it describes. Consider the two sample sentences below.

> James Joyce, author and Dublin native, first performed this song.

> Author and Dublin native James Joyce first performed this song.

In the first sentence, **author and Dublin native** is an appositive phrase and correctly sits between two commas. In the second sentence, that same phrase serves as a title for **James Joyce**, and so no commas are needed. If you did place **James Joyce** between two commas, you'd be isolating the subject from the rest of the sentence.

However, consider the following sentence:

> I was very much looking forward to interviewing the inventor of calculus, Isaac Newton, to hear about his adventures with his new time machine.

In this sentence, the phrase **the inventor of calculus** is *not* a title. We can tell this by observing that we could in fact remove **Isaac Newton** from the sentence and have it still make sense. Because of this, we must have commas around **Isaac Newton**. Do *not* use commas to separate a name from a word or phrase that looks like a title unless it would be clear who or what is being discussed had the name been deleted.

1. This year's prize was awarded to former NFL punter Chris Kluwe.

2. The opinion for the majority was given by the Chief Justice John Roberts.

9   Do NOT *over-punctuate*. The ACT likes to add extraneous commas to sentences in order to confuse you. More commas are not always better, and keep in mind that the ACT focuses on writing things as clearly and simply as possible. Although many comma rules exist, only those described above are tested regularly.

Consider the following sample question.

1. *Kind of Blue* by Miles <u>Davis, is often considered to be one of the greatest albums</u> in the history of jazz.

    A. NO CHANGE

    B. Davis is often considered to be one of the greatest albums,

    C. Davis, is often considered to be one of the greatest albums,

    D. Davis is often considered to be one of the greatest albums

This sentence should not have any commas in it, so while we may be tempted by answer choices **A**, **B**, and **C**, the correct answer is **D**.

Editing Exercises for Commas

Correct the punctuation errors in the sentences below by adding or removing commas.

1. Although he was not previously known to be a great speaker Jonathan impressed the audience with his witty stories.

2. Jonah ran a mile in six minutes and directly afterwards he swam a mile in ten minutes.

3. Washington, who has phenomenal memory won top prize in the Name-the-President contest.

4. Bilbao is a fascinating town but we were too tired to enjoy it.

5. I need a new bookshelf one that holds more.

6. I recently listened to an opera composed by eighteenth century philosopher Jean-Jacques Rousseau.

7. Ian my high school's top basketball player was recruited by several schools.

8. Daily aerobic exercise helps in blood circulation heart-health, and blood pressure control.

9. After quitting gymnastics, Kathryn decided to run cross-country a sport that doesn't require too much experience.

10. Virginia Woolf's greatest novel in my opinion was not *To the Lighthouse* but *Mrs. Dalloway*.

11. One of the reasons I love summer is the weather.

12. One way to help yourself get to bed earlier is to do your homework during your free period.

13. The only person in recorded history to be directly hit by a meteorite, Ann Hodges, was very lucky or very unlucky depending on your point of view.

14. Arti's hastiness to finish her Math teacher argued indirectly caused most of her careless errors.

15. This summer the last one before college is bittersweet for most students and their families.

Semicolons

The **semicolon** (;) is used to separate major sentence elements that hold equal grammatical rank.

`IC; IC` `1`   Though there are other uses for a semicolon, the ACT only tests the idea that you can use a semicolon *between two* **independent clauses** that are NOT joined by a coordinating conjunction (FANBOYS). The two independent clauses should be closely related, but you will never be asked to make a judgment call like whether two clauses are closely related or not.

When used in this fashion, semicolons and periods are *interchangeable* with one another, though, of course, when a period is used, you must capitalize the second clause. If there are two answer choices where the only difference is that one has a semicolon and the other has a period, *neither* can be the correct answer choice!

> Novels written in the 19th century often contain long, complicated sentences; it's one of the ways they're different from present-day books.

NOTE: Use a semicolon or period with transitional words and conjunctive adverbs (*however, thus, therefore, also, finally, then, for example, in fact*, etc.); these words are not coordinating conjunctions.

> Robert wanted to vacation in the mountains; however, his wife preferred a beach vacation.

Correct the sentences below using semicolons properly:

1. When Leslie was young, she could not stand her little sister; now that they are older, they are the best of friends.

2. *Beauty and the Beast* is my favorite Disney movie; however, *The Lion King* is a close second.

Colons

The **colon** (:) is used to call attention to the words following it and can ONLY be used immediately following an independent clause. Correct all errors in the numbered exercises below.

`IC: List` `1`   A colon is used after an independent clause to set off a **list** or a **quotation**.
`IC: Quote`

> As I approached the farm stand, I noticed several delicious smells wafting my way: cinnamon, apples, and pumpkins.

This list can consist of a single item as shown in the following example.

> My friends sat around discussing our favorite opera: *The Marriage of Figaro*.

1. In order to bake my grandmother's favorite cookies tonight, I need to buy the following: flour, baking soda, eggs, and chocolate chips.

2. Barack Obama's campaign centered around three words: "Yes we can."

`IC: IC` `2`   You can use a colon *between* **two independent clauses** when the second *explains* or *clarifies* the first. However, you will *not* be tested on whether the second independent clause specifically explains or clarifies the first. That is, you will not see questions where two independent clauses are separated by a semicolon in one choice and a colon in another.

> The library is quiet when the students are gone: I'll be able to get lots of work done.

1. Mike has not yet made plans for his day off: he is either going hiking or taking his son to the zoo.

2. Summer is my favorite time of year: the weather is nice, the days are long, and school is out.

Dashes

A **dash** (—) can be used in place of a **comma** in some cases, and it can always replace a **colon**. Correct all errors in the numbered exercises below using dashes.

1.   The dash can be used to replace commas that **separate an appositive or a subordinate clause** from the rest of the sentence.

     NOTE: Always keep dashes together and commas together. You will never see a sentence that uses, say, a comma before the appositive and a dash after it.

     Both of the following sentences are correct:

       My cat—who spends most of his time napping—always thinks it's dinner-time.

       My cat, who spends most of his time napping, always thinks it's dinner-time.

     1. The organization of one's pens in a pencil case is—contrary to what you might think—extremely important.

     2. Hector couldn't have guessed—having never even suspected his friend of treachery—that he would be stabbed with a cocktail fork.

2.   The dash can be used *in place of a* **colon**. This works for both of the uses of colons described previously—in between two independent clauses and between an independent clause and a list or quote.

       I invited all my friends to the party—Jack, Jill, Hansel, and Gretel.

       Everyone had a great time at the party—most of the guests didn't leave for days.

     1. George has many pets—a dog, a cat, two birds, and about a dozen fish.

     2. I prefer pancakes to French toast—I think that the latter is often too sweet.

However

The word **however** frequently comes up on the ACT, and it is important to know the three main ways in which it is used, because it can be one of the most confusing words to properly punctuate.

1.   **However** can be used to mean **regardless of**. When used in this fashion, there should be *no* punctuation before or after the word, as shown in the following example.

       However tempted I might be to drink my coffee immediately, my friend told me not to do so.

2.   You can use **however** as a conjunctive adverb, in which case it is used to mean **nevertheless**. In this case, we use it in the same way we do other conjunctive adverbs, such as **thus** or **therefore**.

       I like ice cream; however, I don't eat it every day.

     NOTE: There must be a **comma** placed after the word **however** when the word is used in this way.

3.   **However** can also occur in the middle of a clause. Like appositive phrases and subordinate clauses, interjections like this should be between either two commas or two dashes.

       My friend, however, was the last person to arrive at the party.

       The lawyer—however—avoided prosecution when he turned over incriminating tapes to the special counsel.

Editing Exercises for Commas, Semicolons, Colons, and Dashes

Correct the punctuation errors in the sentences below by adding, changing, or removing punctuation as appropriate. Not all sentences contain errors. Many sentences can be corrected in multiple ways.

1. However out of control her personal life may be, Crighton never lets it interfere with her professional life.

2. Dalby is gifted at Math; however, he has a hard time learning vocabulary.

3. In their desire to win the contract, the firms bid the price too low; thereby they made the project unviable.

4. Roger won the match; hence, he gets the trophy; it matters little that his opponent was injured.

5. After a long and dreary summer spent waiting at the bottom of the pile, Mr. Ripe N. Melon had the thought—or perhaps the flash of intuition—that he would never get consumed.

6. Because I grew up watching my brothers play basketball, I decided to try out for the high school team.

7. Just because I understood the game did not mean I could play; I spent most of the season on the bench.

8. The team with the most NCAA Basketball championships—the UCLA Bruins—was coached by John Wooden for 10 out of the 11 titles they won.

9. Krista moved home after graduation, ready for something new, but after a year at home, she moved to Louisiana to pursue her MBA.

10. Katie plans to stay in Chicago because she loves so much about the city: the beach, the architecture, the parks, and the people.

11. Advertising is a big reason why teens drink so much soda; lack of oversight is another reason.

12. Washington, D.C., the nation's capital, is well known for its monuments; however, some critics bemoan the lack of originality in its architecture.

13. However broad the channel is dug, it will not be able to hold the runoff. ✓

14. Most of us can cook well; the problem is we don't have the time.

15. The décor of her office is, in general, too Spartan for my taste; however, I like the fresh flowers in the vases.

Mixed Punctuation Problem Set

is "The Phonograph an article for "moving picture camera"

In the following exercises, choose the best alternative.

1. Science must have been a much scarier subject a century <u>ago; for much</u> less was known about the universe back then.

- **A.** NO CHANGE
- **B.** ago: and much
- **C.** ago—but much
- **D.** ago: much

2. The best time to start getting in shape was a while <u>ago, but</u> the second best time is now.

- **A.** NO CHANGE
- **B.** ago; but
- **C.** ago, for
- **D.** ago: so

3. The 44th President of the United <u>States, Barack Obama, always seemed to be on excellent terms with Vice President,</u> Joe Biden.

- **A.** NO CHANGE
- **B.** States—Barack Obama, always seemed to be on excellent terms with Vice President Joe
- **C.** States—Barack Obama—always seemed to be on excellent terms with Vice President Joe
- **D.** States Barack Obama always seemed to be on excellent terms with Vice President, Joe

4. The inventor of the moving picture, camera the phonograph, and a long-lasting light bulb, Thomas Edison, held over 1000 patents.

- **A.** NO CHANGE
- **B.** camera, the phonograph, and a long-lasting light bulb, Thomas Edison, held
- **C.** camera, the phonograph, and a long-lasting light bulb Thomas Edison, held
- **D.** camera, the phonograph, and a long-lasting light bulb, Thomas Edison held

5. Riding the subway in the <u>morning I read the newspaper while</u> seated.

- **A.** NO CHANGE
- **B.** morning, I read the newspaper, while
- **C.** morning, I read the newspaper while
- **D.** morning I read the newspaper, while

6. In *Slaughterhouse-Five*, Kurt Vonnegut frequently repeats the same <u>phrase; "so</u> it goes."

- **A.** NO CHANGE
- **B.** phrase, and "so
- **C.** phrase "so
- **D.** phrase: "so

7. Authors can sometimes create significant followings by expanding the world of a novel through the use of <u>sequels: consider</u> the *Harry Potter* series.

- **A.** NO CHANGE
- **B.** sequels; and consider
- **C.** sequels, however, consider
- **D.** sequels: so consider

8. Despite falling in the <u>toilet, my phone still works, unfortunately,</u> I can't say the same about my watch.

   A. NO CHANGE
   B. toilet; my phone still works; unfortunately,
   C. toilet, my phone still works; unfortunately,
   D. toilet; my phone still works, unfortunately,

9. Richard Parker loves going on rafting <u>trips: he has the best time, when</u> he is in the water.

   A. NO CHANGE
   B. trips; he has the best time, when
   C. trips: and he has the best time; when
   D. trips; he has the best time when

10. The Archduke of Covington, Reginald Tipply, enjoys eating <u>fine cheddar cheese on his new dining room table.</u>

   A. NO CHANGE
   B. fine, cheddar, cheese on his new, dining room, table
   C. fine cheddar cheese on his new dining room, table
   D. fine, cheddar cheese on his new, dining, room table

11. <u>John Carpenter never expecting that the *Thing* would find its way to him slept soundly at night.</u>

   A. NO CHANGE
   B. John Carpenter, never expecting, that the *Thing* would find its way to him, slept soundly at night.
   C. John Carpenter, never expecting that the *Thing* would find its way to him—slept soundly at night.
   D. John Carpenter—never expecting that the *Thing* would find its way to him—slept soundly at night.

12. Some older British literature frequently contains <u>long confusing sentences; which can be difficult to read: they</u> can go on and on.

   A. NO CHANGE
   B. long, confusing sentences; these can be difficult to read—they
   C. long confusing, sentences; these can be difficult to read—they
   D. long, confusing sentences; these can be difficult to read, they

13. In early 2017, cave divers discovered a new species of <u>seahorse. In</u> a cave complex off of the Japanese coast.

   A. NO CHANGE
   B. seahorse; in
   C. seahorse: in
   D. seahorse in

14. Julia worked in her kitchen every <u>day—slicing, and dicing,</u> mixing and blending, baking and frying—until she was a master at her craft.

   A. NO CHANGE
   B. day—slicing and dicing,
   C. day, slicing, and dicing
   D. day, slicing and dicing

15. By the time the <u>dangerous stormy weather</u> came in, the umpires had already called the game.

   A. NO CHANGE
   B. dangerous, stormy, weather,
   C. dangerous, stormy, weather
   D. dangerous, stormy weather,

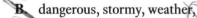

conflicts with #12

Pronouns

There are three types of pronouns: **nominative pronouns** (also known as **subject pronouns**), **object pronouns**, and **possessive pronouns**. Most questions on the ACT involving pronouns test either the difference between subject and object pronouns or the use of pronouns with apostrophes.

Subject pronoun   replaces the subject of a sentence, the noun doing the action.

> Ronda likes to play tennis. <u>She</u> is on the junior-varsity team.

> Maria and Donald went on a walk in the park; <u>they</u> did not have fun.

Object pronoun   replaces the object of a sentence, the noun receiving the action.

> It was Pablo's turn to serve, but Janice had the ball. She passed the ball to <u>him</u>.

> He got here earlier than I did, so Robert is in front of <u>me</u> in line.

Person	Nominative (Subject) Pronoun		Objective (Object) Pronoun	
	Singular	Plural	Singular	Plural
First	I	we	me	us
Second	you	you	you	you
Third	he she it who	they who	him her it whom	them whom

Pronoun Rules

The following rules for pronouns are frequently tested on the ACT. Choose the correct pronouns in the numbered exercises.

1. A pronoun must agree with its antecedent in *number* and *type*.

> Blingley High School had the largest contingent of cheerleaders of any school in the competition, and so it is not surprising that <u>it</u> won the most awards.

> If Ryan wants a good grade, <u>he</u> must bring <u>his</u> books to class.

1. After the students have finished their tests, [he/they] will pick up their final grades.

2. When Judy finishes giving her dog Max a bath, [he/she] will clip his nails.

2. A pronoun *must* have a clear antecedent. You *cannot* use a pronoun if there is confusion as to what it is referring to.

> Sara and Sophia are very well read. ~~She~~ Sara even has a degree in Literature.

1. While the cat chases the mouse, the dog chases [it/the cat].

2. When Jacob and Noah finish their warm-up pitches, [Jacob/he] will take the mound.

3   **Who** is a **subject** pronoun and **whom** is an **object** pronoun. Be careful to not confuse the two!

One rule of thumb is to use **who** when you might otherwise use **he, she** or **they** and use **whom** when you might otherwise use **him, her** or **them**. Check to see if the word **who** or **whom** is doing the action in the sentence. If so, it must be the subject **who**, because only subjects do actions. If not, it must be the object of a verb or preposition, **whom**. Objects receive actions.

Tobacco was first cultivated by Amerindians, from <u>whom</u> Europeans learned about it.

When I needed advice about barbecue, I talked to my friend <u>who</u> lives in North Carolina.

In **questions** involving **who** and **whom**, just answer the question. If you answer it with a subject pronoun (like **he**), use **who**. If you answer with an object pronoun (like **him**), use **whom**. You can also do this with sentences that are not questions by asking the sentence as a question starting with where the word **who** or **whom** is in the sentence, changing the wording as little as possible.

<u>Who</u> likes ice cream? (**He** does)

With <u>whom</u> should I go to the movies? (With **him**)

1. I recently returned from a trip to visit my parents, [who/whom] I haven't seen in a long time.

2. I really enjoyed my conversation with Anthony's wife, [who/whom] is an exceptionally accomplished singer.

3. I used to love Benny [who/whom] loved Martha, [who/whom] I definitely didn't love.

4   Generally, **who** and **whom** are used to describe people while **that** and **which** are used to describe things.

Last night I talked to my brother, <u>who</u> recently got a promotion.

Before us was the famous statue <u>that</u> we had traveled so far to reach.

1. I loved meeting the interesting people [who/which] came to your house this weekend.

2. My house, [whom/which] I painted blue, is at the end of the street.

5   When deciding between the subject and object pronoun, such as **I** versus **me**, in a *list* of **two pronouns**, cross out the other nouns and the **and** to see which pronoun is correct based on which one sounds right when it is by itself.

My mom is going to take ~~Susie and~~ <u>me</u> roller-skating.

Yesterday, I went to go see my brother; ~~he and~~ <u>I</u> like the same kinds of movies.

1. Do you want to come to the park with Larry and [I/me]?

2. Tom and [she/her] came to see Jack and [I/me] after school.

Exercises for Pronouns

Choose the correct pronoun(s) in each of the following sentences.

1. Germany's growth slowed in the late nineteen nineties, the economist argued, because [it/they] had problems with high unemployment.

2. Shaken by her friend's accident, Mother convinced my sister and [I/me] to drive slower.

3. I don't know [who/whom] robbed me, but I do know that all my possessions are gone.

4. He [who/whom] is responsible for the theft shall soon be arrested.

5. The bus drove past [we/us] students without stopping.

6. Have you received the message from [she/her]?

7. Can Leslie and [me/I] please stay for the volleyball game?

8. Arthur has many cats, so it is important that [he/him] keep a lot of milk in the fridge for [him/them].

9. [Who/Whom] among you is afraid of bears?

10. [Who/Whom] do you fear?

11. To [who/whom] should I give the dollar?

12. Jenny and Martha both get cold easily, so mom always keeps extra hats and gloves in the car for [her/them].

13. Our parents told Wendy and [I/me] to be quiet.

14. Nick Carraway was the only friend [who/which] attended Gatsby's funeral.

15. The flowers [that/whom] I gave you for your birthday are fake.

Apostrophes

The **apostrophe** (') is used to show *possession* (ownership) or to indicate a *contraction*. The ACT is mostly concerned with possession although it does test contractions in concert with pronouns. Correctly add or remove apostrophes as necessary in the numbered example sentences.

Possession

Possessive forms are used to indicate ownership of an item or concept. For nouns, we have the following rules:

[1] When a **singular** noun *does not* end in **-s**, add **'s** to show possession.

The girl's coat was hidden under the family's blanket.

1. In many schools, it is the teacher responsibility to track attendance.

2. The students celebrated the School Board decision to build a new gym on campus.

When a **singular** noun ends in **-s**, add **'** *or* **'s** to show possession.

The principal vetoed the class's suggestion for a day off.

The event features many of tennis' biggest stars.

Both of the sentences above are correct, and both ways of punctuating a singular possessive noun are important to know because a correct answer could include either.

3. When I cleaned up after the party, I found James coat and Susan shoes.

4. Dani borrows Bess car when she needs to run errands outside of the city.

[2] When a **plural** noun ends in **-s**, add **'** to show possession.

The debate team met for pizza to celebrate the students' victory.

1. At the track championship, it was all of the schools responsibility to provide volunteers to time the races.

2. After the party, almost all of the girls dresses were covered in cake.

When a **plural** noun *does not* end in **-s**, add **'s** to show possession.

The children's toys were scattered about the playroom.

3. The attendees of the 1851 Women Convention in Akron, Ohio, were privileged to hear Sojourner Truth famous "And Ain't I a Woman?" speech.

4. Even though Stephen is only 15, he is so tall that he needs to shop in the mens department.

Contifications

Contractions

1. In **contractions**, apostrophes are used to take the place of *missing letters*.

It's not raining now, but it was doing so this morning.

Here **it's** is short for **it is**. **It's** can also be short for **it has**.

We can't continue going over the same rules every day.

Here **can't** is short for **cannot**.

Contractions that lead to difficulties often involve pronouns, and the ACT is particularly fond of testing this. In particular, you should be aware of the differences between **possessive adjectives** (or determiners)—such as **its, your, their** and **whose**—and contractions—such as **it's, you're, they're**, and **who's**.

Contraction	Meaning	Possessive	Meaning
it's	it is *or* it has	its	belonging to it
you're	you are	your	belonging to you
they're	they are	their	belonging to them
who's	who is *or* who has	whose	belonging to whom

Correct any errors in the following sentences:

1. My friend who's car I borrowed was somewhat angry when I returned it with one side mirror missing.

2. Its been a long time, but I know a change is going to come.

3. Whatever it's source, the noise outside greatly disturbed you're dog.

NOTE: The words **its'** and **its's** are *not* words in the English language and cannot be correctly used.

Also, although **there**, meaning *in that place*, sounds the same as **their** and **they're**, it is unrelated to a possessive or a contraction.

Editing Exercises for Apostrophes

Add apostrophes where necessary and remove them where they are incorrectly placed. Change words as needed. Not all sentences contain errors.

1. Its heart had stopped beating, but the amphibians tail still quivered with life.

2. The bring-out-the vote effort rejuvenated the community and increased it's involvement in social welfare.

3. Its appetite sated, the leopard wandered off leaving the remains of it's kill to the hyenas.

4. "Its mid-day," mother exclaimed, "and your still in bed!"

5. Harold argued that although Maud was old, she was still beautiful to him: "its in the eyes of the beholder that beauty lies," he said.

6. It was snowing yesterday, but its seventy-five degrees today; its unnerving to have the weather change so suddenly.

7. Your going to have trouble being taken seriously if you dont perfect you're use of apostrophes.

8. These books covers' were torn before they arrived here.

9. On Los Angeles' Rodeo Drive, most shop's are too expensive for me to even look at.

10. Stephen's recently finished film is going to be shown at Sundance this year; he hopes it's content will challenge his audiences thinking.

11. Although I have seen many professional photographers representations of Half Dome, I have seen none that show the peak from my mothers favorite vantage point.

12. Jane Austen's Emma is both a love story and a detective novel.

13. My dogs collar is blue, but both my cousin Joan's dogs collars' are green; when our Chihuahuas play together we can only tell them apart by there collars.

14. Right there is the man who's been causing me so much trouble!

15. Right there is the man who's cats have been causing me so much trouble!

Verb Usage

For a sentence to be correct, the **verb** must agree with the **subject** in *number* (singular or plural) and the verb must be in the correct *tense* (past, present, or future).

Subject–Verb Agreement

To check for subject-verb agreement, follow these steps:

    (1) Locate the verb.

    (2) Find the subject for that verb.

    (3) Place the subject right before the verb and read them together to see if they sound correct.

As can be seen in the following example, when the subjects and verbs in a sentence are adjacent, it isn't difficult to hear whether they agree:

> While many people <u>know</u> about the crime, only two <u>were</u> at the scene and only one <u>saw</u> what happened.

Unfortunately, the ACT rarely tests situations as easy as the one above.

Choose the correct form of the verb in the numbered example sentences following each condition.

1 Watch out for nouns *separated from* the verb by **subordinate clauses** or **prepositional phrases**. Find the subject, then verify subject-verb agreement.

> A long <u>sentence</u>, particularly one in which there are extended subordinate clauses of various sorts placed between the subjects and verbs, <u>is</u> difficult to parse correctly.

    1. The kind note from thirty of Beverly's extended family members [make/**makes**] her smile.

    2. Kanchenjunga, which means "five treasures of the snows," [**is**/are] so called because it consists of five peaks, and [**is**/are] among the highest mountains in the world.

    3. Eloise, along with all of her fellow anxious students, [breathe/**breathes**] a sigh of relief as the teacher announces the postponement of the test.

2 **Collective nouns** (nouns that describe a group of people or things as one unit—**family, team, group, organization**) are always **singular**. You can usually ignore prepositional phrases when determining subject verb agreement.

> A <u>group</u> of my friends <u>is</u> coming over for dinner this weekend.

    1. The litter of puppies that my neighbor's dog had last night [**was**/were] a surprise.

    2. The bouquet of red, white and purple roses [**smells**/smell] so good.

    3. The band that played the most difficult songs [**was the winner**/were the winners].

Verb Tenses

1. Distinguish between **past, present** and **future** tense by the context of the remainder of the sentence or paragraph.

   I ran two miles before I took my ACT. I also ate a hearty breakfast.

   1. We went to the store. We also [go/went] to the movies.

   2. In order to get a good score, Shaun will study hard. He [reviewed/reviews/will review] all his relevant notes from the semester.

2. **Perfect tenses** are used to indicate completed actions or actions whose time is relative to another verb in the sentence. They always use forms of **have**, *never* **of**.

   Present perfect verbs indicate actions that started in the past and are completed or continue in the present, and they use **have** or **has**.

   Past perfect verbs indicate actions that were completed in the past and use **had**.

   Future perfect verbs discuss the past of some future event and use **will have**.

   After working for 45 years, Michael has finally retired from law enforcement.

   The years—especially this year—have not been kind to James.

   The players had tried to keep up through the first half but were listless by the third quarter.

   1. The air [had cooled/cools] to a comfortable seventy degrees before we decided to go for a run.

   2. For the Polar Bear Plunge, I [am jumping/have jumped] into the Chesapeake Bay on January 1st every year for the last six years.

3. **Irregular verbs** that have odd forms for past or perfect tenses are quite common in English. The extremely irregular forms of the verbs **to be** and **to go** usually don't give students difficulty because those verbs are used all the time. It is good to keep in mind that many verbs with an [i] sound in the present and future tenses have an [a] sound in the past tense and a [u] sound in the perfect tenses.

   I swim today. I swam yesterday. I have swum every day for the last two years.

   Dan will begin a new book tomorrow. He began a new book last week. He has begun a new book every Tuesday this summer. He will have begun twelve new books by September.

   1. Brett [had/have] already [drank/drunk] three cups of coffee before breakfast.

   2. I [will have/had] [sang/sung] two songs before my parents make it to the performance.

   3. It [has/had] [came/come] to our attention too late to do anything about it, so we were unable to fix it.

Exercises for Verb Usage

Select the appropriate verb form in each of the following sentences.

1. Lacey, unlike her brothers and sisters, [write/writes] well.

2. Nat Turner, a slave revolt leader with many followers, [are/is] venerated by some as a hero for the fear he sparked in many slave owners.

3. Each one of the twenty-seven desks [has/have] a book on it.

4. Abraham Lincoln, who was raised in the frontier states, [were/was] interested in politics as a child.

5. Each one of the many excellent competitors [has/have] a shot at winning.

6. The triathlon participants had already [swam/swum] for a mile when they were stopped and told that the race had been called off.

7. In a fourth grade recital I [sang/sung] the national anthem in front of the entire school and such was the response that I have never [sang/sung] it since.

8. The all-new Campus Center and the indoor squash court built outside the existing athletic center [was/were] funded by an anonymous alumnus.

9. The statistics recently issued by the Society for Control of Human Population [make/makes] the argument that we need to stop procreating now.

10. The boy by the window on the other side of the soccer and baseball fields [was/were] looking through his binoculars at the pretty girl on her balcony.

11. The largest pride of lions in the Serengeti, which has only three lion cubs, [are/is] on the verge of extinction.

12. The recommendations put forth by the Steering Committee of the corporation [include/includes] educating each employee about the value of diversity.

13. Other animals know to run when the herd of elephants [stampede/stampedes] through the jungle.

14. Behind my house, there [is/are] many trees.

15. Some patients do not respond to the new therapy as well as others [did/do], and some even respond adversely.

Verb Usage, Pronouns, and Apostrophes Problem Set

1. The Boston metro area contains several excellent colleges, including Boston University, Harvard, MIT, and Tufts. Despite <u>Harvard being the oldest college in the country, they are</u> not nearly the largest by number of students, even in the Boston area.

 A. NO CHANGE

 B. it being the oldest college in the country, they are

 C. Harvard being the oldest college in the country, it is

 D. it being the oldest college in the country, it is

2. Andres should submit his application through the digital clearinghouse; <u>its' the best way to get Andres'</u> application in the right hands.

 A. NO CHANGE

 B. it's the best way to get Andres'

 C. it's the best way to get Andre's

 D. its the best way to get Andres's

3. We went to the movies to see the film starring the man <u>whose</u> my favorite actor before I found out that he starred in a really terrible movie.

 A. NO CHANGE

 B. who is

 C. who will be

 D. who was

4. Weather conditions at the Cocoa Santamingo Beach Resort, which can only be accessed by boating across the hidden <u>lagoon, has earned it</u> the nickname, "Home of the Cloudless Sky."

 A. NO CHANGE

 B. lagoon, have earned them

 C. lagoon, have earned the resort

 D. lagoon, has earned the resort

5. Mount Rushmore, despite the tall tales that extend far and wide across websites, magazines, and <u>novel's, does</u> not contain a secret mountain base.

 A. NO CHANGE

 B. novels do

 C. novels, do

 D. novels, does

6. <u>Whom should I take to the new restaurant that Athena, whom</u> I recently befriended, recommended?

 A. NO CHANGE

 B. Whom should I take to the new restaurant that Athena, who

 C. Who should I take to the new restaurant that Athena, whom

 D. Who should I take to the new restaurant that Athena, who

Will their ever be multiple correct answers?

7. A herd of large, black and white, polka-dotted
   <u>cows walk</u> across the field at dinner time.

if so then → ⟶

   A. NO CHANGE
   B. cows walks
   C. cows walking
   D. cows were walking

Otherwise) it has to Be Ⓑ

8. Beth Lemming and Nathan Serez are great
   conversationalists. I always enjoy speaking
   with <u>her and he.</u>

   A. NO CHANGE
   B. she and he
   C. she and him
   D. her and him

9. At a University of Michigan football game,
   Teddy asked if he could get anything for <u>Sally
   and me</u> at the food stand.

   A. NO CHANGE
   B. Sally and I
   C. she and I
   D. she and me

10. Companies that make collectables have an
    effective way to signal that an item is official.
    The use of an embossed logo and a holographic
    sticker has been common practice for years to
    show <u>its a</u> genuine original.

    A. NO CHANGE
    B. that something is a
    C. its' a
    D. that its a

Adjectives and Adverbs

The ACT frequently asks questions testing the ability to distinguish between adjectives and adverbs, and their uses.

Adjective   a word that describes a noun (a person, place, or thing).

> The <u>angry</u> man lay on the <u>cold</u> grass.

> The <u>clear</u>, <u>blue</u> sky was mottled by the <u>occasional</u> cloud.

Adverb   a word that modifies a verb, adjective, or another adverb.

> The <u>very</u> angry man lay <u>uncomfortably</u> on the <u>mildly</u> cold grass.

> The <u>almost</u> blue sky was <u>quickly</u> covered by <u>terrifyingly</u> dark clouds.

To determine whether a given word should be an adjective or an adverb, check to see what word it is modifying or describing. If it is modifying or describing a **noun**, the word should be an **adjective**. If it's modifying or describing a **verb**, **adjective**, or **adverb**, it should be an **adverb**.

NOTE: **Good** is an adjective, and **well** is often used as an adverb.

> I am doing <u>well</u> today because Superman is out there doing <u>good</u> deeds.

Editing Exercises for Adjectives and Adverbs

Correct the following sentences using the appropriate adjectives and adverbs.

1. Math can be real hard for some people; for others it can be real easily.

2. I read the humorously comic strip to my nephew.

3. Natalie runs quick but talks slow.

4. He who reads careful scores good.

5. Ron swats at the quickly fly, but he cannot get it.

Modifiers

A **modifier** is a phrase that alters or describes another word or phrase. A modifier *must* be placed immediately next to the word or phrase that it is modifying. When the modifier starts the sentence, it must modify the subject of the sentence, and that subject must immediately follow the modifier. If a modifier is placed incorrectly, confusing statements can result.

For example, consider the following sentence:

> By a great stroke of luck, the detective saw the would-be assassin as he was about to pull the trigger <u>with his binoculars</u>.

In this sentence, **with his binoculars** is a modifier. The sentence implies that the would-be assassin is going to use the binoculars to pull the trigger. A corrected version follows:

> By a great stroke of luck, the detective saw <u>with his binoculars</u> the would-be assassin as he was about to pull the trigger.

This sentence now correctly makes it clear that the detective used the binoculars to see the assassin.

Now consider another incorrect sentence:

> <u>Humming cheerfully</u>, the boat was rowed into the choppy seas by the oarsman.

This wording implies that the boat was humming cheerfully. A corrected version follows:

> <u>Humming cheerfully</u>, the oarsman rowed the boat into the choppy seas.

This sentence correctly implies that the oarsman was humming cheerfully while he rowed his boat.

Notice in the example above how the incorrect version uses **passive voice**. Passive voice is not itself grammatically incorrect, but when passive voice is used, it is often a clue that there is some other error.

Editing Exercises for Misplaced Modifiers

Correct the following sentences. You may find it necessary to slightly reword the sentence to fix the modifier error.

1. My cousin sold a house to a nice family with no hard wood floors.

2. Our favorite people on Halloween are the ones that give out brownies to the children wrapped in cellophane.

3. Waking up later than planned, the flight was missed by John.

4. After reading the book *Pride and Prejudice*, the movie version seemed dull and lifeless to me.

5. I heard that my roommate intended to throw a surprise party for me while I was outside her bedroom window.

6. Waiting for her brother's game to end, Leslie's impatience rose.

Parallel Structure

When a sentence has a **list** or **comparison** of two or more parts, the different parts need to use the same verb, noun, or prepositional structure. For instance, look at the list in the following sentence:

My classmate Alexander has vacationed in Mexico, Italy, and in India.

The places in the list do not have parallel prepositional structure. There are two ways to correct the error, one where a single **in** caters to all three places and one where each place gets its own **in**.

My classmate Alexander has vacationed in <u>Mexico</u>, <u>Italy</u> and <u>India</u>.

My classmate Alexander has vacationed <u>in Mexico</u>, <u>in Italy</u> and <u>in India</u>.

A parallel structure error can also occur when two or more things in a comparison are not in the same form. For example, look at the following sentence:

I like snowboarding better than to skate.

Snowboarding and **to skate** are not parallel verb forms. There are two ways to correct the error.

I like snowboarding better than skating.

I like to snowboard better than to skate.

Editing Exercises for Parallel Structure

Correct the parallel structure errors in the following sentences.

1. Chris loves writing stories, poems and ~~composing~~ songs.

2. Rick is either playing the fool or he ~~tells~~ jokes.

3. Amanda has trouble with study skills, memory techniques, and managing her time.

4. The recommendations put forth by the committee include making annual standardized tests mandatory after the fourth grade and to randomly sample internal assessments for evidence of grade inflation.

5. Merab has neither played the trombone nor ~~has she~~ played the tuba.

6. Ashley will write the essay, proofread, and e-mail it before tomorrow.

Vocabulary and Homonyms

The following are examples of words that sound similar but have very different meanings. The ACT often tests these, so please watch out!

[1] **would of** vs. **would have**

Would of is always incorrect.

> My friend Alexander, who lives in Greece, ~~would of~~ **would have** visited me when he came to India, but he fell sick.

[2] **set** vs. **sit**

Set means to put down an object. **Sit** means to rest in such a way that your weight is supported by your backside, such as on a chair.

> Before battle, I told Alexander to ~~set~~ **sit** astride his horse Bucephalus, don a helmet with bright plumes, and ride in at the head of his army.

[3] **affect** vs. **effect**

Usually **affect** is used as a verb meaning to influence or impact, and **effect** is used as a noun meaning a result or consequence. You can remember that **affect** starts with the letter **a**, like the word **action**, which is a synonym for verb.

> When he was in Babylon, in modern day Iraq, my friend Alexander was ~~effected~~ **affected** by typhoid. Because of the powerful ~~affects~~ **effects** of the illness, he died.

[4] **then** vs. **than**

Then refers to a time. **Than** is used in comparisons. It helps to remember that the word **time** has the letter **e** and the word **comparison** has the letter **a**.

> Alexander was shorter ~~then~~ **than** his giant horse Bucephalus.

> Alexander defeated Darius, and ~~than~~ **then** he defeated Porus.

[5] **duel** vs. **dual**

A **duel** is a fight. **Dual** means consisting of two things.

> In Mongol, Greek, and Roman cultures, horses often served ~~duel~~ **dual** purposes: steed and companion. You could ~~dual~~ **duel** on your horse or you could, if you were the Roman emperor Caligula, build a house for him and plan to make him consul.

[6] **cite** vs. **site** vs. **sight**

Cite usually means to quote or mention for support. **Site** refers to a location. **Sight** relates to vision.

> My English teacher told me to ~~site~~ **cite** all my sources, including all web**sites** I might use.

> Alexander never lost ~~site~~ **sight** of his principal goal: to conquer the world.

Modifiers, Parallel Structure, and Vocabulary Problem Set

1. To have your cake and eating it too is not possible.

   A. NO CHANGE
   B. Having your cake and eating it too is not possible.
   C. Having your cake and to eat it too is not possible.
   D. Having your cake and eat it too is not possible.

2. Delighted by Santa's generosity, the presents were eagerly unwrapped by the children.

   A. NO CHANGE
   B. Delighted by Santa's generosity, the presents were unwrapped in an eager fashion by the children.
   C. Delighted by Santa's generosity, the children eagerly unwrapped the presents.
   D. The children eagerly unwrapped the presents delighted by Santa's generosity.

3. Hearing the sound of the can opener on the food tin, the wagging of the dog's tail was impatient.

   A. NO CHANGE
   B. tin, the tail of the dog wagged impatiently.
   C. tin, the dog's tail impatiently wagged.
   D. tin, the dog impatiently wagged its tail.

4. Known for his tenacity, Eric's drive impressed his teammates.

   A. NO CHANGE
   B. Eric's teammates were impressed with his drive.
   C. Eric impressed his teammates with his drive.
   D. the drive shown by Eric impressed his teammates.

5. Scientists predict the long-term affects of climate change will include a two-meter rise in sea levels by the end of the century.

   A. NO CHANGE
   B. effects to climate change
   C. affects to climate change
   D. effects of climate change

6. The child is recovering from his surgery much better then predicted by his doctors.

   A. NO CHANGE
   B. then his doctors predicted.
   C. than predicted by its doctors.
   D. than his doctors predicted.

7. Recent research at Stanford suggests that studies sited by lots of other papers are more likely to show evidence of bias.

   A. NO CHANGE
   B. studies sighted by lots of other papers
   C. studies, cited by lots of other papers,
   D. studies cited by lots of other papers

8. Recommendations on electronic devices for children include not using the devices before bedtime and to balance media use with other healthy behaviors.

   A. NO CHANGE
   B. not using the devices before bedtime and balancing media use
   C. to not use the devices before bedtime and balancing media use
   D. not using the devices before bedtime and balance media use

9. Before going to work every morning, Sheila walks her dog Bruno, brushes him, and feeding him his kibble.

   A. NO CHANGE
   B. and she feeds him
   C. and she will feed him
   D. and feeds him

10. A great concern for many of the city's residents, Hurricane Isabel knocked down many power lines, affecting thousands of people.

   A. NO CHANGE
   B. Hurricane Isabel knocked down many power lines, effecting
   C. power lines were knocked down by Hurricane Isabel, effecting
   D. the affect of Hurricane Isabel knocked down power lines for

Rhetorical Skills

There is usually nothing grammatically wrong with any answer choice in a Rhetorical Skills question, so all the choices can sometimes sound correct. Focus on exactly what the question is asking to find the best answer choice.

Broadly speaking, these questions fall into five general styles or asking structures: **yes/yes/no/no**, **reordering**, **best way to achieve a goal**, **least/not**, and **word choice**.

On the following pages you will find a list of the types of questions you will see on an ACT, organized according to these five structures, and a description of how to approach each of them. First review these notes and strategies, and then try the Rhetorical Skills Practice Passage that follows them.

Yes/Yes/No/No Questions

Yes/Yes/No/No refers to the four answer choice options on some of the ACT English questions. These questions can ask about whether the author should make a specific revision, whether a certain sentence should be kept or deleted, whether a sentence or phrase should be added to the passage, or whether the essay as a whole fulfilled a certain goal.

When answering these questions, you should decide on **Yes** or **No**, *physically write down your decision*, and even write down a brief explanation for why you came to that decision. Only then should you look at the two answer choices that correspond to your **Yes/No** decision, and choose the one that most closely matches your own explanation. These questions come in three varieties: main goal, additions, and deletions.

Main Goal

Some questions will ask whether the essay as a whole fulfilled a certain goal. When answering these questions, follow these steps:

(1) Underline the goal in the question.
(2) Decide on **Yes** or **No** before reading through the answer choices.
(3) Write down a brief reason for your **Yes** or your **No**.
(4) Look at the answer choices (only the ones corresponding to your decision) and choose the one that most closely matches what you wrote down.
(5) Read through the other two choices ONLY if the first two you evaluated are both clearly wrong.

Consider the following example:

1. Suppose the writer's goal had been to focus on the path that Smith took to become a musician. Would this essay accomplish that goal?

   A. Yes, because it focuses on how events in Smith's past led to his performance at the Kennedy Center.

   B. Yes, because it focuses on Smith's goals in school growing up.

   C. No, because it focuses on how musicians must balance their careers and families.

   D. No, because it focuses on Smith's most recent performance at the Kennedy Center.

Remember, before you look at the answer choices, you want to decide whether the essay *focused on the path that Smith took to become a musician*. If **Yes**, then decide between **A** and **B** based on the reasons given, and if **No**, then decide between **C** and **D** based on those reasons given.

Additions and Deletions

The ACT English section will contain a handful of questions asking whether or not a sentence (or part of a sentence) should be added to (or deleted from) the essay at a certain point. Most often, the question is testing whether you are paying attention to the context of the paragraph and whether or not the possible addition/deletion is relevant to the passage at that point.

If the sentence (or fragment) is relevant and contributes something worthwhile to the sentence, then add it/keep it. If it seems out of place, irrelevant, or simply a bad fit for the flow of the passage at that point, the correct choice is to delete the sentence or not make the addition.

Consider the following example of an **addition** question:

   2. At this point, the writer is considering adding the following true statement:

> Julie Delano also hiked a 120-mile stretch of the Appalachian Trail in the summer of 2005.

    Should the writer make the addition here?

    A. Yes, because it establishes Julie as a bona fide authority on hiking in the mid-Atlantic region.

    B. Yes, because it provides another example of Julie's accomplishments.

    C. No, because it doesn't indicate whether this hike was as difficult as some of her other undertakings.

    D. No, because it digresses from the main topic of the essay by introducing loosely related information.

If the sentence makes sense and adds worthwhile information to the passage at that point, then decide whether **A** or **B** gives the best explanation of why it should be added. If the sentence is unnecessary, out of place, disrupts the flow, or doesn't make sense at that point in the paragraph, select whether choice **C** or **D** best describes why the sentence should not be added.

Now consider the following **deletion** question:

   3. The writer is considering deleting the following sentence from the passage:

> The cold wind whipped the snow through the trees, obscuring their view down the sloping terrain.

    Should the sentence be deleted?

    A. Yes, because the sentence confuses the reader about what the hunters were doing in the forest.

    B. Yes, because the sentence interrupts the paragraph's focus on the hunters tracking their prey.

    C. No, because the sentence gives the reader a better appreciation of what the hunters were experiencing.

    D. No, because the sentence explains why the hunters had travelled there in the first place.

If the sentence makes sense and adds worthwhile information to the passage at that point, then decide whether **C** or **D** gives the best explanation. If the sentence is unnecessary, out of place, disrupts the flow, or doesn't make sense at that point in the paragraph, select the best answer choice from **A** and **B** based on the reasons given.

NOTE: Every so often the ACT will ask what a passage will *lose* if a preceding or underlined selection is deleted. Though these questions are not presented in the **yes/yes/no/no** style, you can approach them the same way. First decide for yourself what the passage would lose, write it down, and find the choice that best matches what you've written.

Reordering Questions

Reordering questions will ask you to locate the best place for a paragraph within the passage or for a specific sentence within a paragraph.

Paragraphs

You will encounter passages that ask you about the order of the paragraphs in the whole passage. Passages that include these questions will have bracketed numbers above each paragraph, and there will typically be a box at the start of the passage that reads something like "The following paragraphs may or may not be in the most logical order."

The final question for the passage will then be something like the following:

1. For the sake of the logic and coherence of the essay, Paragraph 4 should be placed:

   A. where it is now.
   B. before Paragraph 1.
   C. after Paragraph 2.
   D. after Paragraph 5.

Deciding where to put a paragraph in the whole passage requires paying attention to the transitions between paragraphs and understanding the order of events in the passage. It can often be clear whether or not a paragraph may be a good opener to the passage, like, for example, if it first introduces people or events that are central to the essay. Otherwise, look to put the paragraph near other paragraphs that are closely related to it. Often, a paragraph must be placed in a specific location to best provide a *chronological sequence of events* or to match a *specific transition sentence* at the start or end of another paragraph.

Sentences

Similarly, in some passages there will be questions that ask you to select the best place for a sentence within a certain paragraph. For these questions, there will be bracketed numbers in front of each sentence in a paragraph, which look like this: [1], [2], etc.

At the end of the paragraph there may be a question that asks...

2. For the sake of the logic and coherence of this paragraph, Sentence 3 should be placed:

   A. where it is now.
   B. before Sentence 1.
   C. before Sentence 2.
   D. after Sentence 4.

To decide where to put the sentence, pay close attention to the order of events in the paragraph, as well as *transitions between sentences*. Also be aware of which sentence might sound best starting the paragraph, as that can illuminate which sentence may belong first. There are usually two clear clues to the proper ordering of the sentences, so if you are stuck between two choices, look for a secondary clue.

NOTE: Questions sometimes have answer choices indicating, for example, "before Sentence 2" while others have answer choices saying "after Sentence 2." Underline the **before** or the **after**, and do not simply assume that the sentence will replace the bracketed number.

Best Way to Achieve a Goal

The English section of the ACT will contain many questions that ask you to pick which of the four answer choices best accomplishes something. All of the answer choices will be grammatically correct, but only one will best do what the question asks. If two answer choices contain the same information phrased only slightly differently, both are probably incorrect. For these questions, complete the following steps:

(1) Underline the key words in the question that tell you the goal you're looking for in the correct answer.

(2) Cross out choices, or even words within the choices, that do not meet this specific goal.

(3) Select the choice that best does whatever is being asked for.

Consider the following example:

1. Given that all the choices are true, which one gives the most detail about the visual effects of the fireworks?

   A. She marveled at the incredible fireworks, wishing they would never end.

   B. She gazed at the streaming showers of red, white and blue fireworks streaking through the sky, wishing they would never end.

   C. She wished she could share the amazing experience with Sam, who loved fireworks.

   D. She loved the boom every time the fireworks went off, and wished they would continue for longer.

You should first underline words like **most detail** and **visual** in the question. Answer choice **B** gives the most detail about the visual effects (… streaming showers of red, white, and blue fireworks streaking through the sky…), so this choice is the best of the four.

Least/Not Questions

Most ACT English sections will include a few questions that ask you to pick the LEAST acceptable answer choice or the answer choice that is NOT acceptable. This is tricky because you can get used to selecting the best answer on every question, and then you encounter a question that is essentially asking you to pick the wrong answer. These questions often will capitalize **LEAST** or **NOT** in the wording, but it can still be hard to remember that you are picking the worst option. Use the following steps:

(1) _Underline_ and _circle_ those negative words when you see them in a question.

(2) Cross off answer choices that seem to work well in context.

(3) Select the choice that works the least well. If one choice is substantially different from all of the others, that choice is often the correct answer.

Consider the following example sentence:

1. If the writer wants to illustrate Freddie's doubts about his chances of winning the competition, which choice would be LEAST acceptable?

   A. Freddie's hands shook and his voice quivered as the show drew near.

   B. Freddie couldn't help but think about the advantage that the experience of the other competitors gave them.

   C. Freddie eagerly paced backstage in anticipation of the show.

   D. Freddie felt that familiar nervousness creeping in, wishing he had rehearsed more.

Choice **C** is correct because _eagerly_ shows Freddie's positive attitude. Each one of the other choices **does** indicate Freddie's doubts about his chances of winning and thus is not the LEAST acceptable choice.

Word Choice

Transitional Words

Some of the hardest questions on the ACT English are choices among transitional words (**however, thus, therefore, regardless, nevertheless**, etc.). These are often found between sentences and are completely dependent on the context around them. Like with the other Rhetorical Skills questions, in order to have a good chance at picking the best transitional word, **you must read the sentences on either side of the word in question** and understand the relationship between the sentences. Usually these questions cannot be done effectively by only picking the word that sounds best. The uses of transitional words can fit into a few main categories. Here are some examples of the types of words and phrases you may encounter:

1   Introducing

     These words and phrases are used when the sentence introduces or brings up a new topic.

       Generally, In general, Primarily, Over all, On the whole

2   Concluding

     These words and phrases are used when the sentence finishes a point made in the previous sentence or group of sentences.

       Therefore, So, As a result, Finally, Consequently

3   Connecting

     These words and phrases are used when the sentence draws a conclusion from the previous statement, connects two similar points, or shows examples of the point just made.

       In fact, Similarly, For instance, For example, Next, Meanwhile, In addition

4   Contrasting

     These words and phrases are used when the sentence shows a difference from the previous statement or a contrast exists within the sentence itself.

       However, Alternatively, Though, Although, While, On the other hand, Conversely, Instead, Despite this, Nevertheless, Nonetheless, Still

Some transition word questions will only offer three choices that contain a transition, with the fourth choice being to start the sentence with no transition. In questions like this, **the answer choice that provides no transition is usually correct.** Often, these questions will offer multiple transition words of the same type. You can eliminate all words that essentially have the same meaning.

Consider the following question:

1. Many people debate the correct plural of octopus. <u>Therefore,</u> the actual correct plural is octopuses, although octopi and octopodes are both good enough.

     A. NO CHANGE

     B. Thus,

     C. In conclusion,

     D. DELETE the underlined portion, adjusting the capitalization correctly.

Choice **D** is correct because the second sentence is not causally related to the first, nor is it a conclusion of an argument that has been provided.

Redundancy and Extraneous Information

The ACT promotes a very literal and straightforward approach to writing. Therefore, the English section frequently contains questions involving repetition of phrases or overly convoluted ways of writing simple concepts. The ACT *always* wants things expressed as simply as possible. Therefore, when deciding between multiple answer choices that seem to be correct in terms of grammar and punctuation, **select the shortest choice** unless it introduces a vague pronoun or omits information that is important to the passage.

Consider the following example sentence:

2. Anne <u>walked, ambling along on both of her feet,</u> through the park with her grandparents.

   A. NO CHANGE

   B. strolled and meandered, putting one foot in front of the other,

   C. walked

   D. strolled in a walking manner along

Answer choices **A**, **B**, and **D** are all unnecessarily complicated ways of saying **walked**. You should therefore choose answer choice **C**.

Colloquialisms and Slang

In addition to frowning upon redundancy and overly complicated language, the ACT also discourages overly casual phrasing and even inappropriately technical phrasing.

Consider the following sample:

3. Although I liked the plan, my friend thought it was <u>unlikely to work.</u>

   A. NO CHANGE

   B. way too wacky and weird.

   C. totally crazy and stuff!

   D. unlikely to produce the desired outcome and results.

While choice **D** is clearly too complicated and unnecessarily wordy, choices **B** and **C** are also incorrect. They do not match the tone and style of ACT English passages both because they are too casual and because they use colloquial terms (slang). The correct choice is therefore **A**.

Rhetorical Skills Practice Passage

The Billy Goat Gives Up the Ghost

In American sports, there has been no "curse" on any professional team quite like the championship drought that haunted baseball's Chicago Cubs for over a century. The Cubs won back-to-back World Series championships in 1907 and 1908. Following these wins, <u>meanwhile</u>, the team suffered the longest
₁
championship drought in the history of professional sports. Although the Cubs ascended to the World Series several more times before 1950, they were unable to clinch the championship title <u>again in the first</u>
₂
<u>half of the 20th century.</u> <u>The Boston Red Sox had a</u>
₂   ₃
<u>considerable drought when they failed to win the World</u>
₃
<u>Series championship for 86 years after trading Babe</u>
₃
<u>Ruth to the Yankees in 1919, a drought sometimes</u>
₃
<u>referred to as the 'Curse of the Bambino.'</u>
₃

1. **A.** NO CHANGE
    B. though
    C. nevertheless
    D. similarly

2. **A.** NO CHANGE
    B. again through the first part of the 20th century
    C. again over the course of the 42 years after the 1908 title
    D. DELETE the underlined portion.

3. The writer is considering deleting the underlined sentence. Should the sentence be kept or deleted?

    A. Kept, because it provides necessary context to understand the severity of the Cubs' championship drought.
    B. Kept, because it shows that the Chicago Cubs are not the only team that has suffered a long period without winning a major title.
    C. Deleted, because it takes away from the primary focus of the passage on the championship drought endured by the Chicago Cubs.
    D. Deleted, because it is easily inferred from the rest of the passage.

[1] <u>Championship droughts are hard for fans to</u>

<u>endure.</u> [2] In 1945, the Cubs were in the World Series
4

and led the Detroit Tigers by two games to one.

[3] Partway through the game, William Sianis, owner of

the Billy Goat Tavern, was reportedly asked to leave the

stadium because the smell of his pet goat, Murphy, was

bothering other fans. [4] Game 4 was held at the Cubs'

home stadium, Wrigley Field. [5] Sianis allegedly

responded angrily, declaring, "Them Cubs, dey ain't

gonna win no more." [6] The Cubs went on to lose the

game. [7] Apparently emboldened by the success of his

initial curse, Sianis went on to send the following

telegram to the team's owner: "You are going to lose

this World Series and you are never going to win

another World Series again. [8] You are never going to

win a World Series again because you

insulted my goat." ⬚5

Although the <u>sincerity</u> of these events cannot be
6

confirmed, the 'Curse of the Billy Goat' certainly felt

real to many Cubs fans for years. The Cubs were in the

playoffs several times after 1945, often within one game

of making the World Series; <u>consequently,</u> the team
7

was unable to get to the World Series for 71 years. The

4. Given that all the choices are true, which choice most effectively introduces the paragraph?

    A.   NO CHANGE
    (B.)   The Cubs' unlucky fate was sealed after an alleged incident leading to what became known as the "Curse of the Billy Goat."
    C.   Stories abound of different curses that afflict major athletic teams.
    D.   Owners don't realize the consequences of bringing their pets to athletic events.

5. For the sake of logic and cohesion, Sentence 4 should be placed

    A.   where it is now.
    B.   Before Sentence 2.
    C.   After Sentence 2.
    (D)   After Sentence 5.

6. **(A.)** NO CHANGE
    B.   veracity
    C.   realism
    D.   integrity

7. A.   NO CHANGE
    B.   therefore,
    (C.) however,
    D.   instead,

curse was finally broken by the Chicago Cubs in 2016

when the Cubs edged out the Cleveland Indians in the

deciding game, which required extra innings to

complete. ⊞8 Chicago fans were ecstatic. The city of

Chicago estimated that over five million people

attended the World Series parade and victory

8. The writer is considering adding the following true statement:

> Ordinarily, a baseball game consists of nine innings each of which is divided into halves: the visiting team bats first, after which the home team takes its turn at bat.

Should the writer make this addition here:

A. Yes, because the statement provides necessary information to understanding how the Cubs were able to win.
B. Yes, because the statement explains why the Cubs' win was so remarkable.
C. No, because the statement is irrelevant to the paragraph's discussion of the end of the Cubs' championship drought.
D. No, because the statement suggests that the Cubs used unorthodox methods to win the game.

celebration <u>following the Cubs' win</u>. The longest
                        9
curse in professional sports is over, and no

9. A. NO CHANGE
B. after the triumph of the Cubs
C. in the wake of the Cubs' win
D. DELETE the underlined portion.

goat can stand in Chicago's way! ⊞10

10. Suppose the writer's goal had been to illustrate the impact of fan attendance on the performance of baseball teams. Would this essay accomplish that goal?

A. Yes, because the essay illustrates the impact of one fan's curse on the performance of the Chicago Cubs.
B. Yes, because the essay shows how fan support eventually led to the victory of the Chicago Cubs in 2016.
C. No, because the focus of the essay is on a goat rather than on baseball fans.
D. No, because it relays the story of a single fan who allegedly impacted one baseball team.

Mathematics Test Manual

The Math section is the second of the four multiple-choice sections on the ACT. It consists of 60 questions, and students without extended time are given 60 minutes—or one minute per question—to complete the section. The first questions are fairly simple, but the difficulty increases with the question numbers, and the last ten questions are often very difficult for most students. It is important to have a well-defined number of questions that you aim to answer, and time management is crucial.

Overview

If there's one good thing about standardized tests, it is that they are predictable. In order for test scores to be consistent, the ACT uses the same *type* of questions from test to test. So, in order to do well, all you need is to:

1. Know each type of question, *and*

2. Learn the strategies (quick ways) to solve each type of question accurately.

We've structured this workbook with the most applicable strategies first. Next, we tackle the major types of questions that come up on the ACT:

- Geometry and Graphing
- Numbers and Operations
- Algebra and Functions
- Statistics and Probability
- Trigonometry
- Higher Level Topics

Part I: Strategies

A strategy is just a quick way to solve a problem accurately. Often you can come up with your own quick ways. The trick is to pause for a moment before you start solving and think about the easy way to solve the question. If you're like most students, though, during a timed test like the ACT, you won't even think about pausing.

The people who write the ACT Math test realize that all of us have certain patterned ways of solving questions—the ways we learn in school. In high-pressure situations, we tend to fall back upon these ways that we know so well. Because test-makers want to reward the ability to think creatively under pressure, they devise questions that can seem difficult if you try to solve them in the most obvious way—the way you've learned in school.

One way you can prepare for these questions is to practice alternative strategies as much as you practiced the textbook methods in high school. If you become very familiar with the quick way, it's likely that you'll remember it during the ACT.

Backsolving

Every one of the 60 Mathematics questions on the ACT provides you with answer choices. Because the answer to the question is right there in front of you, you can often simply *try the various answers* until you see which one works.

There are some questions for which it is easiest to start with simple answer choices: 0 and 1, for example, are very quick to plug in and check, and for this reason they are often the best place to start if they are available.

For other questions, you can use the fact that the answer choices are usually in increasing or decreasing order. This is most helpful in cases like the following:

Example 1   For two consecutive even integers, the result of adding the smaller integer to three times the larger integer is 62. What are the two integers?

    A. 14, 16

    B. 16, 18

    C. 18, 20

    D. 20, 22

    E. 22, 24

It is simplest to begin with the middle answer choice, i.e. 18 and 20. Adding the smaller number to three times the larger yields $18 + 3 \times 20 = 78$. This is clearly greater than the 62 you are looking for, so you know that choice **C** is incorrect. However, choices **D** and **E** are *also* incorrect because they will give you something *even larger* than choice **C** does.

You can try choice **B** next, i.e. 16 and 18. Adding the smaller number to three times the larger yields $16 + 3 \times 18 = 70$, which is still too big. You are now actually *done* because you have eliminated *all* answer choices except one, which is **A**.

If you wanted to be extra careful, you could test that answer choice **A** does indeed give you the correct answer: Using 14 and 16 gives us $14 + 3 \times 16 = 62$, which is indeed the answer you are looking for.

Backsolving Problem Set

On the following problem set, focus on backsolving by using your answer choices.

1. If $(x-3)^2 = (2x-1)(x+3)$, which of the following could equal x?

   A. -2
   B. 0
   C. 1
   D. 2
   E. 5

2. When each side of a given square is decreased by 2 inches, the area is decreased by 20 square inches. What is the length, in inches, of a side of the original square?

   A. 3
   B. 4
   C. 5
   D. 6
   E. 7

3. If $\dfrac{4}{3x+1} = \dfrac{2}{2x-2}$, then what is the value of x?

   A. -3
   B. -1
   C. 1
   D. 3
   E. 5

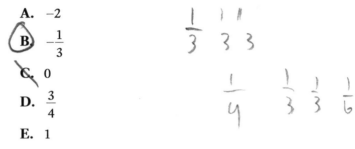

Note: Figure not drawn to scale

4. If x, x^3, and x^2 lie on a number line in that order (as shown above), which of the following could be a value of x?

   A. -2
   B. $-\dfrac{1}{3}$
   C. 0
   D. $\dfrac{3}{4}$
   E. 1

5. If $\dfrac{x^3}{y}$ is an integer but $\dfrac{x}{y}$ is NOT an integer, which of the following could be the values of x and y?

   A. $x=2, y=1$
   B. $x=3, y=9$
   C. $x=4, y=2$
   D. $x=3, y=2$
   E. $x=2, y=3$

x	$f(x)$
-2	8
0	4
1	5
3	13
4	20

6. Which of the following functions is represented in the table above?

~~A.~~ $3x + 4$

~~B.~~ $2x + 3$

~~C.~~ $x^3 - 7$

~~D.~~ $-2x + 5$

(E.) $x^2 + 4$

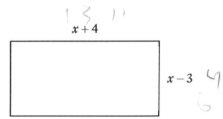

$x + 4$

$x - 3$

7. If the area of the rectangle above is 60, what is the value of x?

A. 5

B. 6

~~C.~~ 7

D. 8

(E.) 9

8. If $3^y = 27$ and $y = \dfrac{1}{2}x$, what is the value of x?

A. 2

B. 3

C. 4

D. 5

(E.) 6

$$4x^2 < (4x)^2$$

9. For what value of x is the statement above FALSE?

A. -4

(B.) 0

C. $\dfrac{1}{4}$

D. 1

E. for no value of x

$$1 \le x^2 \le 9$$

10. Which of the following represents all values of x that satisfy the above inequality?

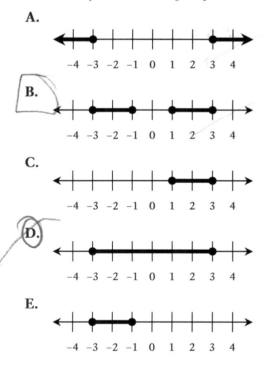

A.

B.

C.

(D.)

E.

11. If $5^{k-4} \times 5^k + 16 = 41,$ what is the value of k?

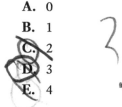

    A. 0

    B. 1

    C. 2

    D. 3

    E. 4

14. If $x^{-\frac{1}{4}} = \frac{1}{3},$ what is the value of x?

    A. −27

    B. −3

    C. 9

    D. 81

    E. 243

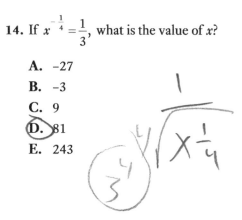

12. For which of the following functions is $f(-2) = f(2)$ true?

    A. $f(x) = x^2 + x$

    B. $f(x) = x^2 + 1$

    C. $f(x) = x + 2$

    D. $f(x) = x^3 + x$

    E. $f(x) = \frac{1}{2}x$

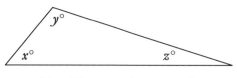

Note: Figure not drawn to scale

15. In the triangle pictured above, $y > 90$ and $x = z + 2.$ If $x, y,$ and z are all integers, what is the largest possible value of z?

    A. 30

    B. 43

    C. 45

    D. 47

    E. 89

$$x + z < 90$$
$$2z + 2 + z < 90$$

13. Which of the following represents all solutions for the inequality $1 < 3 - 2x < 11$?

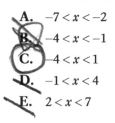

    A. $-7 < x < -2$

    B. $-4 < x < -1$

    C. $-4 < x < 1$

    D. $-1 < x < 4$

    E. $2 < x < 7$

16. What is the solution set for the inequality $|5x - 5| + 2 \leq 7$?

    A. $-2 \leq x \leq 2$

    B. $-2 \leq x \leq 0$

    C. $0 \leq x \leq 2$

    D. $0 \leq x \leq 10$

    E. Empty Set

17. Ashley earned x dollars working at her father's printing shop. She spent $\frac{1}{5}$ of it on clothes, $\frac{1}{4}$ on books for school, and saved the remaining $1100. What is the value of x?

    A. 1200

    B. 1500

    C. 1750

    D. 2000

    E. 2111.11

18. If $\frac{1}{5} + \frac{1}{6} + \frac{1}{7} > \frac{1}{5} + \frac{1}{6} + \frac{1}{x}$, then x could be which of the following?

    A. 4

    B. 5

    C. 6

    D. 7

    E. 8

19. On a high school soccer team, Katharine scored $\frac{1}{3}$ of the team's total goals for the season. Of the remaining goals, Christy scored 15, and the other $\frac{3}{4}$ were scored by various other teammates. How many total goals did the team score this season?

    A. 60

    B. 80

    C. 90

    D. 120

    E. 150

20. Warren is worth $25.6 billion and Bill is worth $23.04 billion. What percent of his net worth would Warren have to donate to Bill so that each is worth the same amount?

    A. 5%

    B. 8%

    C. 23%

    D. 89%

    E. 90%

Plugging in Numbers

Plugging in Numbers is a useful strategy when a question has variables that maintain a constant relationship. By substituting real numbers for variables, you can solve questions arithmetically instead of algebraically.

There are three main steps to Plugging in Numbers.

Choose which number(s) to plug in and write it/them down.

  If there is an equation, plug in on the side where there is more action.

  Usually avoid choosing **0** or **1** as the number you plug in; these will often yield the same result for different choices. For the same reason, try not to use **30°**, **45°**, **60°**, or **90°** for angles.

  Smaller numbers tend to work well in most cases, e.g. **2**, **3**, **4**, or **5**.

  Plug in different numbers for different variables.

  For percent problems use **100**.

  Solve for other variables in equations if necessary.

Write down and BOX your answer.

Plug the number(s) you've chosen into the same variables in the answer choices if applicable. (Note that you *must* try ALL the answer choices)

  Which one(s) matches your answer?

  If multiple answer choices work, try different numbers and repeat steps 1 to 3, though any choice you've eliminated is gone for good.

Example 1   If w is the first of three consecutive odd integers, what is the sum of the two even integers between the smallest and greatest odd integer, in terms of w?

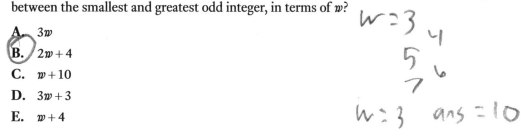

  A. $3w$
  B. $2w + 4$
  C. $w + 10$
  D. $3w + 3$
  E. $w + 4$

Notice the complicated wording in the question. Many students will be confused by the time they get to the part about the even integers. So don't let yourself even get to that part without first plugging in a number.

Choose a number, specifically an odd integer, to plug in for w like, for example, **3**.

If $w = 3$, then the consecutive odd integers are **3**, **5**, and **7**, and the even integers that are between those are **4** and **6**. The sum of **4** and **6** is **10**, so that is the number the correct choice ought to come out to when **3** is plugged in for w.

Plugging in **3** for w in all four choices shows that choice **A** works out to 9, **B** works out to 10, **C** works out to 13, **D** works out to 12, and **E** works out to 7. The answer must be **B**. Notice, had you plugged **1** in for w instead of **3**, choices **B** and **D** would have worked. Such a thing can happen with any number but is more common with numbers like **1** and **0**.

Plugging in Numbers Problem Set 1

1. If $y = 3^x + 3^x + 3^x$, then what is y in terms of x?

   A. 3^{3x}

   B. 9^x

   C. 3^{x^3}

   D. 27^x

   E. 3^{x+1}

   handwritten: X = 3   ans = 81

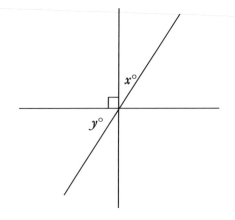

2. If r, s, and t are consecutive odd integers, what is the difference between r and t?

   A. 0

   B. 1

   C. 2

   D. 3

   E. 4

   handwritten: 3 5 7

4. In the figure above, which of the following is equal to x?

   A. $x + y$

   B. y

   C. $90 - x$

   D. $90 - y$

   E. $180 - y$

3. If $-1 < x < 0 < y < 1$, which of the following is the greatest?

   A. xy

   B. $-y$

   C. $-(y^2)$

   D. x^2

   E. 0

   handwritten: X = -1/2   Y = 1/2   0

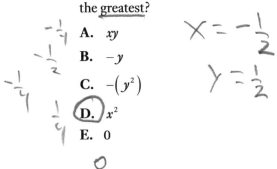

5. If $\dfrac{1}{x} = \dfrac{x}{y}$, which of the following equals xy?

   A. $4x$

   B. $3x^2$

   C. x^3

   D. x

   E. $(2x)^2$

   handwritten: X = 2   Y = 4   A = 8   4 = X   Y = 16

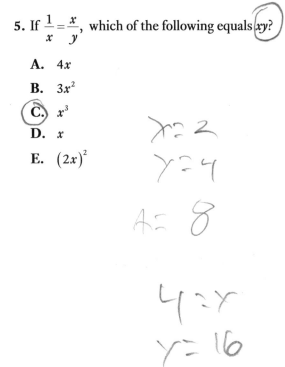

6. Andrew caught three times as many lobsters as crabs. Half of the lobsters he caught were female. If Andrew randomly chooses a shellfish from his catch, what is the likelihood that he picks up a male lobster?

A. $\dfrac{3}{10}$

B. $\dfrac{3}{8}$

C. $\dfrac{5}{12}$

D. $\dfrac{6}{11}$

E. $\dfrac{3}{11}$

(handwritten: C =10, L=30, f=15, m=15, $\frac{15}{40}$)

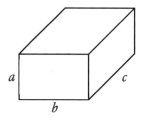

Note: Figure not drawn to scale

9. In the rectangular prism above, $b = 2a$ and $2c = 3b$. What is the volume of the prism?

A. $6a^2$

B. b^3

C. $2b^2c$

D. $6a^3$

E. $\dfrac{b^2c}{4}$

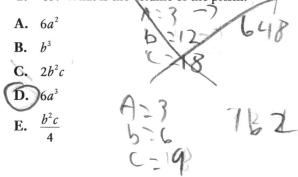

7. If J, K, and L are digits in the positive three-digit integer JKL, what is the decimal equivalent of $JKL \times 10^{-4}$?

A. $0.0JKL$

B. $0.JKL$

C. $J.KL$

D. $JK,L00$

E. $J,KL0,000$

(handwritten: L = poss)

8. If x and y are positive consecutive integers, where $y > x$, which of the following is equal to xy?

A. $3x$

B. $4x$

C. $x^2 + y$

D. $x^2 + x$

E. $y^2 - x$

(handwritten: 3, 4   xy=12   (x)+(x+1) =   5,6 = 30)

10. Ricky had d dollars in the bank. He withdrew $\dfrac{3}{4}$ of d to buy a plane ticket to Paris. He then spent $\dfrac{1}{3}$ of what was left on his lodging for the week. What fraction of the original amount remained in his account?

A. $\dfrac{1}{12}$

B. $\dfrac{1}{6}$

C. $\dfrac{1}{4}$

D. $\dfrac{1}{3}$

E. $\dfrac{1}{2}$

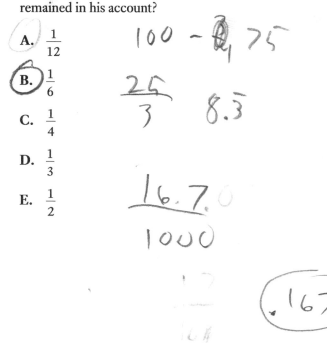

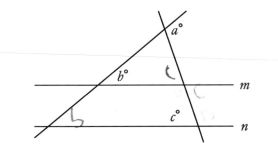

Note: Figure not drawn to scale

11. In the above figure, lines *m* and *n* are parallel. What is the value of *c* in terms of *a* and *b*?

   A. $180-(a+b)$

   B. $180+a-b$

   C. $a+b-180$

   D. $a-b$

   E. $a+b$

12. The sum of two numbers that differ by 2 is *s*. In terms of *s*, what is the value of the greater of the two numbers?

   A. $\dfrac{s-2}{2}$

   B. $\dfrac{s+1}{2}$

   C. $\dfrac{s+1}{2}+1$

   D. $\dfrac{2s+2}{2}$

   E. $\dfrac{s+2}{2}$

$$a+b=x$$
$$ab=y$$

13. Given that the equations above are true, what is $\dfrac{1}{a}+\dfrac{1}{b}$ in terms of *x* and *y*?

   A. xy

   B. $x+y$

   C. $\dfrac{x}{y}$

   D. $\dfrac{y}{x}$

   E. $\dfrac{1}{xy}$

14. If $2a=\dfrac{3b^2}{c}$, what happens to the value of *a* when *b* and *c* are halved?

   A. *a* is halved.

   B. *a* is doubled.

   C. *a* is not changed.

   D. *a* is tripled.

   E. *a* is multiplied by 4.

15. The price of a television was first put on sale at 25 percent off, and then later the new price was increased by 30 percent. The final price was what percent of the initial price?

   A. 90

   B. 95

   C. 97.5

   D. 100

   E. 105

Plugging in Numbers Problem Set 2

1. Chris, Mark, and Trevor are brothers. The average age of Chris and Mark is x. The average age of Mark and Trevor is y. If Chris is 26 years old, how old is Trevor in terms of x and y?

   A. $\dfrac{x+y}{3}$

   B. $13+y-x$

   C. $26+2y-2x$

   D. $26-(y-x)$

   E. $\dfrac{2x+2y}{3}$

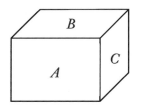

2. If A, B, and C are the areas of the three faces of the rectangular prism (as shown above), in terms of A, B, and C, what is the volume of the prism?

   A. $\sqrt{ABC}$

   B. $A^2B^2C^2$

   C. $\dfrac{A^2B^2}{C^2}$

   D. $\sqrt{\dfrac{AB}{C}}$

   E. $\sqrt{\dfrac{A^2B^2}{C}}$

3. Jan bought 7 CDs for d dollars each. She gave the cashier t ten dollar bills. How many dollars change should Jan receive in terms of d and t?

   A. $t-d$

   B. $10t-7d$

   C. $t-7d$

   D. $10-d$

   E. $t-7$

4. If the average (arithmetic mean) of a, b, and c is z, which of the following is the average of a, b, c and d?

   A. $\dfrac{3z+d}{4}$

   B. $\dfrac{3z+d}{3}$

   C. $\dfrac{z+d}{4}$

   D. $\dfrac{z+d}{3}$

   E. $\dfrac{3(z+d)}{4}$

5. If $a=b^4$ for any positive integer b, and $c=a+a^3$, what is c in terms of b?

   A. $b+b^3$

   B. $b^{12}+b^4$

   C. $b^{10}+b^4$

   D. b^7+b^3

   E. b^5+b^3

6. Yu is taking a test. There are A number of sections, each containing C number of questions. If Yu answers one question, on average, in T minutes, how long will it take her, in hours, to complete the test?

A. $\dfrac{AT}{60C}$

B. $\dfrac{ACT}{60}$

C. $\dfrac{60A}{CT}$

D. $\dfrac{AC}{T}$

E. ACT

7. If x and y are positive consecutive even integers where $y > x$, which of the following is equal to $y^2 - x^2$?

A. $2x$

B. $4x$

C. $2x + 2$

D. $4x + 2$

E. $4x + 4$

8. If the height of a cylinder is increased by 50% and the radius of its base is decreased by 50%, what is the ratio of the old volume to the new volume? (Hint: $V_{\text{Cylinder}} = \pi r^2 h$)

A. $4:9$

B. $8:3$

C. $2:1$

D. $8:1$

E. $4:3$

9. If the sum of the integers from –6 to an odd integer x inclusive is y, where $x > -6$, which of the following shows the relationship between x and y?

A. $y = -5x$

B. $(x+6) = 2y$

C. $x(x+1) = 2(y+21)$

D. $-6 + x = y$

E. $x = 3y$

10. If m is $\dfrac{3}{4}$ of n and n is $\dfrac{4}{5}$ of p, then what is the value of $\dfrac{m}{p}$?

A. $\dfrac{2}{3}$

B. $\dfrac{3}{4}$

C. $\dfrac{3}{5}$

D. $\dfrac{4}{9}$

E. $\dfrac{7}{9}$

11. 30 percent of x is equal to y percent of 50. What is x in terms of y?

   A. $\dfrac{1}{2}y$

   B. $\dfrac{3}{5}y$

   C. $\dfrac{5}{3}y$

   D. $2y$

   E. $\dfrac{10}{3}y$

12. Before starting school, Jennie, Chrisi, and Kim went shopping. Jennie spent $35 more than Chrisi and $15 more than Kim. If Jennie spent j, how much were their total purchases, in dollars, in terms of j?

   A. $j+50$

   B. $3j-50$

   C. $\dfrac{j+50}{3}$

   D. $j+150$

   E. $\dfrac{j+150}{3}$

13. If c percent of $a+b$ is equal to $4b$, what is the value of $\dfrac{a}{b}$ in terms of c?

   A. $\dfrac{c}{25}-1$

   B. $\dfrac{400}{c}-1$

   C. $\dfrac{100}{c}$

   D. $\sqrt{c-1}$

   E. $\dfrac{300}{c}$

14. In a high rise apartment building there is one washing machine for every 6 residents, one dryer for every 5 residents, and a parking space for every 4 residents. If there are x total washers, dryers, and parking spaces, then how many residents live in the high rise building?

   A. $\dfrac{37}{60}x$

   B. $\dfrac{60}{37}x$

   C. $40x$

   D. $120x$

   E. $60x$

15. If k divided by 7 yields a remainder of 5, which of the following, when divided by 7, yields no remainder?

   A. $2k$

   B. $3k$

   C. k^2+3

   D. $k+3$

   E. $k-3$

Calculator Maneuvers

Scrolling

Recall question **11** on the Backsolving Problem Set:

11. If $5^{k-4} \times 5^k + 16 = 41,$ what is the value of k?

    A. 0
    B. 1
    C. 2
    D. 3
    E. 4

If you backsolve this problem, you will simply put each choice in for k until the left side of the equation equals 41. This is significantly simpler both if you use your calculator and if you know all of your calculator's capabilities.

For instance, if you can scroll up on your calculator (most graphing calculators have this ability), you can first, smartly beginning with the middle choice, plug in 2 everywhere you see the letter k:

```
5^{2-4} * 5^2 + 16
```

When you hit enter, the calculator will return a result of 17. This means that 2 is clearly not the correct answer and that k is more likely to be a higher number.

If you next wanted to plug 3 in for k, there is no need to type the entire expression back out again. Just hit the up arrow twice to scroll to the previous entry and hit enter. This will give you an editable version of the expression, so you can go in and change both of your 2s to 3s:

```
5^{2-4} * 5^2 + 16
                            17
5^{3-4} * 5^3 + 16
                            41
```

Since this entry returns the answer 41, you have finished the problem—it must be choice **D**.

Most calculators will allow you to scroll up to many previous entries and answers, even after the calculator has been turned off and back on again.

Catalog

Many calculators will have a function that allows you to view all their operations alphabetically. The TI-84 has this option as the second command above the zero: $\boxed{0}$ ^{CATALOG}. The ALPHA mode will be automatically engaged, so you can jump directly to any letter of the alphabet by simply hitting the button whose letter corresponds to the first letter of the command you are looking for without first having to hit the green $\boxed{\text{ALPHA}}$ button.

Graphing

Graphing calculators allow you to view the graphs of functions, examine the function's points in a table, find intersection points of multiple graphs, calculate intercepts and extrema, and alter your view of the graph in multiple ways. They will even graph parametric equations, conics, and scatterplots, though those can be time-consuming both to learn and to use on a test.

Using the graphing tools can be especially valuable when asked to describe graphic features of functions. Consider the following question:

Example 1   In the function $y = \left| x^2 - 4 \right|$, for how many values of x does $y = 3$?

       A. 0

       B. 1

       C. 2

       D. 3

       E. 4

This question is not simply asking you to *solve* an equation. It's asking you to determine *how many* solutions there are. That is a complicated ask. You might think to sketch the graph of $y = \left| x^2 - 4 \right|$, but that function can be difficult to conceptualize. Your calculator, however, has no trouble conceptualizing it. If you graph both $y = \left| x^2 - 4 \right|$ and $y = 3$ on your calculator, you will see a display that looks like what is shown to the right.

This indicates that there are 4 values of x for which the function has y-values of 3: choice **E**.

Fraction Type

Your calculator should have a feature that allows you to write fractions with a horizontal fraction bar instead of by using the division slash. This simplifies how you go about entering information, particularly when multiple operations need to be done in the numerator or the denominator. The TI-84 has options for fraction types in the MATH menu, but it also has a shortcut to these types if you hit $\boxed{\text{F1}}$.

Shortcut Pop-up Menus

The TI-84 has shortcut pop-up menus for fraction types, hard-to-find operations, matrix building, and enumerated functions that can be accessed by hitting $\boxed{\text{F1}}$, $\boxed{\text{F2}}$, $\boxed{\text{F3}}$, and $\boxed{\text{F4}}$, respectively. Those require you to first hit the $\boxed{\text{ALPHA}}$ key and then use the top row of buttons normally associated with graphing. For example, $\boxed{\text{F3}}$ allows you to build a matrix of any size you choose (rows by columns), which will display on the screen and can be operated on with greater simplicity than if you were to utilize the $\boxed{\text{MATRIX}}$ button.

Graphing Calculator Reference

The following information applies chiefly to the TI-84 suite of calculators, but other graphing calculators have similar features.

The Basics

- The display of numbers is in white. It includes both the decimal point and the negative sign. Be sure not to confuse the negative sign with the subtraction symbol.
- Using the up or down arrows, you can reinsert previous answers or entries. Calculators that don't have this feature require you to use the ENTRY function, $\boxed{\text{2ND}} \rightarrow \boxed{\text{ENTER}}$, to recall entries.
- Caret $\left(\boxed{\wedge} \right)$ is used to raise to a power and is found above the four basic operations.
- $\boxed{x^2}$ can be used to both square or, with $\boxed{\text{2ND}}$, square root.
- The comma $\boxed{,}$ is used when an operation, like $\texttt{lcm}$, is performed on two numbers—you use the commas to separate the numbers.
- Parentheses should be used when operating with negative numbers or fractions to assure the order of operations, PEMDAS, is properly applied.

$\boxed{\text{MATH}}$ button (left column, third from top):

This button will give you four or five menus (MATH NUM CPX PRB FRAC) that will allow you to access many functions. These include:

▷ $\texttt{Frac}$: This will change a rational decimal to a fraction in lowest terms.

$\sqrt[3]{\ }$ and $\sqrt[x]{\ }$: These will take the specified root of the number you type inside the radical.

$\texttt{logBase(}$: You can calculate a logarithm in any base; you will see $\log_\square \left(\square \right)$.

$\texttt{abs(}$: Use this to take the absolute value of an expression.

$\texttt{lcm(}$: You can find the least common multiple of two numbers separated by a comma.

$\texttt{gcd(}$: You can find the greatest common divisor (factor) of two numbers separated by a comma.

$\texttt{nPr}$: This button sets up permutations: n things taken r at a time when order matters.

$\texttt{nCr}$: This button sets up combinations: n things taken r at a time when order doesn't matter.

$\texttt{!}$ (factorial): This multiplies a whole number by each whole number below it all the way down to 1.

Trigonometric and Logarithm Functions and Imaginary Numbers

- $\boxed{\text{SIN}}$, $\boxed{\text{COS}}$, and $\boxed{\text{TAN}}$ operate on angles to find trig ratios.
- $\boxed{\text{2ND}} \rightarrow \boxed{\text{SIN}}^{\text{SIN}^{-1}}$, $\boxed{\text{COS}}^{\text{COS}^{-1}}$, and $\boxed{\text{TAN}}^{\text{TAN}^{-1}}$ operate on trig ratios to find angles.
- $\boxed{\text{LOG}}$ means $\log_{10}$ and $\boxed{\text{LN}}$ means $\log_e$; otherwise use $\texttt{logBASE(}$ in $\boxed{\text{MATH}}$ menus.
- You can access the imaginary base number, i, using $\boxed{\text{2ND}} \rightarrow \boxed{.}$.

Graphing

$\boxed{\text{Y=}}$: Use to input functions where y has been isolated.

$\boxed{\text{WINDOW}}$: Use to adjust horizontal and vertical minima and maxima of graph screen and set scale for how frequently axes hash marks are shown.

$\boxed{\text{ZOOM}}$: Use to adjust view.

ZBox : to create, with the cursor, a rectangle whose interior will be enlarged

ZStandard : to return to basic window from –10 to 10 in each direction

ZTrig : produces a helpful window for trigonometric curves that approximates two cycles of a sine or cosine graph (with hash marks at critical points)

ZFit : adjusts window to show as much of inputted graph(s) as possible

$\boxed{\text{TRACE}}$: Have the cursor follow graph(s) in graph screen as the x and y values are reported at the bottom (use up and down arrows to toggle through multiple graphs).

$\boxed{\text{TABLE}}$ ($\boxed{\text{2ND}} \rightarrow \boxed{\text{GRAPH}}$) : You can view a list of x and y coordinates for inputted functions.

$\boxed{\text{CALC}}$ ($\boxed{\text{2ND}} \rightarrow \boxed{\text{TRACE}}$) : Use the following functions to calculate

zero : an x-intercept (or root); you will need to use the cursor to set left and right boundaries for the root you're looking for.

minimum and maximum : turning points (again, between left and right boundaries).

intersect : the intersection point between two curves nearest where the cursor selects the curves (toggle using up and down arrows to select the curves) .

NOTE: It is often easier to graph complicated functions and calculate their roots, turning points or transformations than to use algebraic methods like factoring or formulas.

Calculator Problem Set

Utilize the functions of the calculator to help you answer the questions in the following set.

1. What is the value of $\dfrac{3xy^2 - 17}{5\sqrt{z}}$ when $x = -4, y = -3,$ and $z = 625$?

   A. $-\dfrac{1279}{125}$

   B. -1

   C. $\dfrac{91}{125}$

   D. 1

   E. $\dfrac{1279}{125}$

2. If $a = \dfrac{37}{11}b$ and $b = \dfrac{13}{17}c,$ what is a in terms of c?

   A. $\dfrac{25}{14}c$

   B. $\dfrac{5}{2}c$

   C. $\dfrac{481}{187}c$

   D. $\dfrac{629}{143}c$

   E. $-4c$

3. What is the value of $\left|-4\right| - \left|20 - 33\right|$?

   A. -17

   B. -9

   C. 9

   D. 17

   E. 57

   absolute value symbol

4. The expression $\dfrac{3 + \dfrac{3}{5}}{2 + \dfrac{1}{10}}$ is equal to:

   A. $\dfrac{12}{7}$

   B. $\dfrac{9}{5}$

   C. $\dfrac{22}{7}$

   D. $\dfrac{22}{5}$

   E. $\dfrac{32}{7}$

5. What is the product of the complex numbers $(-6 + 5i)$ and $(6 + 5i)$?

   A. -61

   B. -10

   C. $25i$

   D. $-36 + 25i$

   E. 61

6. What is the sum of i^3 and i^5?

   A. -1

   B. $-i$

   C. 0

   D. i

   E. 1

7. If the least common multiple of 34 and 85 is a and the least common multiple of 33 and 12 is b, what is the least common multiple of $a - b$ and 57?

A. 3

B. 14

C. 19

D. 114

E. 798

8. Which of the following expressions is NOT equal to 1?

A. $\log 10$

B. $\ln e$

C. $\sin 90°$

D. i^4

E. $\tan 180°$

9. Which of the following equations is correct?

A. $_{10}P_4 = {}_{10}P_6$

B. $_{10}P_4 = {}_{10}C_6$

C. $_{10}C_4 = {}_{10}C_6$

D. $_{10}P_4 = {}_{10}C_4$

E. $_{10}P_4 = 6!$

10. For what value of x will the graphs of $y = x^3 - 2x^2 - 30$ and $y = \sqrt{x}$ intersect?

A. $\sqrt[6]{30}$

B. 2

C. 4

D. 6

E. They never intersect

11. If $\log_x y = 3$ and $\log_2 512 = x$, what is the value of y?

A. 2

B. 8

C. 9

D. 64

E. 729

12. The graphs of $y = -|x|$ and $y = \sqrt[3]{x}$ share which of the following quadrants?

A. I only

B. I and III

C. III only

D. III and IV

E. II and IV

13. What is the maximum value of

    $f(x) = -\left|(x-a)^2 - b\right| + c$ for each set of

    positive real numbers a, b, and c?

    A. a

    B. b

    C. c

    D. $a - b$

    E. $-c$

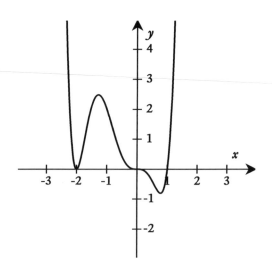

14. What are the equations of the vertical
    asymptotes for the graph of the function

    $y = \dfrac{2x-4}{x^2-4}$?

    A. $x = 2$ and $x = -2$

    B. $x = 2$ only

    C. $x = -2$ only

    D. $x = 0$ and $x = 2$

    E. $x = 0$, $x = 2$ and $x = -2$

15. The graph in the standard xy-coordinate plane
    above is the graph of which of the following
    functions?

    A. $a(x) = x(x+2)(x-1)$

    B. $b(x) = x^2(x+2)^3(x-1)$

    C. $c(x) = x^3(x+2)^2(x-1)$

    D. $d(x) = x^2(x-2)^3(x+1)$

    E. $e(x) = x^3(x-2)^2(x+1)$

Measuring

Oftentimes the figures of graphs or geometric shapes on an ACT test are drawn to scale. Unless specifically noted with a phrase such as "Figure not drawn to scale," you can assume that they are to scale. Because of this, there will be many opportunities to eliminate two, three, or even all four of the wrong choices simply due to their not matching how the diagram looks.

It is even possible, in some cases, to use a piece of paper, like your answer sheet, to mark the length of one part of the figure, and then accurately compare that length to the lengths of other parts of the figure. This can be particularly helpful if you are stuck, if you want to limit the choices to gain a better understanding of the problem, or if you want to confirm an answer you obtained mathematically.

Consider this example:

Example 1   A circle with center O has within it rhombus $DBEG$ and rectangle $ACHF$. All four points of rhombus $DBEG$ lie on the perimeter of rectangle $ACHF$. What is the radius of the circle?

   A. $\sqrt{93}$

   B.   13

   C.   14

   D.   17

   E. $\sqrt{485}$

The geometry involved in properly solving this problem can become cumbersome, having to do with obscure rules of circles and quadrilaterals that will show that a radius, like $\overline{OC}$ for example, can be viewed as a diagonal of a rectangle, like $BOEC$ (which itself is a rectangle because diagonals of rhombi are perpendicular), and since diagonals of rectangles have the same measure, $OC = BE = 17$.

If you didn't follow all of that, don't despair—many math teachers have trouble following it. You have a wonderful alternative:

   Take a piece of paper, like the answer sheet you will use to bubble in your answers, and place a corner at point B while laying the edge along $\overline{BE}$. If you make a mark where E meets the paper, you have just created a ruler with a measurement of 17 units on it. Label that mark 17. Likewise, you can rotate the paper so it lies along $\overline{BC}$ and get a second mark for 14.

   If you then put the corner of your paper at point O and check to see where the circle crosses the paper, it should indicate a radius that hits right about at the 17 mark (and certainly larger than 14).

   Examining the choices allows you to confidently choose choice **D** since 17 is the only viable choice according to your measurement.

Measuring Problem Set

The following problems can be solved either with or without measuring. Either use measuring to find the answer, or, if you can solve without measuring, use measuring to confirm your solution.

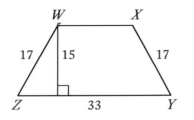

1. Trapezoid *WXYZ* has a height of 15 as shown. If the longer base has length 33 and both non-parallel sides have length 17, what is the length of *WX*?

   A. 12

   B. 13

   C. 17

   D. 21

   E. 24

2. Burks is experimenting with a graphing program. He instructs the program to draw a set of points, over a certain domain, that are all equidistant from a center point and have the quality that $x = \sqrt{4y - 2 - y^2}$. The graph below on the *xy*-coordinate plane represents the portion of a circle which results from his instructions and his domain restriction. What is the center point of the circle?

   A. (0,0)

   B. (1,0)

   C. (2,0)

   D. (0,2)

   E. (0,3)

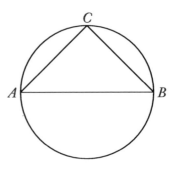

3. In the circle above, $AC = CB$ and $\overline{AB}$ is a diameter. What is $m\angle A$?

   A. 20°

   B. 30°

   C. 45°

   D. 60°

   E. 90°

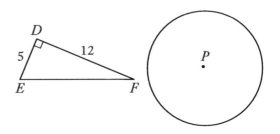

4. In the figure above, right triangle *DEF* can be superimposed over circle *P* such that all three of its vertices lie exactly on the circumference of the circle. What is the diameter of circle *P*?

   A. 5

   B. 7

   C. 13

   D. 16

   E. 20

Part II: Geometry and Graphing

Many students taking the ACT are a year or more removed from a dedicated Geometry class, so there is a tendency to feel uncertain or rusty at the first sign of a diagram or geometric concept. The abundance of formulas in both Geometry and Coordinate Geometry also leads to anxiety. This section is designed to prompt you to reboot those geometric and graphing concepts and formulas and then apply them in tailored problem sets.

First, fill in as much as you can in the *Geometry Nuts and Bolts* and *Coordinate Geometry and Graphing Nuts and Bolts* exercises. Any concept you cannot remember can be retrieved from the answer key to this book or looked up online.

The *Nuts and Bolts* exercises are each followed by two problem sets, the second more complicated than the first. Working through these sets will allow you to practice both using the formulas and recognizing when strategies like *backsolving* and *plugging in numbers* are appropriate. You'll also find that, when diagrams are shown, the *measuring* strategy can be very useful, as long as figures do not have a label that indicates they are not drawn to scale.

When no diagram is available, it is almost always a good idea to draw one yourself. Label, directly on your diagram, any information you can, and keep asking yourself, "What else can I find?" Often, you need to obtain a side length, angle measure, or coordinate pair that you are not actually asked for in order to discover the thing that you *are* asked for.

Geometry Nuts and Bolts

Angle Relationships

If two lines intersect, what is the relationship between…

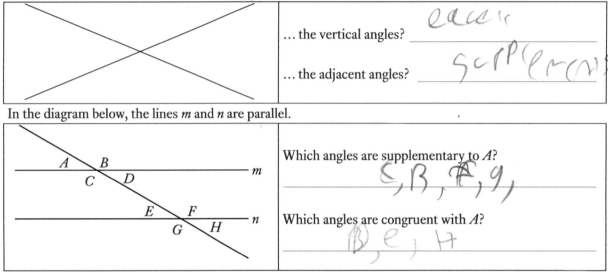

… the vertical angles?	*equal*
… the adjacent angles?	*supplement*

In the diagram below, the lines *m* and *n* are parallel.

	Which angles are supplementary to *A*? *E, B, F, g,*
	Which angles are congruent with *A*? *B, e, H*

Sums of Interior Angles

What is the sum of the interior angles in a…

triangle?	180
quadrilateral?	360
pentagon?	540

General Polygon Formulas for Interior Angles

Formula for sum of interior angles for a polygon with *n* sides	$(n-2) \times 180$
Measure of each interior angle for a regular polygon with *n* sides	$\dfrac{(n-2)}{N} \times 180$

Formulas to remember

	Area of a triangle: $\frac{1}{2}BH$
	Area of a rectangle: BH Perimeter of a rectangle: $2L+2W$
	Area of a square: S^2 Perimeter of a square: $4S$
	Area of a parallelogram: BH
	Volume of a rectangular solid: ABC Surface area of a rectangular solid: $2ab+2bc+2D$ Length of the diagonal in a rectangular solid: $a^2+b^2+c^2$
	Area of a trapezoid: $\frac{1}{2}H(b_1+b_2)$
	Circumference of a circle: $D\pi$ Area of a circle: πR^2
	Volume of a right circular cylinder: $\pi R^2 H$

Triangles

State the Pythagorean Theorem and its use	$A^2 + B^2 = C^2$ finding the Hypotenuse
Name 3 common sets of Pythagorean Triples	(3 , 4 , 5) (5 , 12 , 13) (8 , 15 , 17)

Draw each of the following		
An Isosceles Triangle	An Equilateral Triangle	A pair of similar triangles

In what proportion are the sides of an isosceles right (45-45-90) triangle?	1 : 1 : $\sqrt{2}$
In what proportion are the sides of a 30-60-90 triangle?	1 : $\sqrt{3}$: 2

What is the relationship between the largest side of any triangle and the other two sides?	it is less then the sum of other sides
In a triangle, what is true about the side opposite the largest angle? ...opposite the smallest angle?	Large Side = opposite Large angle ; same

Circles

How do you find the length of the arc of a circle?	$\frac{\emptyset}{360}$ $2\pi R$
How do you find the area of a sector?	$\frac{\emptyset}{360}$ $2\pi R^2$
What is the relationship between the degree measure of an **inscribed angle** and the degree measure of the arc it intercepts?	$\frac{1}{2}$ arc
What is the relationship between the degree measure of a **central angle** and the degree measure of the arc it intercepts?	arc

Geometry Problem Set 1

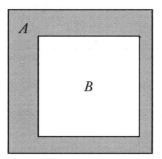

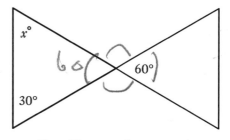

Note: Figure not drawn to scale

1. Square *A* with side length 5 completely encloses square *B* with side length 3.5. What is the area of the shaded region in the figure?

   A. 12.25

   B. 12.75

   C. 17.5

   D. 21.25

   E. 25

3. What is the value of *x*?

   A. 30

   B. 60

   C. 90

   D. 120

   E. 180

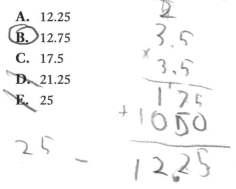

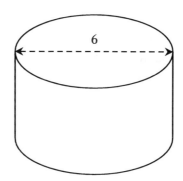

Note: Figure not drawn to scale

2. What is the surface area of the rectangular solid pictured above?

   A. 24

   B. 72

   C. 108

   D. 120

   E. 144

4. If the diameter of the right circular cylinder pictured above is half its height, what is its volume?

   A. 18π

   B. 72π

   C. 108π

   D. 208π

   E. 216π

5. The measures of three angles of a triangle are $39°$, $63°$, and $3x°$. What is the value of x?

    A. 18

    B. 26

    C. 39

    D. 78

    E. 86

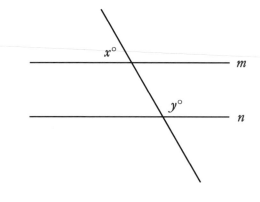

7. If m and n are parallel and $y = 2x$, what is $y - x$?

    A. 30°

    B. 60°

    C. 90°

    D. 120°

    E. 150°

6. What is the length of the edge of a cube that has the same volume as a rectangular solid with dimensions 2, 4, and 8?

    A. 4

    B. 6

    C. 8

    D. 12

    E. 16

8. In triangle ABC, side $AB = 7$ and side $BC = 4$. Which of the following could NOT be the length of side AC?

    A. 3

    B. 4

    C. 7

    D. 9

    E. 10

9. Which of the following could NOT be the lengths of the sides of a triangle?

   A. 3, 4, 5

   B. 6, 6, 8

   C. 5, 12, 14

   D. 4, 4, 8

   E. 3, 5, 7

10. An equilateral triangle with side length of $2a + 3$ and a square with sides of length $2a$ have equal perimeters. What is the measure of one side of the triangle?

    A. 3

    B. 4.5

    C. 6

    D. 9

    E. 12

11. In $\triangle NOP$, $PN = NO$ and $m\angle O = 30°$. What is the value of $m\angle N$?

    A. 30°

    B. 60°

    C. 90°

    D. 120°

    E. 150°

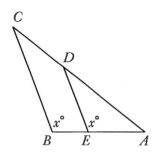

Note: Figure not drawn to scale

12. If $CB = 10$, $AD = 9$, and $DE = 6$, what is CD?

    A. 3

    B. 4

    C. 6

    D. 7.5

    E. 15

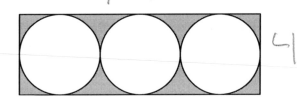

13. If three circles each with a radius of 2 are inscribed in the rectangle shown above, what is the area of the shaded region?

    A. 48

    B. 12π

    C. $48 + 12\pi$

    D. $12\pi - 48$

    E. $48 - 12\pi$

15. What is the diameter of the base of a right circular cylinder with height 5 and volume 80π ?

    A. 2

    B. 4

    C. 8

    D. 10

    E. 16

14. If the sides of a rectangle with area 24 are scaled down to half the original size, what will the new area be?

    A. 4

    B. 6

    C. 8

    D. 12

    E. 16

16. If the measure of each interior angle of a regular polygon is 150°, how many sides does the polygon have?

    A. 2.4

    B. 6

    C. 8

    D. 10

    E. 12

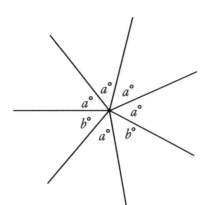

Note: Figure not drawn to scale

17. In the figure, if $a = 58,$ what is the value of b?

   A. 35

   B. 58

   C. 64

   D. 70

   E. 162.5

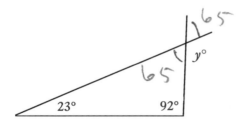

Note: Figure not drawn to scale

18. What is the value of y in the figure?

   A. 27

   B. 63

   C. 92

   D. 113

   E. 115

19. A trapezoid has an area of 80 square inches. If its height is 5 inches and one base is 19 inches, what is the length, in inches, of the other base?

   A. 3

   B. 12

   C. 13

   D. 16

   E. 25

20. In $\triangle ABC$, $m\angle A = 31°$ and $m\angle B = 68°$. Which of the following is true about the sides of $\triangle ABC$?

   A. $AB < AC < BC$

   B. $BC < AC < AB$

   C. $AC < AB < BC$

   D. $AC < BC < AB$

   E. $BC < AB < AC$

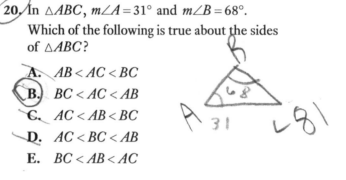

Geometry Problem Set 2

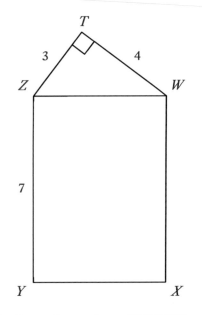

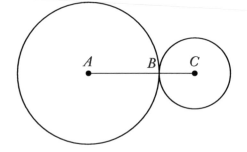

1. In the figure shown above, if *WXYZ* is a rectangle, what is the area of polygon *TWXYZ*?

   A. 12
   B. 35
   C. 41
   D. 47
   E. 50

3. In the figure above, two circles are externally tangent at point *B* and *AC* = 9. If the radius of the larger circle is twice that of the smaller, what is the area of the smaller circle?

   A. 2π
   B. 3π
   C. 4π
   D. 6π
   E. 9π

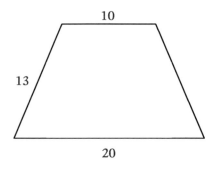

2. If the circumference of a circle is $\dfrac{8\pi}{5}$, what is the radius of the circle?

   A. $\dfrac{1}{5}$

   B. $\dfrac{1}{2}$

   C. $\dfrac{4}{5}$

   D. $\dfrac{6}{5}$

   E. $\dfrac{8}{5}$

4. What is the area, in square units, of the isosceles trapezoid above?

   A. 5
   B. 12
   C. 130
   D. 180
   E. 240

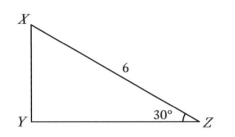

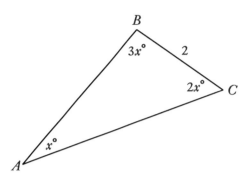

5. If $m\angle XYZ = 90°$, what is the area of triangle XYZ?

   A. $6\sqrt{3}$

   B. $\dfrac{9\sqrt{2}}{2}$

   C. $\dfrac{9\sqrt{3}}{2}$

   D. $9\sqrt{2}$

   E. $9\sqrt{3}$

Note: Figure not drawn to scale

7. In triangle ABC, what is the length of side AC?

   A. 4

   B. $2\sqrt{3}$

   C. 3

   D. 2

   E. $\sqrt{3}$

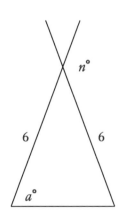

6. What is the value of a in terms of n?

   A. $180 - n$

   B. $180 - \dfrac{n}{2}$

   C. $\dfrac{n}{2}$

   D. $90 + n$

   E. $90 - n$

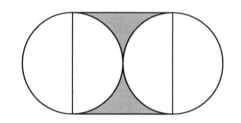

8. The radius of each of the circles above is 1. What is the area of the shaded region?

   A. $2\pi - 4$

   B. $8 - 2\pi$

   C. $4 - \pi$

   D. $4 - 2\pi$

   E. $\pi - 2$

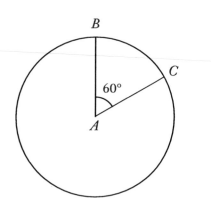

9. What is the area of sector ABC pictured in the circle above if A is the center of the circle and $AC = 3$?

    A. $\dfrac{\pi}{2}$

    B. $\dfrac{2\pi}{3}$

    C. $\dfrac{9\pi}{12}$

    D. π

    E. $\dfrac{3\pi}{2}$

10. In triangle ABC, the measure of angle B is equal to two-thirds of the sum of the measures of angles A and C. What is the measure of angle B?

    A. 60

    B. 72

    C. 90

    D. 108

    E. 120

11. In the circle above, $AC = BC$ and $\overline{AB}$ is a diameter with length $10\sqrt{2}$. What is the perimeter of $\triangle ABC$?

    A. 10

    B. 20

    C. $10 + 10\sqrt{2}$

    D. $20 + 10\sqrt{2}$

    E. 50

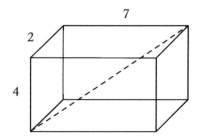

12. What is the length of the diagonal of the rectangular solid shown?

    A. $\sqrt{53}$

    B. $\sqrt{69}$

    C. 9

    D. 13

    E. 53

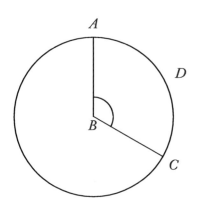

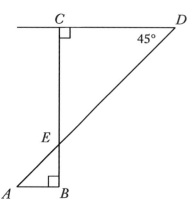

13. What is the length of arc $\overset{\frown}{ADC}$ if B is the center of the circle, $AB = 3,$ and $m\angle ABC = 120°$?

A. π

B. 2π

C. 3π

D. 6π

E. 9π

15. If BE is 6 and CE is 16, what is the length of AD?

A. $11\sqrt{2}$

B. $11\sqrt{3}$

C. 22

D. $22\sqrt{2}$

E. $22\sqrt{3}$

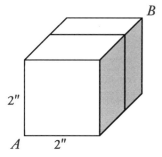

14. A rectangular prism is comprised of two identical cubes of side 2 inches. What is the length in inches of AB?

A. $3\sqrt{2}$

B. $2\sqrt{5}$

C. $2\sqrt{6}$

D. 5

E. 8

16. A triangle is inscribed within a cylinder of volume 250π such that two of the vertices of the triangle form the diameter of one base of the cylinder, and the third vertex lies directly above that diameter on the other base of the cylinder. The height of the cylinder is 10. What is the area of the triangle?

A. 25

B. 50

C. 100

D. 200

E. 250

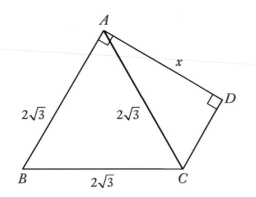

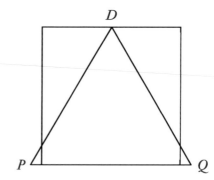

17. *ABC* is an equilateral triangle with each side equal to $2\sqrt{3}$. If $m\angle BAD = m\angle ADC = 90°$, what is the length of side *AD*?

   A. $\sqrt{2}$

   B. $\sqrt{3}$

   C. 3

   D. $3\sqrt{3}$

   E. 6

19. $\triangle PDQ$ is equilateral and each of its sides measures $\sqrt{12}$. What is the area of the square?

   A. $4\sqrt{3}$

   B. 9

   C. $6\sqrt{3}$

   D. 12

   E. 18

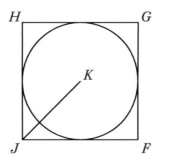

18. A circle with center K is inscribed in square *HGFJ*. $\overline{JK}$ bisects $\angle HJF$ and has the length of 2. What is the radius of the circle?

   A. 1

   B. $\dfrac{\sqrt{2}}{2}$

   C. $\sqrt{2}$

   D. 2

   E. $2\sqrt{2}$

20. What is the measure of an exterior angle of a regular hexagon?

   A. 30°

   B. 60°

   C. 90°

   D. 120°

   E. 180°

Coordinate Geometry and Graphing Nuts and Bolts

What is the equation of a line in slope–intercept form?	$y = mx + B$	
What do *m* and *b* represent?	*m* $slope$	*b* $y-int$

Intercepts

How do you find the *y*-intercept of a line?	set $x = 0$
How do you find the *x*-intercept of a line?	set $y = 0$

Slope, Midpoint and Distance

What is the formula for the slope of a line connecting two points in the coordinate plane?		$\dfrac{y_1 - y_2}{x_1 - x_2}$	
What is the slope of a horizontal line?	0	What is the slope of a vertical line?	undefined
What is the relationship between the slopes of two lines that are parallel?		$=$	
What is the relationship between the slopes of two lines that are perpendicular?		negative recipicle	
What is the formula for the midpoint between two points in the coordinate plane?		$\dfrac{x_1 + x_2}{2}, \dfrac{y_1 + y_2}{2}$	
What is the formula for the distance between two points in the coordinate plane? From where is this derived?		$D = \sqrt{(x_2 - x_1)^2 + (y_2 - y_1)^2}$	

Circles and Parabolas

What is the equation of a circle?	$(x - H)^2 + (y - K)^2 = R^2$
What is the equation of a parabola in vertex form?	$y = a(x - H)^2 + K$

Transformations

What happens to the point (x, y) when…	
	… it is reflected across the *x*-axis $\quad x, -y$
(x, y)	… it is reflected across the *y*-axis $\quad -x, y$
	… it is reflected across the origin $\quad -x, -y$

Coordinate Geometry and Graphing Problem Set 1

1. Point A has the geometric coordinate of $(5, 4)$. Point B can be found at $(5, 7)$. What is the distance between point A and point B?

   A. -3

   B. 0

   C. 3

   D. $2\sqrt{3}$

   E. $3\sqrt{2}$

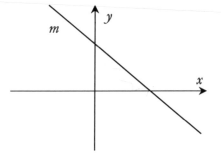

3. Which of the following could be the equation of the line m shown in the diagram above?

   A. $y = x + 3$

   B. $y = -x - 1$

   C. $y = 2x + 2$

   D. $y = -8x - 2$

   E. $y = -x + 3$

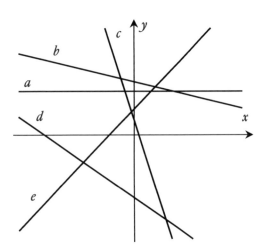

2. Place the above lines in order of *increasing* slopes:

   A. a, b, c, d, e

   B. d, c, b, e, a

   C. c, d, b, a, e

   D. c, e, d, b, a

   E. a, e, b, d, c

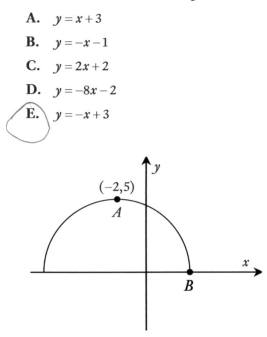

4. Point A is the peak of the semi-circle shown. What is the x-coordinate of point B?

   A. 2

   B. 3

   C. 4

   D. 5

   E. 6

5. Line t has a positive slope and passes through the point (2, 4). Which of the following could NOT be true?

   A. Line t passes through the origin.

   B. Line t has a negative y-intercept.

   C. Line t has a positive y-intercept.

   D. Line t has an x-intercept of 2.

   E. Line t has an x-intercept of –2.

7. The line that passes through (–5, 3) and has a slope of $-\dfrac{1}{2}$ also passes through (3, q). What is q?

   A. 1

   B. –1

   C. –2

   D. –3

   E. –5

8. What is the reflection of the point (3, 5) across the x–axis?

   A. (5, 3)

   B. (–3, –5)

   C. (–5, 3)

   D. (–5, –3)

   E. (3, –5)

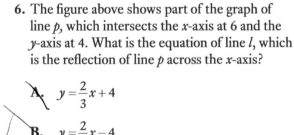

6. The figure above shows part of the graph of line p, which intersects the x-axis at 6 and the y-axis at 4. What is the equation of line l, which is the reflection of line p across the x-axis?

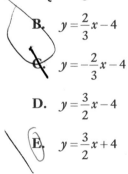

   A. $y = \dfrac{2}{3}x + 4$

   B. $y = \dfrac{2}{3}x - 4$

   C. $y = -\dfrac{2}{3}x - 4$

   D. $y = \dfrac{3}{2}x - 4$

   E. $y = \dfrac{3}{2}x + 4$

9. What is the equation of a line parallel to and three units to the right of the y-axis?

   A. $x = 3$

   B. $x = -3$

   C. $x = 0$

   D. $y = 3$

   E. $y = -3$

10. What is the equation of the line perpendicular to $y = 2x + 4$ that passes through (4, 6)?

   A. $y = 2x + 6$

   B. $y = -2x + 8$

   C. $y = -\dfrac{1}{2}x - 8$

   D. $y = -\dfrac{1}{2}x + 8$

   E. $y = -\dfrac{1}{2}x + 4$

11. If a and k are both positive for the graph $y = a(x-h)^2 + k$, which of the following points CANNOT lie on this graph?

A. $(-2, 1)$

B. $(2, 1)$

C. $(-1, 2)$

D. $(1, 2)$

E. $(2, -1)$

12. In the xy-coordinate plane, what is the distance between points $D(-13, 9)$ and $E(11, 16)$?

A. 7

B. 24

C. 25

D. 31

E. 84

13. $\overline{PQ}$ lies in the xy-coordinate plane. What are the coordinates of the midpoint of $\overline{PQ}$ if P is located at $(-7, -1)$ and Q is located at $(12, 9)$?

A. $(2.5, 4)$

B. $(2.5, 8)$

C. $(5, 5)$

D. $(5, 8)$

E. $(9.5, 5)$

14. The midpoint of a line segment in the xy-plane is $(-1, 12)$. If one endpoint of the segment is $(3, 8)$, what is the other endpoint?

A. $(-5, 10)$

B. $(-5, 16)$

C. $(1, 4)$

D. $(1, 10)$

E. $(7, 4)$

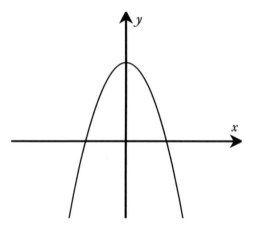

15. The graph above represents $f(x)$. The area underneath $f(x)$ and above the x-axis is 7. What is the area underneath $f(x-1)$ above the x-axis?

A. 5

B. 6

C. 7

D. 8

E. 10

Coordinate Geometry and Graphing Problem Set 2

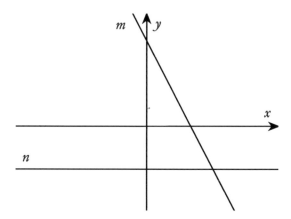

3. If the graphs $y = 3x^2 - 4$ and $y = mx + 2$ intersect at $(2, b)$, what is the value of m?

A. -2

B. 0

C. 3

D. 4

E. 6

1. What is the area of the triangle bounded by the y-axis, m, and n if m is given by $y = 6 - 3x$ and n by $y = -3$?

A. 4.5

B. 9

C. 13.5

D. 18

E. 27

4. Two endpoints of a diameter of a circle in a coordinate plane are $(-2, 13)$ and $(-14, 17)$. How far is the center of the circle from the origin?

A. 8

B. 15

C. 17

D. 25

E. 60

2. In the xy-coordinate plane, the point $(-8, 3)$ is shifted 10 units up and 12 units to the right. What are the coordinates of the new point?

A. $(2, -9)$

B. $(2, 15)$

C. $(4, -9)$

D. $(4, 13)$

E. $(18, 15)$

5. The line k in the xy-coordinate plane is given by the equation $3x + 2y = 12$. Line j has a slope that is twice the slope of line k and a y-intercept that is half the y-intercept of line k. What is the equation of line j?

A. $y = 3x + 3$

B. $y = -3x + 3$

C. $y = -3x - 3$

D. $y = -3x + 12$

E. $y = 3x + 12$

6. What is the *y*-intercept of a line in the *xy*-coordinate plane that contains the points $(5, 10)$ and $(2, 1)$?

A. $\left(0, \dfrac{5}{3}\right)$

B. $(0, -5)$

C. $\left(\dfrac{5}{3}, 0\right)$

D. $(3, -5)$

E. $(3, 0)$

7. A circle in the *xy*-coordinate plane is tangent to both the *x*-axis and the *y*-axis. If the center of the circle is $(4, 4)$, which of the following points is located on the circle?

A. $(8, 8)$

B. $(8, 4)$

C. $(6, 6)$

D. $(2, 0)$

E. $(-4, 0)$

8. What are the center and radius of the circle whose equation is $(x+3)^2 + (y-2)^2 = 13$?

A. Center $= (3, -2)$; Radius $= 13$

B. Center $= (3, -2)$; Radius $= \sqrt{13}$

C. Center $= (-2, 3)$; Radius $= \sqrt{13}$

D. Center $= (-3, 2)$; Radius $= 13$

E. Center $= (-3, 2)$; Radius $= \sqrt{13}$

9. What is the equation of a circle with center $(2, 3)$ that passes through the point $(1, 1)$?

A. $(x+2)^2 + (y+3)^2 = 5$

B. $(x+2)^2 + (y+3)^2 = \sqrt{5}$

C. $(x-2)^2 + (y-3)^2 = 5$

D. $(x-2)^2 + (y-3)^2 = \sqrt{5}$

E. $(x-2)^2 - (y-3)^2 = 5$

10. What is the center of the circle given by the equation $x^2 - 10x + y^2 + 6y + 2 = 0$?

A. $(5, -3)$

B. $(-5, 3)$

C. $(-5, -3)$

D. $(10, -6)$

E. $(-10, 6)$

Part III: Numbers and Operations

Questions involving number types, relationships, or operations require a mathematical vocabulary. To answer them successfully, you'll also want to be comfortable with much of what your calculator has to offer as well as strategies like **backsolving** and ***plugging in numbers***. Use the problem sets that follow to strengthen your skills of identifying and implementing strategy where appropriate.

This section includes notes and problem sets on topics that emphasize arithmetic fluency:

- Number Terms and Comparisons
- Ratios and Proportions
- Sequences
- Percent

Often, these topics will bleed into other areas like Algebra or Statistics, but they are rooted in their exploration of relationships between numbers.

Number Terms

The following definitions make translating arithmetic and algebra problems easier. Pay particular attention to the subtle differences in the various types of numbers.

Whole number   any number without a fractional or negative part {0, 1, 2, 3...}

Digit   one of the whole numbers 0–9 which has a place value in larger numbers or decimals

Integer   any positive or negative whole number; those numbers that get labels on a number line

Multiple of _n_   a number that is divisible by the integer _n (4, 12, and 88 are all multiples of 4)_

Factor of _n_   an integer by which _n_ is divisible _(the positive factors of 6 are 1, 2, 3, and 6)_

Rational number   a number that can be expressed as the ratio (fraction) of two integers

Irrational number   any non-repeating, non-terminating decimal, like π or $\sqrt{2}$

Prime number   a positive integer with exactly two positive factors, 1 and itself

Real number   any number, positive or negative, that falls along a continuous number line

Remainder   the amount left over when one integer is divided by another

Exponent   a number which indicates how many times another number is multiplied by itself

Root   a number which is multiplied by itself a number of times to produce another number

Absolute value   the distance a quantity is from zero (always non-negative)

Set   a collection of distinct elements, usually depicted within braces and separated by commas

Sequence   an ordered set of numbers that follow a rule

Consecutive   following in unbroken order

Comparing Numbers: Smaller vs. Greater

Some problems ask you to find the least or smallest number out of a group of numbers or to compare two numbers and determine which one is smaller. These are easiest to answer by converting the numbers to decimals on your calculator.

COMPARISON TRICK: Subtract any two numbers on your calculator. If the answer is positive, the first number in your subtraction must have been larger.

Negatives

Negative numbers are always smaller than positive numbers; however, unlike positive numbers, the "larger" the negative number, the _smaller_ it is. For instance, although 100 is larger than 50, –100 is _smaller_ than –50. One way to clear this up is to plot the numbers on a traditional number line: the farther to the left a number sits, the smaller it is; the farther to the right a number sits, the larger it is.

$$-100 \quad -50 \quad 0 \quad 50 \quad 100$$

Number Terms Problem Set

1. If h is a negative integer, which of the following could be h?

  A. −2.5
  B. −2
  C. −0.5
  D. 0
  E. 3

2. Which of the following does not equal the cube of an integer?

  A. −8
  B. 0
  C. 1
  D. 9
  E. 27

3. When the integer h is divided by 11, the remainder is 4. Which of the following is a possible value of h?

  A. 33
  B. 34
  C. 35
  D. 36
  E. 37

4. If the remainder is 3 when a positive integer b is divided by 9, what is the remainder when $b + 4$ is divided by 9?

  A. 3
  B. 4
  C. 5
  D. 6
  E. 7

5. How many odd numbers between 30 and 40 have precisely two distinct prime factors?

  A. 1
  B. 2
  C. 3
  D. 4
  E. 5

6. If n is the number of terms in a series of consecutive positive integers, for what value of n will the sum of the series always be even?

  A. 2
  B. 3
  C. 4
  D. 5
  E. 6

7. How many positive three-digit integers have 9 as their middle digit?

  A. 19
  B. 20
  C. 90
  D. 100
  E. 900

8. On a number line, point P is at −2 and is 12 units away from point Q. What are the possible locations for point Q on the number line?

  A. −14 and 10
  B. −14 and 14
  C. −10 and 10
  D. −10 and 14
  E. 10 and 14

9. Which of the following is NOT a factor of 3003?

    A. 3

    B. 7

    C. 9

    D. 11

    E. 13

10. If the sum of 5 consecutive integers is 100, then what is the greatest of these integers?

    A. 16

    B. 18

    C. 20

    D. 22

    E. 24

11. If a is a two-digit number whose tens digit is three times its units digit, which of the following must be true?

    A. a is a multiple of 3

    B. a is a multiple of 6

    C. a is odd

    D. a is greater than 30

    E. a is less than 60

12. If n is the product of three prime numbers, each of which are greater than 2, whose *sum* is also a prime number, then what is the smallest possible value for n?

    A. 19

    B. 30

    C. 105

    D. 165

    E. 385

13. What is the least common multiple of 5, $3x$, $7y$, and $2xy$?

    A. xy

    B. $35xy$

    C. 210

    D. $210xy$

    E. $210x^2 y^2$

14. Which of the following numbers is NOT a real number?

    A. $-\sqrt{49}$

    B. $\sqrt{-49}$

    C. $\dfrac{-10}{\sqrt{49}}$

    D. $\dfrac{-10}{\sqrt{7}}$

    E. $\sqrt{7}$

15. If 20 more than a is negative and 25 more than a is both positive and prime, which of the following could be the value of a?

    A. -26

    B. -25

    C. -22

    D. -21

    E. -20

Ratios and Proportions

Ratios

A **ratio** is the size or number of one thing in relation to another.

Example 1   If x:y is in the ratio of 1:2, then if $x = 1$, $y = 2$. But if $x = 2$, $y = 4$.

Try it 1 Give three pairs of numbers in the ratio 2:5.

A part-to-part ratio   compares the quantities of two different items: for example, 5 apples to 11 oranges.

A part-to-whole ratio   compares the quantity of one item to the total number of items: for example, 5 apples to 16 total pieces of fruit.

Proportions

There are several ways to solve ratio problems, but the most straightforward is to use proportions.

A **proportion** is an equation showing that two ratios are equal. To solve a proportion, you can cross-multiply and solve for the given variable.

Example 2   The ratio of pencils to pens in Jared's backpack is 3:4. If Jared has 12 pens, how many pencils does he have?

$$\frac{3 \text{ pencils}}{4 \text{ pens}} = \frac{x \text{ pencils}}{12 \text{ pens}}$$

$\frac{3}{4} = \frac{x}{12}$ can be solved by cross-mulitplying. You get $4x = 36$, so to solve for x, divide each side by 4 and $x = 9$. Thus, Jared has 9 pencils.

Sometimes, it may be necessary to rewrite a part-to-part ratio as a part-to-whole ratio.

Example 3   Tyra needs 42 baked goods for the school bake sale. Her friend asked her to bring five times more brownies than cookies. How many brownies does she need to bake?

The ratio of brownies to cookies is 5:1, so the ratio of brownies to total baked goods is 5:6 (the 6 comes from 5+1). Since she needs 42 baked goods, you can set up and solve the following proportion where x = the number of brownies.

$$\frac{5}{6} = \frac{x}{42} \qquad \rightarrow \qquad 6x = 210 \qquad \rightarrow \qquad x = 35$$

Therefore, Tyra needs to bake 35 brownies.

Sometimes you will see a proportion question where you are asked to find the ratio of two of the variables.

Example 4   If $\dfrac{x}{6} = \dfrac{y}{15}$, what is the ratio of x to y?

You can cross-multiply, so $15x = 6y$. Then solve for x: $x = \dfrac{6}{15}y = \dfrac{2}{5}y$. Now divide both

sides by y, so $\dfrac{x}{y} = \dfrac{2}{5}$.

Proportionality: Direct and Inverse

There are two types of proportionality: direct and inverse. It is important to understand what each means and how to recognize each one.

Directly Proportional

If y is directly proportional to x, then $y = kx$, where k is a constant.

Example 5   Assume y is directly proportional to x. If x is 3 when y is 12, then what is x when y is 32?

$y = kx$ or $12 = 3k$. Therefore, $k = 4$, and when y is 32, we solve for x as follows: $32 = 4x$, so $x = 8$.

Inversely Proportional

If y is inversely proportional to x, then $y = \dfrac{k}{x}$, where k is a constant.

Example 6   Assume y is inversely proportional to x. If x is 3 when y is 6, then what is x when y is 24?

Solve using $y = \dfrac{k}{x}$, or $6 = \dfrac{k}{3}$. Solving for k, you get $k = 18$. Now we know that $y = \dfrac{18}{x}$, and we

can solve for x with $y = 24$. $y = 24 = \dfrac{18}{x}$ so $x = \dfrac{18}{24} = \dfrac{3}{4}$.

Ratios and Proportions Problem Set

1. If the ratio of boys to girls in the class is 3:5 and there are 48 students, how many of them are girls?

   A. 5

   B. 13

   C. 26

   D. 30

   E. 48

4. If $\dfrac{x}{3} = \dfrac{y}{14}$, what is the ratio of x to y?

   A. 14:3

   B. 3:14

   C. 11:1

   D. 12:2

   E. 5:6

2. In a bag of red and blue candies, the ratio of red candies to blue candies is 3:4. If the bag contains 120 blue candies, how many red candies are there?

   A. 30

   B. 50

   C. 60

   D. 90

   E. 100

5. The weight of a box of 50 pencils is 9 ounces. What is the weight, in ounces, of 15 pencils?

   A. 2.3

   B. 2.7

   C. 4.6

   D. 12

   E. 30

3. If I can walk $\dfrac{5}{7}$ of the way to Ian's house in 30 minutes, how long will it take me to walk the rest of way to Ian's house at the same rate?

   A. 6 minutes

   B. 10 minutes

   C. 12 minutes

   D. 14 minutes

   E. 21 minutes

6. Joe makes enough hot chocolate for 7 people by mixing 17 tablespoons of mix with 6 cups of milk. If Joe wants to make hot chocolate for 21 people, how much milk does he need?

   A. 7 cups

   B. 8.5 cups

   C. 18 cups

   D. 21 cups

   E. 51 cups

7. Sarah opened up a bag of only green, orange, and blue M&Ms. If the ratio of the colors were 2:1:4 respectively, how many M&Ms could have been in the bag?

   A. 8
   B. 34
   C. 54
   D. 62
   E. 77

8. The ratio of boys to girls in a class is 2:3. If one-fifth of the girls in the class get A's on a Math test, what is the ratio of the number of boys to the number of girls who did not get A's?

   A. 4:5
   B. 5:6
   C. 6:5
   D. 5:4
   E. 10:7

9. ACME sells hats in only three colors: black, blue and red. The colors are in the ratio of 3:4:5. If the store has 20 blue hats, how many hats does it have altogether?

   A. 40
   B. 55
   C. 60
   D. 65
   E. 70

10. Jake, Anna, and Josh pooled their money to buy a birthday gift for their mom, sharing the cost in a ratio of 3:4:5. If the gift cost $45, how much did Anna contribute?

   A. $9.00
   B. $10.00
   C. $13.50
   D. $15.00
   E. $22.50

11. If Joan has exactly 25 minutes of homework for every 40 minutes of class, how many hours of homework does she have on a day when she has 6 hours of class?

   A. 2 hrs 15 min
   B. 2 hrs 45 min
   C. 3 hrs
   D. 3 hrs 15 min
   E. 3 hrs 45 min

12. If the ratio of fish to birds in the pet store is 7:2 and the ratio of birds to ferrets is 7:1, what is the ratio of fish to ferrets?

   A. 49:2
   B. 2:1
   C. 1:1
   D. 14:7
   E. 14:3

13. Nitin has 30 beans, 18 of which are red and 12 of which are blue. Jill has 20 beans, all of which are either red or blue. If the ratio of the red beans to the blue beans is the same for both Nitin and Jill, then how many blue beans does Jill have?

    A. 6
    B. 8
    C. 10
    D. 12
    E. 16

14. I carefully mix my cereal each morning so that the bowl contains O's, sugar flakes, and honey puffs in the ratio of 2:5:7. If my bowl contains ½ cup of O's, how many cups of honey puffs does it contain?

    A. 1 cup
    B. $\frac{5}{4}$ cup
    C. $\frac{7}{4}$ cup
    D. $\frac{3}{2}$ cup
    E. $\frac{7}{2}$ cup

15. x is inversely proportional to y. If x is 4 when y is 3, what is y when x is 6?

    A. 1
    B. 2
    C. 5
    D. 7
    E. 12

16. If $a = 9$ when $b = 3$ and a and b are directly proportional, what does a equal when $b = 21$?

    A. 3
    B. 7
    C. 21
    D. 63
    E. 72

17. If r and q are directly proportional and $\frac{r}{q} = 4$, what is q if $r = 28$?

    A. 2
    B. 3
    C. 6
    D. 7
    E. 14

18. A machine can fill 150 chip bags in one hour. At this rate, how many chip bags can the machine fill in 12 minutes?

    A. 15

    B. 20

    C. 22.5

    D. 30

    E. 50

19. If m is inversely proportional to n and $m = 12$ when $n = 5$, what is the value of n when $m = 6$?

    A. 2.5

    B. 3

    C. 9

    D. 10

    E. 60

20. Which of the following represents the graph of a directly proportional function?

A straight line with positive slope passing through the origin.

A straight line with a negative slope passing through the origin.

A straight line with a positive slope and a positive y-intercept.

    A. I only

    B. I and II

    C. I and III

    D. II and III

    E. III only

Sequences

A sequence is simply a list of terms whose order and elements are governed by a specific rule. Some sequence questions can best be answered by recognizing and applying a certain pattern. With such questions, it is useful to identify how "deep" the pattern goes (how many terms until the pattern repeats), and then determine what postion in the pattern you are looking for.

Other sequence questions use a formula applied to each term. There are two main types of formulaic sequence types about which questions are frequently asked on the ACT: Arithmetic and Geometric.

Arithmetic Sequences

Arithmetic sequences have a **common difference** between subsequent terms. Note that this difference may be *positive* or *negative*.

Example 1   The sequence 1, 4, 7, 10, 13, … has a common difference of 3.

Example 2   the sequence 24, 19, 14, 9, 4, … has a common difference of –5.

The formula for the nth term of an arithmetic sequence is

$$a_n = a_1 + d(n-1) \text{ where}$$

a_n = the nth term in the sequence

a_1 = the first term in the sequence

d = the common difference

The sum of the first n terms in an arithmetic sequence is equal to the product of n and the average of the first and nth terms, given by

$$S_n = \frac{a_1 + a_n}{2}n$$

Geometric Sequences

Geometric sequences have a **common ratio** between subsequent terms. This common ratio may be any number, positive or negative.

Example 3   The sequence 2, 6, 18, 54, … has a common ratio of 3.

Example 4   The sequence $3, 1, \frac{1}{9}, \frac{1}{27}, \ldots$ has a common ratio of $\frac{1}{3}$.

The formula for the nth term of a geometric sequence is

$$a_n = a_1 r^{n-1} \text{ where}$$

a_n = the nth term in the sequence

a_1 = the first term in the sequence

r = the common ratio in the sequence

Sequences Problem Set

$$0, 1, 1, 2, 3, 5, \ldots$$

1. The sequence shown above is made up of what are known as Fibonacci numbers, where each term is the sum of the previous two terms. What is the 10th term of this sequence?

    A. 8
    B. 13
    C. 34
    D. 36
    E. 55

2. Simon repeatedly gives commands in the following order: jump, clap, crouch, snap. What will be Simon's 789th command?

    A. snap
    B. crouch
    C. clap
    D. jump
    E. roll over

$$1, 1, 2, 3, \ldots$$

3. In the above sequence, each term after the second term is the sum of the two terms that immediately precede it. How many of the first 1000 numbers in the sequence are odd?

    A. 333
    B. 500
    C. 665
    D. 666
    E. 667

$$13, 17, 21, 25, 29, \ldots$$

4. What is the 83rd term of the sequence shown above?

    A. 333
    B. 337
    C. 341
    D. 345
    E. 349

$$-25, -23, -21, \ldots$$

5. What is the sum of the first 25 terms of the sequence shown above?

    A. −25
    B. −15
    C. 0
    D. 15
    E. 25

$$1, 5, 9, 13, \ldots$$

6. What is the difference between the 20th and the 10th terms of the sequence shown above?

    A. 4
    B. 24
    C. 36
    D. 40
    E. 48

7. How many positive integers less than 300,000 are common multiples of 30, 40 and 50?

A. 250

B. 499

C. 500

D. 999

E. 1000

10. The fraction $\frac{1}{13}$ can be represented as the repeating decimal 0.076923076923… . What is the 70th digit after the decimal point in this decimal representation?

A. 2

B. 3

C. 6

D. 7

E. 9

8. The first three terms of a geometric sequence are 2, 3, and $\frac{9}{2}$. What is the fourth term in the sequence?

A. 5

B. 6

C. $\frac{27}{4}$

D. 9

E. $\frac{27}{2}$

4, 14, 34, 74, …

9. Each term after the first term in the sequence above is determined by first adding a to the preceding term and then multiplying by m. What is the value of a?

A. 1

B. 3

C. 4

D. 7

E. 10

Percent

Percent problems can most easily be solved with your calculator using the direct translation method, where you convert words into mathematical operators. **What** or **what percent** can be written as x, **of** as a multiplication symbol, and **is** as an equal sign. Remember to write percents in decimal form when they appear in equations. You can do this by moving the decimal point two places to the left and dropping the percent symbol. Here are a few examples:

Example 1   What is 35% of 50?

What becomes x

is becomes =

35% becomes 0.35

of becomes the multiplication symbol

$x = 0.35 \cdot 50$

$x = 17.5$

Example 2   40% of what number is 80?

$0.40 \cdot x = 80$

$x = 200$

Example 3   63 is what percent of 72?

$63 = x \cdot 72$

$0.875 = x$

Since the question asked for a percent, remember to convert 0.875 into 87.5%.

Example 4   80% of the times Isha ate at McDonald's last year, she ordered a Big Mac. If she ordered a Big Mac 36 times, how many times did Isha eat at McDonald's?

$0.80 \cdot x = 36$

$x = 45$

Sales tax   an additional amount you pay for goods or services based on a set tax rate (percent).
Use this formula: (**Total Price**) = (**original price**) $\times$ (1$\pm$**tax rate as decimal**).

Example 5   A dress is priced at $229. The sales tax is 5%. What is the total cost of the dress, including tax?

$\text{Cost} = 229(1 + 0.05)$

$= 229(1.05) = 240.45$

Discount and mark-up   A discount is a decrease in price, and a mark up is an increase in price.

These work similarly to a sales tax, and you can use the formula
New Price = Original×(1±**%change**).

As with sales tax, the change should be given as a *decimal*.

Example 6   A book that was originally $15 is marked "10% off." What is the new price?

$$\text{New price} = 15(1-0.10)$$
$$= 15(0.90) = 13.50$$

Example 7   Erwin has been a lifeguard the past three summers. In the second summer, his salary increased 5% from the first summer. In the third summer, his salary increased 8% from the second summer. What percent greater was his salary in the third summer than his salary in the first summer?

If Erwin's first-summer salary is represented by x, you can calculate the second-summer salary to be $x(1+0.05) = 1.05x$, and, consequently, you can calculate the third-summer salary to be $1.05x(1+0.08) = 1.05x(1.08) = 1.134x$. Since $1.134 = 1 + \%\text{change}$, the percent change is 0.134 or 13.4%. Erwin's salary in the third summer is a 13.4% increase from his salary in the first summer. Notice, this is different than the straight 13% increase you would get if you simply added 5% and 8

Percent change   Percent change can be found as a decimal using the formula $\text{change} = \dfrac{\text{new-original}}{\text{original}}$.

Then convert to a percent, paying attention to whether the change is postitive or negative.

Example 8   A pair of jeans is on sale for $33.75. The usual cost is $45. What is the percent discount?

$$\text{Percent change} = \frac{33.75-45}{45} = \frac{-11.25}{45} = -0.25$$

The percent change is negative because it is a discount, so the jeans are 25% off.

Percent Problem Set

1. What is 46% of 1200?

 A. 420
 B. 456
 C. 460
 D. 552
 E. 600

2. 30 is 12% of what number?

 A. 3.6
 B. 40
 C. 250
 D. 280
 E. 300

3. What is $\frac{1}{5}$ of 40% of 600?

 A. 48
 B. 60
 C. 64
 D. 120
 E. 240

4. If 35% of x is 7, what is 75% of x?

 A. 5.25
 B. 14
 C. 15
 D. 20
 E. 21

5. 30% of 90 is 25% of which number?

 A. 75
 B. 85
 C. 95
 D. 108
 E. 120

6. If Keenan only answered 18 questions right on the test and he got a 60%, how many questions were on the test?

 A. 10
 B. 12
 C. 15
 D. 26
 E. 30

7. Sarah has 20 pens and 30 pencils. If 15% of the pens are red and 30% of the pencils are red, then what is the percentage of red writing utensils?

 A. 12%
 B. 32.2%
 C. 24%
 D. 33.3%
 E. 41%

8. A $30 soccer ball is on sale for 15% off. If 6% sales tax is added to the sale price, what is the cost of the ball?

 A. $25.50
 B. $27.03
 C. $27.30
 D. $27.72
 E. $28.62

9. An employee earns $800 per week, but must pay the following taxes: 16% Federal Income Tax, 5% State Income Tax, and 7% Payroll Tax. How much, in dollars, is remaining after all taxes are taken out?

   A. 520
   B. 576
   C. 772
   D. 828
   E. 1024

10. The Merriweather Mockingbirds won 17.5% of their games and lost 33 games. How many games did they play?

    A. 35
    B. 40
    C. 42
    D. 50
    E. 50.5

11. Ned read 60% of a book. Melanie read 25% of the same book. If Ned read 300 pages, how many fewer pages did Melanie read?

    A. 75
    B. 100
    C. 125
    D. 175
    E. 215

12. A suit originally priced at $200 is discounted to $170. What is the percent of discount on this suit?

    A. 15%
    B. 17%
    C. 30%
    D. 70%
    E. 85%

13. Isaac works at a restaurant. He earns $5 an hour plus 20% tip on all the food he sells. If he earned $72 in 6 hours, how many dollars worth of food did he sell?

    A. 42
    B. 30
    C. 142
    D. 210
    E. 365

14. What is 35% greater than the number 35% less than 320?

    A. 280.8
    B. 320
    C. 367.6
    D. 435
    E. 556.87

15. A movie grossed $33 million in its first weekend and $30 million in its second weekend. Approximately what is the percent decrease?

    A. 1%
    B. 3%
    C. 9%
    D. 11%
    E. 15%

16. Roberta is a photographer. At the start of October, Roberta has 150 photos, which is 20% more than the number of photos she had at the start of September. How many photos did she take in the month of September?

    A. 25
    B. 50
    C. 110
    D. 125
    E. 135

17. A hotel charges $126 per night for a room. Customers who wish to park their cars are charged an additional $14 per night. For a two-night stay with parking, what percentage of the cost is parking?

    A. 5%
    B. 10%
    C. 11%
    D. 14%
    E. 22%

18. If the Smiths paid a total of $86.77 at the restaurant including the 20% tip, about how much did they pay without tip?

    A. $53.12
    B. $64.22
    C. $72.31
    D. $76.55
    E. $90.25

19. A textbook is sold at a 30% discount. After a 5% sales tax, the total price is $102.73. What was the original pre-tax price of the book?

    A. $65.43
    B. $99.99
    C. $109.99
    D. $139.77
    E. $169.23

20. A number is decreased by 30%. The resulting number is then increased by 40%. Which of the following would result in the same final answer?

    A. Decrease the original by 10%
    B. Decrease the original by 2%
    C. Increase the original by 2%
    D. Increase the original by 10%
    E. Increase the original by 35%

Part IV: Algebra and Functions

When Algebra problems have multiple choices, there are almost always opportunities to use strategies like ***backsolving*** or ***plugging in numbers***. Still, algebraic techniques, such as translating word problems, factoring, and applying exponent rules, are always worth practicing and refining. With such problems, you can assess whether "doing the algebra" is more efficient and then consider using a strategy either as a check or as an alternative if the algebra gets messy.

This section includes notes and problem sets on topics that emphasize algebra skills and function notation:

- Algebraic Expressions, Equations, and Inequalities
- Word Problems
- Functions
- Exponents
- Absolute Value
- Distributing and Factoring

Algebraic Expressions

Words and phrases associated with

Addition   sum, plus, increased by, added to, more than, greater than

Subtraction   difference, minus, decreased by, subtracted from, less than (be careful of the order)

Multiplication   product, times, multiplied by, for every, of (for fractions), twice (two times)

Division   quotient, ratio, divided by, over, rate

Inequalities   is less than $(<)$, is greater than $(>)$, no more than $(\leq)$, no fewer than $(\geq)$, at most $(\leq)$, at least $(\geq)$, between (for example, $2 < x < 9$)

Terminology

Variable   a letter that represents a number or set of numbers

Constant   a number that is unassociated with a variable

Coefficient   a number multiplied by a variable

Term   a constant or a product of a coefficient and variables (also known as a monomial)

Equation   a statement that two expressions have the same value

Inequality   a statement that expressions have a relationship using $<$, $>$, $\leq$, $\geq$, or $\neq$

Evaluating an expression

You may be asked to evaluate an expression when variables hold particular values. For example, to evaluate the expression $-2x^3 + 5x$ when $x = 2$, substitute 2 for x in the expression. Remember to follow PEMDAS (parentheses, exponents, multiplication/division, addition/subtraction):

Example 1 $-2(2)^3 + 5(2) = -2(8) + 10 = -16 + 10 = -6$

Simplifying an expression

To simplify an expression, first distribute any negative signs (subtraction symbols) if necessary. Then, rearrange the expression so like terms are grouped. **Like terms** are terms that contain the same variables raised to the same power. For example, $4x$ and $-x$ are like terms because they both have x even though the coefficients are different. To combine like terms, add their coefficients. For example, $4x + (-x) = 3x$.

Example 2 $3n + 4m - 10n - 11 + m = (3n - 10n) + (4m + m) - 11 = -7n + 5m - 11$

Example 3 $3 - (4y + 5) - 7y = 3 - 4y - 5 - 7y = (-4y - 7y) + (3 - 5) = -11y - 2$

Algebraic Expressions Problem Set

1. If a, b, and c are all odd integers, which of the following is NOT necessarily an odd integer?

   A. $a + b + c$

   B. $a \times b \times c$

   C. $b - c - a$

   D. $a \times b + a + b$

   E. $a \times b + a \times c$

2. Charlie has built houses for 5 years less than twice as long as Molly has. If Molly has built houses for n years, which of the following expressions represents the number of years for which Charlie has built houses?

   A. $n - 5$

   B. $n + 5$

   C. $2n - 5$

   D. $2n + 5$

   E. $5 - 2n$

3. Kaili ran for m minutes yesterday. If Javi ran 5 minutes less than half as long as Kaili, how many minutes did Javi run in terms of m?

   A. $5 - \dfrac{1}{2}m$

   B. $5 + \dfrac{1}{2}m$

   C. $\dfrac{1}{2}m - 5$

   D. $2m - 5$

   E. $5m - \dfrac{1}{2}$

4. $y + 12$ is how much greater than $y - 9$?

   A. 3

   B. 12

   C. 21

   D. 22

   E. 31

5. Giorgio has a pocket full of quarters and dimes. If he has q quarters and d dimes, how much money does he have in cents?

   A. $q + d$

   B. $25q + 10d$

   C. $\dfrac{q}{25} + \dfrac{d}{10}$

   D. $\dfrac{25}{q} + \dfrac{10}{d}$

   E. $35(q + d)$

6. How many hours are there in d days and h hours?

   A. $24h + d$

   B. $24d + h$

   C. $(d + h)24$

   D. $\dfrac{d + h}{24}$

   E. $\dfrac{d}{24} + h$

7. If g is 3 less than the product of x and y, which of the following is an expression for g in terms of x and y?

   A. $x + y - 3$

   B. $3 - (x + y)$

   C. $3 - xy$

   D. $\dfrac{x}{y} - 3$

   E. $xy - 3$

8. Of the c cookies in a batch, s were sugar cookies. Which expression represents the fraction of cookies in the batch that were NOT sugar cookies?

   A. $\dfrac{s}{c}$

   B. $\dfrac{c}{s}$

   C. $\dfrac{c - s}{s}$

   D. $\dfrac{c - s}{c}$

   E. $\dfrac{s - c}{c}$

9. Which of the following equations is equivalent to the statement:
"When a number n is cubed, the result is 45 more than the product of 3 and m"?

   A. $3n = 45 + 3m$

   B. $3n = 45 + m^3$

   C. $n^3 = 45 - 3m$

   D. $n^3 = 45 + m^3$

   E. $n^3 = 45 + 3m$

10. If $d = c(c + 5)$, then $d - 2 = ?$

   A. $c^2 + 3c$

   B. $c^2 + 7c$

   C. $c^2 + 5c - 2$

   D. $c^2 - 5c + 2$

   E. $c^2 + 3$

11. What is the value of the expression $-ab + b^3 - 1$ if $a = 3$ and $b = -2$?

   A. -15

   B. -3

   C. 1

   D. 13

   E. 15

12. What is the value of $\dfrac{p}{q} - \dfrac{p}{q^2}$ when $p = 5$ and $q = -2$?

   A. $-\dfrac{15}{4}$

   B. $-\dfrac{15}{8}$

   C. $-\dfrac{10}{6}$

   D. $-\dfrac{5}{4}$

   E. $\dfrac{5}{4}$

13. If $\dfrac{a}{b} = 2$ and $\dfrac{c}{a} = 3$, what is the value of

$\dfrac{a+b+c}{a}$?

   A. 3.5

   B. 4

   C. 4.5

   D. 5

   E. 6

14. Which of the following is a simplified form of the expression $2 - (4 - 7y) - y$?

   A. $-2 + 6y$

   B. $2 - 6y$

   C. $-2 + 7y$

   D. $2 - 7y^2$

   E. $-2 - 8y$

15. Which of the following is a simplified form of the expression $3(5 + 7x) + 4 - 2x$?

   A. $8x + 12$

   B. $19x + 19$

   C. $17x + 15$

   D. $26x + 4$

   E. $32x$

Linear Equations and Inequalities

Solving Linear Equations and Inequalities

To solve an equation or inequality, you must isolate the variable. You may first need to simplify the expressions on both sides of the equation by distributing and/or combining like terms. Then, add or subtract to get the variable on one side and the constant terms on the other side. Finally, multiply or divide to isolate the variable.

Example 1 $-3(x+5) = x - 3$

$$-3x - 15 = x - 3 \quad \Rightarrow \quad -12 = 4x \quad \Rightarrow \quad \frac{-12}{4} = \frac{4x}{4} \quad \Rightarrow \quad -3 = x$$
$$+3x \qquad +3x$$

NOTE: Follow the same procedure with an inequality, but if you multiply or divide both sides by a negative number, you must flip the inequality symbol.

Literal Equations

A literal equation consists primarily of variables. You may be asked to solve for one of the variables in a literal equation. Isolate the variable the same way you would to solve a linear equation.

System of Equations

A system of linear equations in two variables consists of two equations and can be written in the following form, where $A, B, C, D, E,$ and F are constants: $Ax + By = C$
$$Dx + Ey = F$$

A **solution** to a linear system like this is an ordered pair (x, y) that satisfies both equations.

Infinite solutions   When one equation is just a multiple of the other, there will be infinitely many solutions.

No solutions   When the left side of one equation is a multiple of the left side of the other, but the right sides don't have the same relationship, there are no solutions.

One solution   If neither of the scenarios above is true, then there is a single solution (x, y).

Substitution Method

1. Solve one equation for one of its variables.
2. Substitute the expression from step 1 into the other equation and solve for the other variable.
3. Substitute the value obtained in step 2 into the equation from step 1 and solve.

Follow the steps to solve the linear system below.

Example 2 $-3x + 2y = 4$
$$4x + y = -9$$

Step 1	Step 2	Step 3
$4x + y = -9$	$-3x + 2y = 4$	$y = -4x - 9$
$y = -4x - 9$	$-3x + 2(-4x - 9) = 4$	$y = -4(-2) - 9$
	$-3x - 8x - 18 = 4$	$y = 8 - 9 = -1$
	$-11x = 22$	The solution is $(-2, -1)$.
	$x = -2$	

In the second step, if you get an equation that is never true, like $16 = 6$, there is no solution. If you get an equation that is always true, like $12 = 12$, there are infinitely many solutions.

Elimination Method

1. Multiply one or both equations by a constant so the coefficients of one variable are opposites.
2. Add the equations from step 1 to eliminate a variable, and solve for the remaining variable.
3. Substitute the value obtained in step 2 into one of the original equations and solve.

Follow the steps to solve the linear system below.

Example 3 $2x + 3y = 11$
$$5x - 2y = -20$$

Step 1	Step 2	Step 3
$2(2x + 3y = 11)$	$4x + 6y = 22$	$2x + 3y = 11$
$3(5x - 2y = -20)$	$15x - 6y = -60$	$2(-2) + 3y = 11$
	$19x = -38$	$3y = 15$
	$x = -2$	$y = 5$
		The solution is $(-2, 5)$.

Linear Equations and Inequalities Problem Set

1. If $6 + 3x = 27$, then $4x = ?$

    A. 7

    B. 24

    C. 28

    D. 44

    E. 144

2. If $5x + 4 = -4 + x$, then $x = ?$

    A. -8 $4x \cancel{10} = -8$

    B. -2

    C. 0

    D. 2

    E. 8

3. If $-6x - 11 = -2x + 5$, then $x = ?$

    A. -4

    B. -2 $-11 = 4x + 5$

    C. -1.5

    D. 2 $-16 = 4x$

    E. 4

4. If $\frac{x}{4} - 1 = -4$, then $x = ?$

    A. -20

    B. -12

    C. 4

    D. 12

    E. 20

5. If $8(x - 10) = -18$, then $x = ?$

    A. $-\dfrac{49}{4}$

    B. $-\dfrac{31}{4}$

    C. 0

    D. $\dfrac{31}{4}$

    E. 9

6. If $4(x + 2) + 5x = 3(x - 1) + 7$, then $x = ?$

    A. -12 $9x + 8 = 3x - 3 + 7$

    B. -2

    C. $-\dfrac{4}{3}$ $6x + 8 = \cancel{6}\ 4$

    D. $-\dfrac{2}{3}$ $6x = -\cancel{x}\ 4$

    E. $\dfrac{7}{3}$

7. What is the value of x if $\frac{1}{7}x + \frac{1}{3}x = 10$?

    A. 10

    B. 21

    C. 42

    D. 64

    E. 100

$\dfrac{3}{21}x + \dfrac{7}{21}x = 10$

$\dfrac{10}{21}x = 10$

8. What is the solution to $a - 6 \leq 15 + 8a$?

   A. $a \leq -3$

   B. $a \geq -3$

   C. $a \geq 3$

   D. $a \geq 1$

   E. $a \geq -\dfrac{21}{9}$

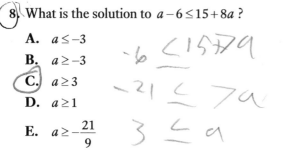

9. What is the solution to $28 - k \geq 7(k - 4)$?

   A. $k \leq 0$

   B. $k \geq 0$

   C. $k \leq 7$

   D. $k \leq \dfrac{28}{3}$

   E. $k \leq 8$

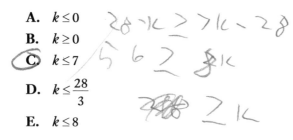

10. The area of a triangle is $A = \dfrac{1}{2}bh$. Which of the following expressions gives the value of b in terms of A and h?

   A. $b = \dfrac{2A}{h}$

   B. $b = \dfrac{A}{2h}$

   C. $b = 2Ah$

   D. $b = \dfrac{1}{2}Ah$

   E. $b = \dfrac{2}{Ah}$

11. If $ax + b = c$, which of the following expressions gives the value of x in terms of a, b, and c?

   A. $c - b - a$

   B. $\dfrac{c - b}{a}$

   C. $\dfrac{c + b}{a}$

   D. $\dfrac{c}{a} - b$

   E. $\dfrac{c - a}{b}$

12. The formula for surface area of a rectangular solid is given by $S = 2lw + 2wh + 2lh$,where l is the length, w is the width, and h is the height. In terms of l, w, and S, which of the following is an expression for h?

   A. $S - 2lw - 2w - 2l$

   B. $\dfrac{S - 2lw}{2}$

   C. $\dfrac{S - 2lw}{2w + 2l}$

   D. $\dfrac{S}{2} - lw$

   E. $\dfrac{S}{2lw + 2w + 2l}$

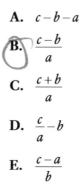

$$2x + y = 20$$
$$6x - 5y = 12$$

$$-3x + 2y = -16$$
$$9x - 6y = 48$$

13. What is the solution to the system of equations shown above?

    A. $(-6, 7)$

    B. $(0, 2)$

    C. $(2, 0)$

    D. $(3, 14)$

    E. $(7, 6)$

15. What is the solution to the system of equations shown above?

    A. $(0, -8)$ only

    B. $(2, -5)$ only

    C. $(0, -8)$ and $(2, -5)$

    D. There are infinitely many solutions

    E. No solution

$$-5x - 8y = 17$$
$$2x - 7y = -17$$

14. What is the solution to the system of equations shown above?

    A. $(-8.5, 0)$

    B. $(-5, 1)$

    C. $(1, -2.75)$

    D. $(5, 1)$

    E. $(5, 6)$

Algebraic Word Problems

Students often find word problems quite intimidating and don't know where to start. Break down your approach by following these steps:

Define your variable(s). Use a variable to represent any unknown quantity. Often this quantity will be the answer to the question.

Translate the words into an equation(s). Remember the lists of words that indicate addition, subtraction, multiplication, and division referenced earlier.

Solve for the variable(s).

Answer the question. The solution to the equation is often, but not always, the answer to the original question.

Example 1   Because of a traffic detour, Sophia returns home from college on a route that is 12 miles longer than the route she used driving to college. If the round trip was 202 miles, how many miles was the shorter route that she took when she drove from home to college?

A. 89

B. 95

C. 101

D. 107

E. 113

Step 1 is to define the variable. Let x = the distance of the route from home to college (in miles). Since the return route is 12 miles longer, let $x + 12$ = the distance of the route from college to home (in miles).

Step 2 is to write an equation. Since the round trip is the sum of the distances of the two routes, you can express it as: $x + (x + 12) = 202$.

Step 3 is to solve for x. Combine like terms to get $2x + 12 = 202$ and isolate x:

$2x = 190$

$x = 95$

Step 4 is to answer the question: how many miles was the shorter route that she took when she drove from home to college? Remember that you defined x as the distance of the route from home to college, so 95 miles is the answer.

Algebraic Word Problems Problem Set

1. When twice a number is decreased by five the result is 279. What is the number?

   A. 56.2

   B. 81

   C. 137

   D. 142

   E. 144.5

2. A 5-foot board is cut into two pieces so that one piece is 10 inches longer than the other. What is the length of the shorter piece, in inches?

   A. 15

   B. 22

   C. 25

   D. 35

   E. 50

3. Fiona makes $12 an hour working at Freezy's Ice Cream Parlor, but on Sundays she makes 1½ times her regular pay. How much money did Fiona earn last week if 7 of the 30 total hours she worked were on Sunday?

   A. $276.00

   B. $286.50

   C. $360.00

   D. $402.00

   E. $412.50

4. The number of hours that were left in a day was one-fifth of the number of hours already passed. How many hours were left in the day?

   A. 2

   B. 3

   C. 4

   D. 6

   E. 8

5. Jennifer, Julie and Jack all are carrying pencils to school. Jennifer has 2 fewer than 3 times the number of pencils as Julie, and Julie has 3 more than one third as many pencils as Jack. Jack has 9 pencils. How many pencils does Jennifer have?

   A. 8

   B. 10

   C. 12

   D. 16

   E. 18

6. For two consecutive odd integers, the result of adding the larger integer and four times the smaller integer is 87. What are the two integers?

   A. 15, 17

   B. 16, 17

   C. 17, 19

   D. 21, 22

   E. 21, 23

7. Beth wants to fence in a rectangular play area for her dog. She has 82 feet of fencing and wants the length of the play area to be 9 feet longer than the width. What should the length be?

   A. 16

   B. 20

   C. 25

   D. 32

   E. 34

8. Calvin is seven times as old as his son. The sum of Calvin's age and his son's age is 48. How old is Calvin?

   A. 28

   B. 35

   C. 36

   D. 40

   E. 42

9. A certain type of candy contains only red, green, and blue pieces. In the mix, the amounts of red and green pieces are equal, and the amount of blue pieces is twice the amount of the red pieces. How many green pieces are in a bag of 60 pieces of this candy?

   A. 10

   B. 15

   C. 20

   D. 25

   E. 30

10. Kelly bought 4 more cases of soda than cases of juice. There are 10 bottles of soda in each case of soda and 20 bottles of juice in each case of juice. If the number of bottles of soda that Kelly bought equals the number of bottles of juice that she bought, how many bottles of soda did Kelly buy?

   A. 20

   B. 40

   C. 80

   D. 120

   E. 160

11. Charlie and Sara begin working at the same time. Charlie's starting salary is $50,000 with an annual raise of $2,500. Sara's starting salary is $68,000 with an annual raise of $1,600. If x represents the number of years since each started working, which of the following equations could be used to determine the number of years until Charlie and Sara's salaries will be equal?

   A. $50,000 + 2,500x = 68,000 + 1,600x$

   B. $50,000x + 2,500 = 68,000x + 1,600$

   C. $2,500x = 1,600x + x$

   D. $2,500x + 1,600x = 18,000$

   E. $900x = 118,000$

12. One cell phone plan charges $12 a month plus $.20 for every text. Another plan charges $30 a month plus $.05 for every text. For how many texts will these two plans be equal, assuming the owner is only using the phone for texting?

   A. 4

   B. 60

   C. 90

   D. 100

   E. 120

13. At the cafeteria, Mike buys 3 soups, 2 salads and a soda for $8.75. Jane buys 2 soups, a salad, and a soda for $5.25. What is the cost of one soup and one salad?

   A. $3.25

   B. $3.50

   C. $3.75

   D. $4.00

   E. $4.55

14. Kim's wallet is full of $5 and $10 bills. She has 25 bills totaling $230. How many $10 bills does she have?

   A. 4

   B. 10

   C. 14

   D. 20

   E. 21

15. A science test consists of 40 questions and is worth 100 points. Multiple-choice questions are worth 2 points each, and short-answer questions are worth 4 points each. How many multiple-choice questions are on the test?

   A. 5

   B. 10

   C. 20

   D. 30

   E. 32

Functions

A function consists of a dependent and an independent variable such that for each value of the independent variable, there is only one value of the dependent variable. Functions are often named $f(x)$ or simply y, in which case y is the dependent variable and x is the independent variable.

Sometimes, funny-looking symbols, like $\otimes$ or $\lozenge$, are used to indicate arithmetic instructions to be performed on two numbers. These work just like functions—simply plug in where the definition directs you.

Consider the function $f(x) = 3x - 2$. Questions on the ACT often involve tables showing the values produced by a function. The table on the right shows selected values for $f(x) = 3x - 2$. The two examples below use this function.

x	$f(x)$
–3	–11
–2	–8
–1	–5
0	–2
1	1
2	4
3	7

Example 1   What is the value of $f(6)$?

$$f(6) = 3(6) - 2 = 16$$

Example 2   What is the x-value for which $f(x) = 13$?

$$f(x) = 3x - 2 = 13. \text{ So } 3x = 15, \text{ and } x = 5.$$

Try It!

The set of questions below refers to the functions $f(x) = 3x - 2$ and $g(x) = \dfrac{x}{2} + 4$.

The set of questions below refers to the function $f(x) = x^2 + 2$.

Try it 1 What is the value of $g(2)$?

Try it 4 What is $f(a)$?

Try it 5 What is $f(2a)$?

Try it 2 For what value of x does $g(x) = 10$?

Try it 6 What is $f(3a - 1)$?

Try it 3 For what value of x does $f(x) = g(x)$?

Compostite Functions and Inverses

A composite function can be written either as $f(g(x))$ or $f \circ g(x)$. You obtain the output by first plugging the x-value into the interior function ($g(x)$ in this case), and then plugging the result of that into the outer function.

Function inverses, usually denoted $f^{-1}(x)$, undo one another. To create an inverse of a function, switch the x and y values, and then solve for y.

Functions Problem Set

1. If $f(x) = -2x^3 + x$, then $f(-2) = ?$

    A. -18

    B. -14

    C. 14

    D. 16

    E. 18

2. If $f(x) = 3x^2$ and $f(a) = 12$, what is the value of a?

    A. -2 only

    B. 2 only

    C. -2 or 2

    D. -4 or 4

    E. 432 only

3. Let a function of two variables be defined by $f(x, y) = x - xy + y^2$. What is the value of $f(2,5)$?

    A. -3

    B. -1

    C. 3

    D. 17

    E. 37

4. If $g(x) = 3x - 4$ and $f(x) = 2x + 3$, what is the value of $f(3) - g(3)$?

    A. -13

    B. -4

    C. 0

    D. 4

    E. 13

5. A ball is thrown up from a height of 4 feet. The equation describing the ball's height after t seconds is $h(t) = 4 + 10t - 16t^2$. What is the ball's height after 0.4 seconds?

    A. It will have hit the ground

    B. 1.6 feet

    C. 5.44 feet

    D. 10.56 feet

    E. 14.4 feet

6. If $f(x) = -4x + 1$, then $2f(x) - 2 = ?$

    A. $-2x - 1$

    B. $-2x$

    C. $-8x - 2$

    D. $-8x + 2$

    E. $-8x$

7. If $f(x) = 3x + 5$ and $g(x) = \dfrac{1}{2}x - \dfrac{5}{2}$, for what value of x does $f(x) = g(x)$?

A. -3

B. -1

C. $-\dfrac{5}{2}$

D. 3

E. 5

8. If $m(x) = 30x + c$ where c is a constant and $m(3.5) = 123$, what is the value of c?

A. 12

B. 13

C. 18

D. 19

E. 20

$123 \cdot 3.5 = 30x + c$

$123 = 30 \times 3$

$123 = 30(3.5) + c$

x	$f(x)$	$h(x)$
0	–2	12
1	1	6
2	3	13
3	4	8
4	6	14
5	9	10
6	13	15

9. In the table above, for which value of x is $h(x) = f(3x)$?

A. 0

B. 1

C. 2

D. 3

E. 4

10. The function $f(x)$ is defined by the equation $f(x) = 10x - 2$. If $f(3a) = 88$, then $a =$

A. 0

B. 3

C. 6

D. 9

E. 10

11. If $f(x) = 3x + 2$ and $3f(n) = 51$, then what is the value of $f(n-3)$?

A. 8

B. 9

C. 10

D. 11

E. 12

12. If $f(x) = mx - 13$ and $f(7) = 71$, what is m?

A. 4

B. 7

C. 11

D. 12

E. 14

13. If $f(x) = 6x - \dfrac{1}{2}$ and $g(x) = \dfrac{1}{6}x + 3$, what is $f(g(2))$?

    A. 6.5

    B. 13

    C. 15.4

    D. 19.5

    E. 22.4

15. For all numbers p and q, let $p \otimes q$ be defined as $p \otimes q = p^2 + 3pq + q^2$. What is the value of $(2 \otimes 1) \otimes 3$?

    A. 16

    B. 45

    C. 72

    D. 208

    E. 229

14. For which of the following functions is $f(a) = f(-a)$ for all a?

    A. $f(x) = x^2 + x$

    B. $f(x) = x^3 - x$

    C. $f(x) = x - 4$

    D. $f(x) = 2$

    E. $f(x) = 2x^3 - 4x + 2$

16. Let $x \oplus y$ be defined as $x \oplus y = x^2 + y$ for all real numbers x and y. What is $3 \oplus 4 - 4 \oplus 3$?

    A. –9

    B. –6

    C. 6

    D. 13

    E. 19

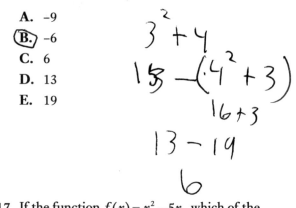

17. If the function $f(x) = x^2 - 5x$, which of the following is equal to $f(f(x))$?

    A. $2x^2 - 10x$

    B. $x^4 + 25x^2$

    C. $x^4 - 10x^3 + 25x^2$

    D. $(x^2 - 5x)^2 - 5(x^2 - 5x)$

    E. $(x - 5)^4 - 5(x - 5)^2$

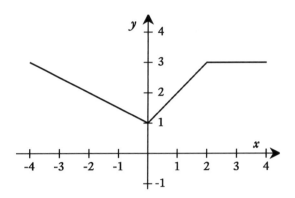

18. The function $y = f(x)$ is shown in the graph above. What is $f(f(-2))$?

    A. -4

    B. 2

    C. 3

    D. 9

    E. none of these

19. If $f(x) = x^3$, $g(x) = 2x + k$, and $(-1, 125)$ is a point on the graph of $y = f(g(x))$, which of the following could be the value of k?

    A. -3

    B. -1

    C. 3

    D. 5

    E. 7

20. What is the inverse of the function
$$f(x) = \frac{2}{x} - 4?$$

    A. $f^{-1}(x) = 2(x + 4)$

    B. $f^{-1}(x) = \frac{x}{2} - 4$

    C. $f^{-1}(x) = -\frac{2}{x} + 4$

    D. $f^{-1}(x) = \frac{x + 4}{2}$

    E. $f^{-1}(x) = \frac{2}{x + 4}$

Exponents

The following rules of exponents should be reviewed.

$$a^0 = 1 \qquad\qquad a^{-x} = \frac{1}{a^x}$$

$$a^x a^y = a^{x+y} \qquad\qquad \frac{a^x}{a^y} = a^{x-y}$$

$$\left(a^x\right)^y = a^{xy} \qquad\qquad a^{1/x} = \sqrt[x]{a}$$

$$a^x \cdot b^x = (ab)^x$$

Try It!

Solve for x. If you want to test your understanding of the rules above, do not use a calculator:

1. $5^3 \cdot 5^6 = 5^x$

2. $\dfrac{7^5}{7^3} = 7^x$

3. $\left(8^2\right) = 2^x$

4. $2^{-4} = x$

5. $27^x = 3$

6. $3^{-2} \cdot 4^{-2} = x^{-2}$

7. $\left(\left(2^2\right)^2\right)^2 = 2^x$

8. $3 \cdot 3^2 \cdot 3^{-1} = 3^x$

9. $\dfrac{9^9}{9^{-9}} = 3^x$

10. $4 \cdot 8 \cdot 16 = 2^x$

11. $\dfrac{2^4 \cdot 3^4}{6^2} = x$

12. $\left(81^{1/2}\right)^3 = 3^x$

Exponents Problem Set

1. If $x, y,$ and z are all positive numbers such that $x^2 = y^{12}z^4$, what is x *in terms of y and z*?

A. y^{10}

B. $y^6 z^2$

C. $y^{12} z^4$

D. $y^{12} z^2$

E. $y^6 z^4$

2. If $x^{-1/3} = \dfrac{1}{3}$, what is the value of x?

A. -9

B. -3

C. $\dfrac{1}{9}$

D. 27

E. 81

3. If $3^x = 5$, then $3^{3x} = ?$

A. $\dfrac{5}{3}$

B. 5

C. 10

D. 25

E. 125

4. $\left(64m^6 n^3 p^{12}\right)^{\frac{1}{3}} =$

A. $4m^2 np^4$

B. $64m^6 np^4$

C. $4m^6 n^3 p^{12}$

D. $4m^6 np^{10}$

E. $4m^6 np^4$

5. $\dfrac{\left(x^2\right)^5 \cdot \left(x^4\right)^3}{x^2} =$

A. x^{11}

B. x^{12}

C. x^{20}

D. x^{60}

E. x^{118}

6. For positive a and b, if $a^3 = b^6$, what is a in terms of b?

A. b

B. b^2

C. b^{-3}

D. $b^{-1/2}$

E. $b^{1/2}$

7. $\dfrac{\left(3^x \cdot 3\right)^3}{9^x} =$

    A. 3^{6x}

    B. 3^3

    C. 3^{3-x}

    D. 3^{4x}

    E. 3^{x+3}

10. If $z = a^3 k^2$ and $a = c^2 r^5$, then what is z in terms of k, c, and r?

    $c^2 r^5 k^2$

    $c^4 r^{10} k^2$

    $c^6 r^{15} k$

    $c^6 r^{15} k^2$

    $c^5 r^8 k^2$

8. If $4^{x+1} = 64$, what is x?

    A. 0

    B. 1

    C. 2

    D. 3

    E. 4

11. If $125 \cdot (5^x) = 5^y$, what is x in terms of y?

    A. $y - 3$

    B. $3y$

    C. $y + 3$

    D. $\dfrac{y}{3}$

    E. y^3

9. If $\dfrac{4^x}{2^3 \cdot 2^4} = 2$, what is the value of x?

    A. 0

    B. 2

    C. 4

    D. 6

    E. 8

12. If $4^x = y$, which of the following equals $16y$ in terms of x?

    $4^{x/2}$

    4^{2x}

    4^{2+x}

    4^{x^2}

    64^x

13. If a, b, and c are positive numbers and $a^4b^2c^3 < a^3b^2c^4$, which of the following must be true?

    I. $c > a$
    II. $c > b$
    III. $a > b$

  A. I only

  B. II only

  C. III only

  D. I and II only

  E. II and III only

14. If $a^{\frac{1}{3}} = b^4$ and $b^{-2} = c^3$, what is a in terms of c?

  A. c^{-18}

  B. c^{27}

  C. $c^{-\frac{1}{2}}$

  D. c^6

  E. c^{-2}

15. Which of the following has the greatest value?

  A. 2^{400}

  B. $\left(2 \cdot 2^3\right)^{300}$

  C. 8^{300}

  D. 4^{350}

  E. $\left(4 \cdot 2^2\right)^{200}$

Absolute Value

The absolute value of a number represents that number's distance from zero. A number can never be a negative distance from zero; therefore, the absolute value of any number is always positive.

Examples:

Example 1 $|4| = 4$ *Example 2* $|7 - 5| = 2$ *Example 3* $|x| = |-x|$

Example 4 $|-4| = 4$ *Example 5* $|5 - 7| = 2$ *Example 6* $|x - y| = |y - x|$

As shown above, 4 and –4 are both four units away from zero on a number line, and 7 and 5 are 2 units away from each other no matter which number is written first.

Try it!

Try it 1 $|-9| - (-8) =$ *Try it 2* $\big||-2| - |-3 - 3|\big| =$

Absolute Value Graphs

Absolute value functions have a characteristic feature: the graphed line never falls below the *x*-axis, unless it is shifted downward, because an absolute value can never be negative.

Absolute value signs often result in part of a function being *reflected* over the *x*-axis.

Example 7 $y = |x|$ *Example 8* $y = |x| - 1$ *Example 9* $y = \big||x| - 1\big|$

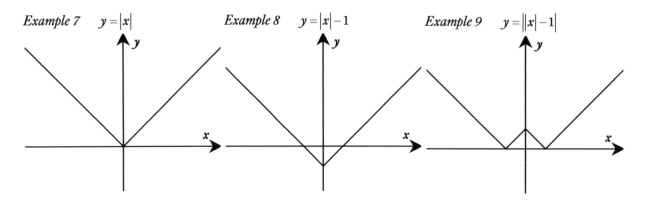

When solving an algebraic problem with an absolute value, you can write out two separate equations.

Example 10 $|x - 9| = 3$

$$x - 9 = 3 \qquad x - 9 = -3$$
$$x = 12 \qquad x = 6$$

For absolute value questions, it is almost always easiest to work backwards from the answer choices by backsolving. This is particularly true when dealing with questions involving inequalities and absolute value.

Absolute Value Problem Set

1. What is the value of $-3|3-8|+|-2^3|$?

    A. -23

    B. -9

    C. -7

    D. 7

    E. 23

2. If $|3x-9|<0$, which of the following is a possible value of x?

    A. 4

    B. 3

    C. 0

    D. -2

    E. No possible value.

3. If $x<0$ and $|x-y|=6$, what is the value of x when $y=-3$?

    A. -9

    B. -6

    C. -3

    D. 3

    E. 9

4. If $f(x)=|3x-12|-3$, for what value(s) of x does $f(x)=0$?

    A. 3 only

    B. 5 only

    C. -5 and 5

    D. -3 and 5

    E. 3 and 5

5. If $|2x-5|<7$, what are all the values of x that satisfy this inequality?

    A. $-1<x<6$

    B. $-6<x<6$

    C. $-8<x<8$

    D. $-3<x<8$

    E. $1<x<6$

6. If $3<x<9$, which of the following is true about all possible values of x?

    A. $|x-6|>3$

    B. $|x-6|<3$

    C. $|x+6|<3$

    D. $3<|x+6|<9$

    E. $|x+3|<9$

7. For what value of c does $|c-6|=-2c$?

    A. -6

    B. -4

    C. -2

    D. 2

    E. 6

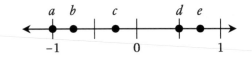

8. What is the value of $|c - d|$?

    A. *a*

    B. *b*

    C. *c*

    D. *d*

    E. *e*

9. Which of the following functions has no positive *y*-values?

    A. $y = |x| - 1500$

    B. $y = \left| \dfrac{x}{15} - 1000 \right|$

    C. $y = |-150x - 10|$

    D. $y = -15|x - 100|$

    E. $y = 15 - |x - 100|$

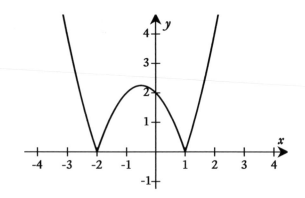

10. Which of the following could be the function represented by the figure above?

    A. $y = x^2 + x - 2$

    B. $y = |x^2 + x - 2|$

    C. $y = |x^2 - 2|$

    D. $y = \left| \left| x - \dfrac{1}{2} \right| - 2 \right|$

    E. $y = \left| x - \dfrac{1}{2} \right| + 2$

Distributing and Factoring

Distributing

Any term that is multiplied by an entire expression may also be multiplied by each of the terms within the expression before addition or subtraction is carried out.

$$a(b+c-d) = ab + ac - ad.$$

FOIL

This term is an mnemonic device to help you remember how to *double distribute* when multiplying two binomials:

$$(a+b)(c+d) = \underbrace{ac}_{\text{Firsts}} + \underbrace{ad}_{\text{Outers}} + \underbrace{bc}_{\text{Inners}} + \underbrace{bd}_{\text{Lasts}}$$

Some students learn to double distribute using a 2×2 box structure instead. Either way, and no matter the sizes of the polynomials being multiplied, you must be sure to multiply each term of one of the polynomials by each term of the other polynomial.

Factoring

Factoring means breaking an expression up into its component factors. One way to factor a polynomial is to pull out a common factor, which is like reversing the process of a single distribution.

Example 1 $6x^8 - 9x^3 + 12x^2 = 3x^2(2x^6 - 3x + 4)$

Factoring can also entail reversing the process of FOIL.

Example 2 $x^2 - 5x - 36 = (x-9)(x+4)$

It helps to remember a few formulas for perfect squares of binomials and for the difference of two squares:

$$\left.\begin{array}{l}(x+y)^2 = x^2 + 2xy + y^2 \\ (x-y)^2 = x^2 - 2xy + y^2\end{array}\right\} \text{The perfect square formulas}$$

$$x^2 - y^2 = (x+y)(x-y)\big\} \text{The difference of two squares}$$

Example 3   Factor the following polynomial: $2x^3 + 8x^2 + 8x$

   The first step is to look for common factors to pull out. In this case, $2x$ goes into each term, so write $2x^3 + 8x^2 + 8x = 2x\left(x^2 + 4x + 4\right)$

   The next step is to see if the expression fits a formula or if you can easily reverse FOIL. This particular polynomial has a factor that is a perfect square of $(x+2)$ because $(x+2)^2 = x^2 + 4x + 4$, so the complete factoring of the polynomial can be written as

   $$2x^3 + 8x^2 + 8x = 2x\left(x^2 + 4x + 4\right) = 2x(x+2)^2.$$

Distributing and Factoring Problem Set

1. Which of the following expressions is equivalent to $-7x(2x^3 - 5x + 3)$?

   A. $-14x^3 + 35x - 21$

   B. $-14x^4 - 5x + 3$

   C. $-14x^4 - 35x^2 + 21x$

   D. $-14x^4 + 35x^2 - 21x$

   E. $-5x^4 - 12x^2 - 4x$

2. Which of the following is a factor of $x^2 - 6x + 5$?

   A. $x - 1$

   B. $x - 2$

   C. $x - 3$

   D. $x - 6$

   E. $x + 5$

3. Which of the following expressions is equivalent to $(x - 4)(3x + 1)$?

   A. $3x^2 - 6x - 4$

   B. $3x^2 - 13x - 4$

   C. $3x^2 - 11x - 4$

   D. $3x^2 - 3x - 4$

   E. $3x^2 + 13x - 4$

4. The polynomial $6x^2 + 7x - 20$ is equivalent to the product of $3x - 4$ and which of the following?

   A. $2x - 16$

   B. $2x - 5$

   C. $2x + 5$

   D. $3x - 5$

   E. $3x + 5$

5. The expression $(5a - 7b^2)(5a + 7b^2)$ is equivalent to:

   A. $10a$

   B. $10a - 14b^2$

   C. $10a^2 - 14b^2$

   D. $25a^2 - 49b^4$

   E. $25a^2 + 49b^4$

6. Where $\dfrac{x + 3}{x^2 - 2x - 15}$ is defined, it is equivalent to which of the following expressions?

   A. $-\dfrac{3}{x - 15}$

   B. $\dfrac{1}{x - 5}$

   C. $\dfrac{3}{x + 5}$

   D. $\dfrac{1}{x + 5}$

   E. $\dfrac{x + 3}{(x - 3)(x + 5)}$

7. For all x and y, $(3x + y)(x^2 - y) = ?$

   A. $3x^3 - 2y$

   B. $3x^3 - y^2$

   C. $3x^3 - 3xy - y^2$

   D. $3x^3 - 4xy + x^2 y^2$

   E. $3x^3 - 3xy + x^2 y - y^2$

8. The expression $m^4 n^3 (m + mn)$ is equivalent to:

   A. $2m^4 n^3$

   B. $m^4 n^3 + m^4 n^4$

   C. $m^5 n^3 + m^5 n^4$

   D. $m^5 + m^5 n^4$

   E. $m^5 n^4 + m^5 n^5$

9. Which of the following is equivalent to
   $25m^2 - 81n^{10}$?

   A. $(5m - (3n)^4)(5m + n^6)$

   B. $(5m - 9n^5)(5m + 9n^2)$

   C. $(5m^2 - 9n^5)(5m + 9n^2)$

   D. $(5m + 9n^5)(5m - 9n^5)$

   E. $(5m - 9n^5)(5m - 9n^5)$

10. Which of the following is equivalent to
    $(5x - 3)^2$?

    A. $10x - 6$

    B. $25x^2 - 9$

    C. $25x^2 + 9$

    D. $25x^2 - 15x - 9$

    E. $25x^2 - 30x + 9$

11. For $x^2 \neq 36$, $\dfrac{(x + 6)^2}{x^2 - 36} = ?$

    A. $-\dfrac{1}{6}$

    B. $\dfrac{1}{x - 6}$

    C. $\dfrac{1}{x + 6}$

    D. $\dfrac{x + 6}{x - 6}$

    E. 1

12. If $a^2 = b^2 + 80$, which of the following
    expressions must equal 80?

    A. $2(a + b)$

    B. $a^2 + b^2$

    C. $b^2 - a^2$

    D. $(a - b)(a - b)$

    E. $(a + b)(a - b)$

13. Which of the following is equivalent to
$3a(2a-b)^2$?

   A. $6a^2 - 3ab^2$

   B. $7a^2 - 7ab + 4ab^2$

   C. $12a^3 - 12a^2b + 3ab^2$

   D. $18a^3 - 9a^2b$

   E. $36a^4 - 36a^3b + 9a^2b^2$

14. Which of the following is NOT a factor of
$x^5 - x^3$?

   A. x

   B. x^3

   C. $x-1$

   D. $x^2 - 1$

   E. $x^3 - 1$

15. If $9x^2 - 4y^2 = a(3x + 2y)$, then what is the
value of a, in terms of x and y ?

   A. $x - y$

   B. $x + 2y$

   C. $3x - 2y$

   D. $3x + 2y$

   E. $3x^2 - 2y^2$

Part V: Statistics and Probability

Statistical measurements, like average and median, and probability concepts come up sporadically in math classes, but it is quite rare for a student to take a dedicated Statistics course. Nevertheless, using data to interpret, synthesize and predict the complex systems that govern our world is perhaps the most widespread application of mathematics.

In recent years, ACT Math sections have more consistently tested complicated statistics and probability concepts like standard deviation and permutations. It is becoming more important to have a foundation of understanding in such topics so that you can more confidently approach problems toward the end of the Math section.

On the following pages, you will find notes and problem sets for both the simpler and the more complex concepts of data analysis:

- Basic Statistics of Central Tendency
- Distributions and Statistics of Spread
- Probability
- Arrangements

Statistics

A statistic is a measurement that informs you about a·certain element of a set of data. Graphs and tables can present statistics in a meaningful way. Some statistics give a representation of the data in a single snapshot by presenting a measurement of, for example, the center or spread of a set.

Measurements of Central Tendency

The arithmetic mean, or **average**, of a set can be found using $\dfrac{\text{sum of a set of numbers}}{\text{amount of numbers in the set}}$. You can also use a variation of this formula when the average is known: $\text{Sum} = (\text{Average}) \times (\text{\# of Things})$.

The **median** is the middle number of a set when the set is placed in numerical order. If the set has an even number of elements, then the median is the average of the two middle numbers.

The **mode** is the number that occurs most often in a set.

Example 1   A class of 11 students received the following scores on a recent quiz:

$$98, 87, 57, 100, 76, 90, 85, 76, 80, 63, \text{ and } 79$$

The **average** score is $\dfrac{98+87+57+100+76+90+85+76+80+63+79}{11} = 81.$

The **median** score is the middle of $57, 63, 76, 76, 79, \mathbf{80}, 85, 87, 90, 98,$ and 100, which is 80.

The **mode** score is 76, since there are two students who received that score and every other score is represented only once.

Example 2   A team of six wrestlers weigh in at an average weight of 155 pounds. When a wrestler leaves the team, the new average weight is 146 pounds. What was the weight of the wrestler who left the team?

Since the six wrestlers averaged 155 pounds, their total weight equals $6 \times 155 = 930$. When the one wrestler leaves, there will be five wrestlers remaining with a total weight of $5 \times 146 = 730$. The difference between those two totals is 200, so the wrestler who left must have weighed **200** pounds.

$1.46 = \dfrac{5x}{}$

Statistics Problem Set 1

1. Dan's average score on 8 tests is 89. What is the sum of his scores on all 8 tests?

A. 78
B. 89
C. 657
D. 712
E. 915

2. Mr. Gerver computes his students' test grades by deleting the lowest test score and averaging the remaining test scores for the semester. If one of Mr. Gerver's students scored 68, 78, 86, 87 and 93 on her tests this semester, what will her test grade be?

A. 68.8
B. 82.0
C. 82.4
D. 86.0
E. 86.5

21, 17, 59, 38, 37, 27, 86, 18, 21

3. What is the median of the 9 scores above?

A. 21
B. 27
C. 36
D. 37
E. 38

4. When John, Max, and Samantha pool their DVDs, they discover they own a total of 98. If Max owns 34 of them, how many DVDs do John and Samantha each own, *on average*?

A. 32
B. 34
C. 36
D. 38
E. 40

5. In the figures above, what is the average of a, b, c, d, e, and f?

A. 30
B. 60
C. 75
D. 80
E. 90

6. Leo and Don both receive an 88 on a test. Mike receives an 89 and Raffy receives a 93. April scores a 94. Arrange the mean, median and mode of their scores in ascending order.

A. Mean, mode, median

B. Mode, mean, median

C. Median, mode, mean

D. Mode, median, mean

E. Mean, median, mode

9. If the six players on the Varsity A team average 12 points per game and the nine players on the Varsity B team average 5 points per game, what is the combined average of the players on both teams?

A. 117

B. 8.5

C. 7.8

D. 6.8

E. 4.5

7. If set A consists of three positive integers $x, y,$ and z such that $x < y < z,$ which of the following could NOT affect set A's median?

A. Decreasing x

B. Decreasing z

C. Decreasing y

D. Increasing y

E. Increasing x

10. If $3a = 3b + 3c + 12,$ then what is the average of b and c?

A. $\dfrac{-b + 3c - 4}{2}$

B. $\dfrac{a - 4}{2}$

C. $\dfrac{a + 4}{2}$

D. $\dfrac{a}{2}$

E. $\dfrac{a + b + c}{3}$

8. The average of 20 numbers is 38. When two of the numbers, 40 and 18, are discarded, what is the average of the remaining set of numbers?

A. 38

B. 39

C. 40

D. 41.5

E. 42

11. In his first five basketball games, Jack has the most points per game on his team, with scores of 23, 20, 31, 22, and 24. How many points must Jack score in his sixth game to maintain the same average points per game after six games that he had after five games?

   A. 20

   B. 22

   C. 24

   D. 27

   E. 30

14. In a set of seven integers, the average is 9, the median is 10, there are two 11's, and the only mode is 4. Which of the following is true about the set?

   A. The largest integer is 19

   B. The largest integer 22

   C. The sum of the integers is 70

   D. 9 is in the set

   E. 10 is not in the set

$$8, 7, 9, 10, 10, 9, 8, 9, 10, m, 10$$

12. For the numbers listed above, 10 is the only mode and the median is 9. Each of the following could be the value of m EXCEPT

   A. 10

   B. 9

   C. 8

   D. 7

   E. 6

15. Rich jogged m days in May, a days in August, and s days in September, averaging x jogging days per month over those three months. If he jogged j days a month in both June and July, how many days a month did Rich average jogging over the five-month period?

   A. $\dfrac{x+j}{2}$

   B. $\dfrac{m+a+s+j}{4}$

   C. $\dfrac{3x+j}{4}$

   D. $\dfrac{3x+j}{5}$

   E. $\dfrac{3x+2j}{5}$

13. If $x + 1$ is the average (arithmetic mean) of 20, x, x, 12, and 30, what is the value of x?

   A. 9

   B. 12

   C. 19

   D. 20

   E. 29

Distributions and Measurements of Spread

The ways in which numbers in a data set are distributed can be presented using different kinds of **tables**, **graphs**, **Venn diagrams**, or even individual numbers.

Frequency Table

When the number of times an individual number (or interval of numbers) appears in a set is displayed in a table, this is called a frequency table. This can make the work of finding statistics, like the mean, median, and mode, much simpler for large sets.

Age	Number of Students
14	120
15	103
16	97
17	79
18	22

Example 1 Find the average, median, and mode of the ages of students at Jefferson High School, shown in the table on the right.

The **average** can be calculated by multiplying each age by its frequency, adding those totals, and then dividing by the 421 students at the school:

$$\frac{(14 \cdot 120) + (15 \cdot 103) + (16 \cdot 97) + (17 \cdot 79) + (18 \cdot 22)}{421} = 15.477.$$

The **median** will be the 211th student since 211 is the middle of 421 numbers. The youngest 120 students are 14 years old and the next 103 students are 15 years old. That will put the total over 211, so the 211th student is **15** years old.

The **mode** is **14** because 14 years old has the highest frequency.

In rare cases, you may be asked for the **expected value** of a discrete random variable. This is just a weighted average and would be calculated just like the calculation for average in the previous example. It is a little confusing because no student is exactly 15.477 years old, but expected values can be very useful in representing long-run probability problems.

Measurements of Spread

A measurement of spread helps to represent how the numbers are dispersed.

Range is found by subtracting the lowest data point from the highest data point.

Standard deviation is a number that measures how spread out the data points are from the average. You will not be asked to calculate the standard deviation of a set, but you will want to recognize that a large standard deviation means the numbers in the set are very spread out while a small standard deviation means the numbers are bunched toward the middle.

Example 2 The sets $A = \{72, 73, 74, 76, 76, 76, 78\}$ and $B = \{53, 64, 74, 76, 78, 88, 92\}$ have the same **average** of 75, but set A has a **range** of **6** and a **standard deviation** of **1.93**, while the much more spread out set B has a **range** of **39** and a **standard deviation** of **12.39**.

Statistics Problem Set 2

Number of pets	Number of students
0	4
1	2
2	3
3	4
4	0

1. The table above shows the number of pets each student in Mrs. Bell's Math class has. What is the total number of pets owned by the class?

   A. 10

   B. 13

   C. 15

   D. 18

   E. 20

Number of hours practiced	Number of students
0	2
2	3
4	10
6	4

2. The 19 students in an orchestra are getting ready for their recital. The chart above shows how many musicians practiced for 0, 2, 4, or 6 hours the week before the recital. A new musician ends up joining the orchestra before the performance. How many hours must this musician practice so that the new average (arithmetic mean) equals the mode hours practiced?

   A. 2

   B. 4

   C. 6

   D. 8

   E. 10

3. Which of the following sets has the smallest standard deviation?

   A. 1, 5, 5, 5, 9

   B. 1, 3, 5, 7, 9

   C. 5, 6, 7, 8, 9

   D. 7, 7, 8, 8, 8

   E. 0, 10, 20, 30, 40

2, 4, 6, 8, 10, 12, 14

4. If the 2 and the 14 were removed from the set of numbers above, which of the following would change from the original set?

     I. The median

     II. The mean

     III. The standard deviation

   A. I only

   B. III only

   C. I and II only

   D. I and III only

   E. I, II, and III

5. If 23 were added to each of the following sets, which set would have its standard deviation *lowered*?

   A. 10, 15, 15, 20

   B. 23, 23, 23, 23

   C. 21, 22, 24, 26

   D. 25, 30, 30, 35

   E. 35, 35, 35, 35

Total Annual Precipitation (inches)

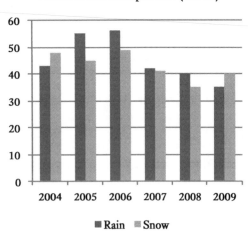

■ Rain   ■ Snow

Jelly Beans

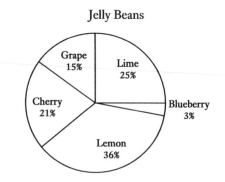

Questions 6 and 7 both refer to the graph above, which shows the total rainfall and snowfall for Orangetown, USA.

6. For which year was the percent change of total rainfall the greatest from the previous year?

   A. 2005
   B. 2006
   C. 2007
   D. 2008
   E. 2009

8. The circle chart above shows the distribution of jelly beans in a bag Michael just purchased from the candy store. If Michael gives half of his lemon jelly beans and 20% of his lime jelly beans to his sister, which of the following represents the greatest percentage of the remaining beans in the bag?

   A. Cherry
   B. Lemon
   C. Blueberry
   D. Lime
   E. Grape

7. 10 inches of snow is equivalent to 1 inch of rain. In what year was the total precipitation (including rainfall and snowfall) the greatest?

   A. 2004
   B. 2005
   C. 2006
   D. 2007
   E. 2008

Number of Pets (X)	Probability $P(X)$
0	0.60
1	0.30
2	0.08
3	0.02

9. There are 100 students in Mira's graduating class. The table above shows the probability distribution of the number of pets each student has. What is the mean number of pets per student?

   A. 0

   B. 0.25

   C. 0.52

   D. 1

   E. 1.5

Years of Language Classes (X)	Frequency
0	10
1	30
2	40
3	40

10. The frequency distribution table above shows the number of years of high school language classes taken by the 120 11th graders in Bryson High School by the end of the 11th grade, as represented by the variable X. What is the expected value of the discrete random variable X?

   A. 0

   B. $\dfrac{1}{2}$

   C. 1

   D. $\dfrac{23}{12}$

   E. 3

Outcome	Probability $P(X)$
–$1 (no prize)	0.920
$9	0.079
$99	0.001

11. The probability distribution table above shows the probability of the three possible outcomes in Scratch Card lottery where the cost of the ticket is $1. Each of the outcomes in the table is the value of the prize less the value of the ticket. What is the expected value, in dollars, of the lottery?

   A. –0.11

   B. 0

   C. 0.50

   D. 0.79

   E. 1

12. Newsaw Tinit proposes that you play a game with him. If you roll a fair die and get a 5, then you win $1, and if you roll a 6, you win $2. If any other number comes up, you have to pay $1. What is the expected value, <u>rounded to the nearest cent</u>, of playing the game?

   A. –25

   B. –17

   C. 0

   D. 50

   E. 100

13. There are 600 students in 8th grade at J. M. Hendrix Middle School. Students take French, Spanish, both, or neither language. 250 students take neither, 300 take French, and 100 take Spanish. How many students take both languages?

    A. 25

    B. 50

    C. 75

    D. 100

    E. 150

14. At a summer camp, 20 campers participate in painting and 30 campers participate in crafts. If 10 kids did both painting and crafts, and 5 kids did neither activity, how many total students are at the camp?

    A. 35

    B. 40

    C. 45

    D. 50

    E. 55

15. The following stem and leaf plot shows the high temperature in °F for every day last July in the town of Thermidor. If a day with temperatures above 95°F is considered unsafe for the elderly, infants, and sick people, then what percentage, rounded to the nearest whole number, of days in this month were considered *safe*? (Note that July has 31 days.)

7	9
8	4 6 8 8 9 9
9	0 0 2 3 3 3 4 5 7 7 7 7 9 9
10	0 0 1 1 1 2 5 8
11	0 1

Example: $8|4 = 84$

    A. 45%

    B. 48%

    C. 52%

    D. 55%

    E. 58%

Probability

Single Event Probability

The probability of something happening can be calculated by dividing the number of desired outcomes that are possible by the total number of possible outcomes.

Example 1   There are five red balls, three green balls, and two blue balls in a bag. If you draw a ball from the bag (without looking inside the bag), what is the probability that you will draw a green ball?

The probability of a green ball being selected is $\dfrac{\text{the number of green balls}}{\text{the total number of balls}} = \dfrac{3}{10}$.

A **probability fraction** can be converted into a **decimal** or a **percent**, but it will always be between 0 and 1. The probability of an impossible event equals 0, and the sum of all possible probabilities for an event must be 1.

Independent Events

When multiple events have no effect on one another, they are independent. If you flip a coin and roll a die, for example, those two events do not influence each other in any way. In fact, if you were to flip a coin several times, even those flips would be independent of one another.

Example 2   If you roll eight straight 3s on a fair die, the probability that you will roll a 3 on your ninth roll is still equal to $\dfrac{1}{6}$, the same that it was for every single prior roll.

Or Questions

If you are asked for the probability that one of two different things happen, and those two things are mutually exclusive, this is called an **or** problem, and you simply **add** the probabilities.

Example 3   The probability of rolling a 3 **or** a 5 on a fair die is $\dfrac{1}{6}+\dfrac{1}{6}=\dfrac{2}{6}$.

And Questions

When you wish to find the probability that two different independent events occur in conjunction, this is called an **and** problem, and you can simply multiply the probabilities.

Example 4   The probability of flipping heads on a fair coin **and** rolling a 3 on a fair die is $\dfrac{1}{2}\times\dfrac{1}{6}=\dfrac{1}{12}$.

Dependent Event Probability

When an event occurs multiple times **without replacement**, each event is dependent upon the previous events, and you must subtract relevant outcomes from the numerator and denominator.

Example 5   The probability of drawing two Jacks and then one Queen, all without replacement, from a 52-card deck that has four cards of each suit is $\dfrac{4}{52}\times\dfrac{3}{51}\times\dfrac{4}{50}$.

Probability Problem Set

1. If a number is chosen at random from the list below, what is the probability that it will be greater than 6?

   2, 3, 4, 5, 6, 7, 8, 9

   A. $\frac{1}{4}$

   B. $\frac{3}{8}$

   C. $\frac{1}{2}$

   D. $\frac{5}{8}$

   E. $\frac{3}{4}$

2. David has 10 baseball cards, 4 football cards, and 5 hockey cards. How many more hockey cards will David need to acquire to have a $\frac{1}{3}$ probability of randomly selecting a hockey card from all his sports cards?

   A. 2
   B. 3
   C. 4
   D. 7
   E. 9

3. Which of the following have equal probabilities when rolling a fair six-sided number cube?

   A. Rolling a 6 or rolling an odd number

   B. Rolling a 5 or rolling an even number

   C. Rolling an even number or rolling a number greater than 4

   D. Rolling an even number or rolling a number less than 4

   E. Rolling a prime number or rolling a multiple of 3

4. Mrs. Groom's class has 36 students, all of whom have either brown eyes, blue eyes or green eyes. When Mrs. Groom calls on a student, there is a $\frac{1}{4}$ probability the student has blue eyes and a $\frac{1}{6}$ probability the student has green eyes. How many brown-eyed students are in Mrs. Groom's class?

   A. 9
   B. 10
   C. 15
   D. 21
   E. 26

5. Of the 34 shirts in a closet, the most common color is blue. What is the probability that a shirt randomly selected from the closet is *not* blue?

   A. $\frac{1}{34}$

   B. $\frac{8}{17}$

   C. $\frac{1}{2}$

   D. $\frac{9}{17}$

   E. Cannot be determined

6. Mr. Sagevsal is rolling a fair die. He has already rolled two sixes. What are his chances of rolling a third six on his next roll?

   A. $\left(\dfrac{1}{6}\right)^3$

   B. $\dfrac{1}{6}+\dfrac{1}{6}+\dfrac{1}{6}$

   C. $\dfrac{1}{18}$

   D. $\left(\dfrac{1}{6}\right)^2$

   E. $\dfrac{1}{6}$

7. Woody, the magician, is randomly choosing a volunteer from the audience. If there are 440 men in the auditorium and he has a $\dfrac{10}{21}$ chance of picking a male, how many people are there in the audience?

   A. 400
   B. 764
   C. 840
   D. 924
   E. 1004

8. There are three red blocks and five other blocks in a bin. A worker grabs two of these blocks at random. If the first block removed is not red, what is the probability of the second block being a non-red block?

   A. $\dfrac{2}{7}$

   B. $\dfrac{1}{2}$

   C. $\dfrac{4}{7}$

   D. $\dfrac{5}{7}$

   E. $\dfrac{5}{8}$

9. A jar contains 20 total jelly beans. 10 of the jelly beans are blue, 7 are red, and 3 are green. Nancy withdrew one jelly bean at random, ate it, and then withdrew another jelly bean at random. What is the probability that Nancy withdrew two red jelly beans?

   A. $\dfrac{7}{20}+\dfrac{7}{20}$

   B. $\dfrac{7}{20}+\dfrac{6}{19}$

   C. $\dfrac{7}{20}\cdot\dfrac{7}{20}$

   D. $\dfrac{7}{20}\cdot\dfrac{6}{20}$

   E. $\dfrac{7}{20}\cdot\dfrac{6}{19}$

10. Mr. Monk is a pianist. If there are 5 black keys and 7 white keys, and Mr. Monk closes his eyes and plays two random notes (which could be the same) what is the probability that he plays two black keys?

   A. $\dfrac{35}{144}$

   B. $\dfrac{25}{49}$

   C. $\dfrac{5}{7}$

   D. $\dfrac{25}{144}$

   E. $\dfrac{49}{144}$

Arrangements

The Fundamental Counting Principle

The Fundamental Counting Principle is used in problems where you are asked to find the number of possibilities of picking one element from each of two or more sets to form a new set. In such problems, you could just model the information, if the numbers are small enough, by writing out all of the possibilities.

Example 1   Ms. Avery has four shawls—orange, purple, green, and white—to go with her three wigs which are red, auburn, and blonde. How many different shawl-and-wig pairs can she wear to work?

You can write out the possible combinations using the information in the table to the right:

Shawls	Wigs
(O)range	(R)ed
(P)urple	(A)uburn
(G)reen	(B)londe
(W)hite	

OR, OA, OB   PR, PA, PB

GR, GA, GB   WR, WA, WB

Each shawl can be combined with three different types of wigs, giving you a total of 12 possible combinations of shawls and wigs that Ms. Avery can wear to work. Notice that you could have taken a short cut and just multiplied 4×3 to get the same answer.

For any problem like this, you can write down **slots** for every event for which choices get made, fill each slot with the amount of choices you have for that category, and then multiply to get your answer.

Example 2   From a group of 20 teachers, 6 administrators, and 4 custodians, you can figure out how many teams could be made consisting of 1 teacher, 1 administrator, and 1 custodian by making slots for each and multiplying: $\underset{T}{20} \times \underset{A}{6} \times \underset{C}{4} = 480$.

Permutations and Combinations

A **permutation** is a slot problem except that there is a single category that diminishes as you choose.

Example 3   You can figure out how many ways you can fill four roles in a scene if you have nine actors to choose from by making slots for each role and multiplying: $\underset{A}{9} \times \underset{B}{8} \times \underset{C}{7} \times \underset{D}{6} = 3024$.

The above example could be represented using the notation $_9P_4$ since there are 9 in the original pool and 4 choices to be made. Most calculators have a permutation option under a probability menu (MATH $\rightarrow$ PRB on the TI-84) written as $_nP_r$. There you may also see !, for **factorials**, and $_nC_r$, for **combinations**.

A factorial is just a permutation brought all the way down to 1, so $5! = 5 \times 4 \times 3 \times 2 \times 1$.

Combinations divide the order out of permutations when the order doesn't matter.

Example 4   If instead of actors to fill roles, where the order of selection clearly matters, you wanted to find how many 4-person committees you could make from 9 people, you could calculate:

$$\frac{9 \times 8 \times 7 \times 6}{4 \times 3 \times 2 \times 1} = \frac{_9P_4}{4!} = {_9C_4} = 126.$$

The order doesn't matter when you choose a committee, so it helps to remember to use a **COM**bination to solve a **COM**mittee problem.

Arrangements Problem Set

1. A restaurant allows you to pay one fixed price if you select one appetizer, one main course and one dessert from a list that has 4 appetizers, 7 main courses and 5 desserts. How many different meals could you have with this deal?

   A. 17
   B. 16
   C. 28
   D. 140
   E. 280

2. Kim mixes and matches all of her jeans, shirts, and hats to make different outfits. She can make a total of 36 different outfits that are one pair of jeans, one shirt, and one hat. Which of the following could NOT be the number of hats that Kim has?

   A. 3
   B. 4
   C. 5
   D. 6
   E. 9

3. Shaun has a white shirt, a blue shirt, a red shirt, a purple shirt, and a black shirt. He also has a black tie, a gray tie, and a blue tie. How many different shirt-and-tie combinations can he wear if he wears one of each?

   A. 5
   B. 8
   C. 10
   D. 15
   E. 720

4. Maryland license plates contain 6 characters: any combination of 3 letters, followed by 3 numerical digits. The letters and digits may repeat, but the first digit cannot be 0. How many millions of different license plates can be made, rounded to the nearest million, using these stipulations?

   A. 15
   B. 16
   C. 17
   D. 18
   E. 19

5. A basketball team has 5 starting players. The coach wants to have the starters announced in a different order every game. How many games could the team play without repeating the order in which the starting players are announced?

   A. 5
   B. 15
   C. 25
   D. 120
   E. 3125

6. Han, Luke, Chewy, Anakin, Leia, Lando and Yoda ran a race. How many arrangements of first, second and third place could there be if you know that Chewy came in first and Yoda came in last (seventh)?

   A. 3
   B. 7
   C. 20
   D. 42
   E. 210

7. If the letter U cannot be first or second, how many distinct four-letter arrangements can be made using all four letters in the word JUMP?

   A. 4
   B. 6
   C. 12
   D. 22
   E. 24

8. What is the value of $\dfrac{n!}{(n-3)!}$ in terms of n?

   A. $n(n-2)$

   B. $\dfrac{n}{n-2}$

   C. $n(n-1)(n-2)$

   D. $n(n-3)$

   E. $\dfrac{n}{n-3}$

9. What is the value of $\dfrac{8!}{5!3!}$?

   A. 1
   B. 8
   C. 28
   D. 56
   E. 2688

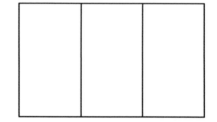

10. A new country is designing its flag. It wants three colored stripes. The outside stripes can be the same color or different colors, but the interior stripe must be unique. If it has ten colors to choose from, how many different flags can it design?

    A. 1000
    B. 900
    C. 810
    D. 720
    E. 560

11. Which of the following is equivalent to $_{10}P_3$?

    A. 10×3

    B. $10 \times 9 \times 8$

    C. $10 \times 9 \times 8 \times 7 \times 6 \times 5 \times 4 \times 3$

    D. $\dfrac{10!}{3!}$

    E. $\dfrac{_{10}C_3}{3!}$

12. How many 3-letter arrangements can you make from the letters in the word SOFTWARE if each letter can be used only once?

    A. 3

    B. 8

    C. 24

    D. 56

    E. 336

13. How many distinct committees of 8 people can be made from a seminar group of 25 people?

    A. 25×8

    B. $_{25}P_8$

    C. $_{25}C_8$

    D. $\dfrac{25!}{8!}$

    E. 25^8

14. From a team of 6 Mathletes, 2 will be chosen to represent the team at the annual Chaos Theory Conference. How many different pairs of two Mathletes can be chosen?

    A. 6

    B. 12

    C. 15

    D. 30

    E. 36

15. In a league tennis tournament each player plays every other player once. If there are 21 matches, how many players are in the tournament?

    A. 4

    B. 5

    C. 6

    D. 7

    E. 8

Part VI: Trigonometry

The ACT Math section always has four or five trigonometry questions, not as many as you'll see highlighting algebra, geometry, or data analysis but still a significant number. Usually, there will be two or three questions that can be answered with basic right-triangle trig (often called SOH-CAH-TOA trig), and two or three others pulled from a wide array of higher trig topics.

Though a graphing or scientific calculator is not technically necessary on the ACT because answer choices will often display calculations instead of complicated decimals, it can be very helpful to use the trig buttons for sine, cosine and tangent on your calculator to determine whether an answer choice even makes sense— just be sure that if you mean to calculate in degrees, your calculator is in "degree mode." If a diagram is given, you can compare a calculated answer to what the diagram could plausibly support. This is similar to the *measuring* strategy.

After reviewing the notes in this section, try the two problem sets. The first set includes the types of trigonometry questions you might see in the first 40 questions on an ACT Math section, while the second set is a sampling of the kinds of higher-level trig questions found toward the end of the Math section.

Trigonometry Basics and Formulas

The most important thing to remember for trigonometry is SOH–CAH–TOA:

$$\sin\theta = \frac{\text{opposite}}{\text{hypotenuse}}$$

$$\cos\theta = \frac{\text{adjacent}}{\text{hypotenuse}}$$

$$\tan\theta = \frac{\text{opposite}}{\text{adjacent}}$$

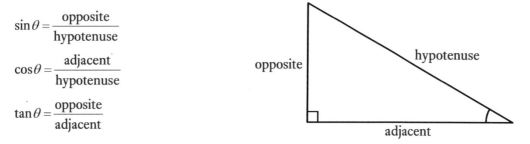

Knowing how to use **inverse functions** to find an angle when given the sine, cosine, or tangent is also important.

$$\sin^{-1}(x) = \arcsin(x) = \theta \Rightarrow \sin(\theta) = x$$
$$\cos^{-1}(x) = \arccos(x) = \theta \Rightarrow \cos(\theta) = x$$
$$\tan^{-1}(x) = \arctan(x) = \theta \Rightarrow \tan(\theta) = x$$

Formulas

There are two trigonometry identities (formulas) you should memorize:

$$\sin^2\theta + \cos^2\theta = 1 \qquad \tan\theta = \frac{\sin\theta}{\cos\theta}$$

Other trigonometric identities are tested less commonly:

$$\csc\theta = \frac{1}{\sin\theta} \qquad \sec\theta = \frac{1}{\cos\theta} \qquad \cot\theta = \frac{1}{\tan\theta} = \frac{\cos\theta}{\sin\theta}$$

Law of Sines and Law of Cosines

The **Law of Sines** and the **Law of Cosines** are often tested, so familiarity with the two formulas and their use is important. These formulas apply to non-right triangles, as shown:

Law of Sines: $\dfrac{\sin A}{a} = \dfrac{\sin B}{b} = \dfrac{\sin C}{c}$

Law of Cosines: $c^2 = a^2 + b^2 - 2ab\cos C$
$$b^2 = a^2 + c^2 - 2ac\cos B$$
$$a^2 = b^2 + c^2 - 2bc\cos A$$

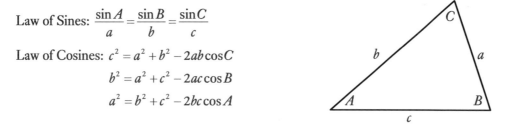

Radians

A radian is a portion of the circumference of a circle equivalent to the length of one radius of that circle. Radian measurement is another way to measure the size of an angle.

$$\pi \text{ radians} = 180°$$

The Unit Circle

The unit circle has the equation $x^2 + y^2 = 1$. Any angle θ measured from the positive x-axis will have a terminal side that intercepts the unit circle at a point with $x = \cos\theta$ and $y = \sin\theta$.

Coterminal Angles

When two angles, measured from the positive x-axis, share a terminal side, they are coterminal angles. The difference between coterminal angles is always a multiple of $360°$ (or 2π radians). For example, $20°$, $380°$, $740°$, and $-340°$ are all coterminal angles.

Graphing Trigonometric Functions

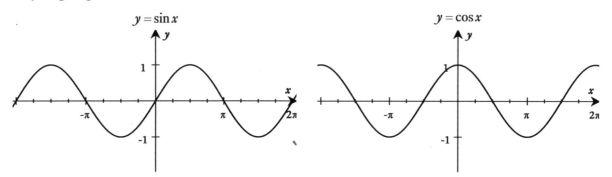

For $y = a\sin b(x - h) + k$ and $y = a\cos b(x - h) + k$:

$|a|$ = **Amplitude**   the height of the peak of the graph above its midline

$|b|$ = **Frequency**   how many cycles of the wave occur in a 2π span

$\dfrac{2\pi}{|b|}$ = **Period**   width of a full cycle, or wavelength

(h, k) = **Shift**   horizontal and vertical movement from the basic graph ($y = k$ will be the midline)

Trigonometry Problem Set 1

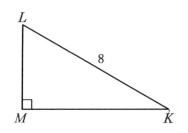

1. In the right triangle *KLM* pictured above, $\sin K = \frac{1}{2}$. What is the length of side *LM*?

A. 3
B. 4
C. 5
D. 8
E. 16

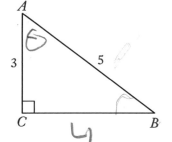

2. In the figure above, which of the following is equal to $\frac{3}{5}$?

A. $\sin A$
B. $\cos A$
C. $\tan A$
D. $\cos B$
E. $\tan B$

3. In $\triangle ABC$, $\angle A$ is a right angle. Which of the following is equal to $\tan B$?

A. $\frac{AC}{BC}$
B. $\frac{BC}{AC}$
C. $\frac{AB}{AC}$
D. $\frac{AC}{AB}$
E. $\frac{AB}{BC}$

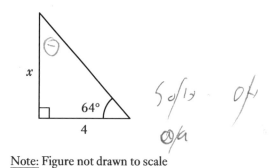

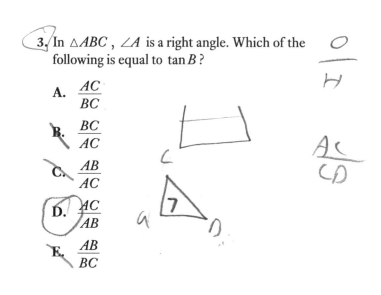

Note: Figure not drawn to scale

4. In the triangle above, what is the value of *x*?

A. $4\sin 64°$
B. $\frac{4}{\sin 64°}$
C. $\frac{4}{\cos 64°}$
D. $4\tan 64°$
E. $\frac{4}{\tan 64°}$

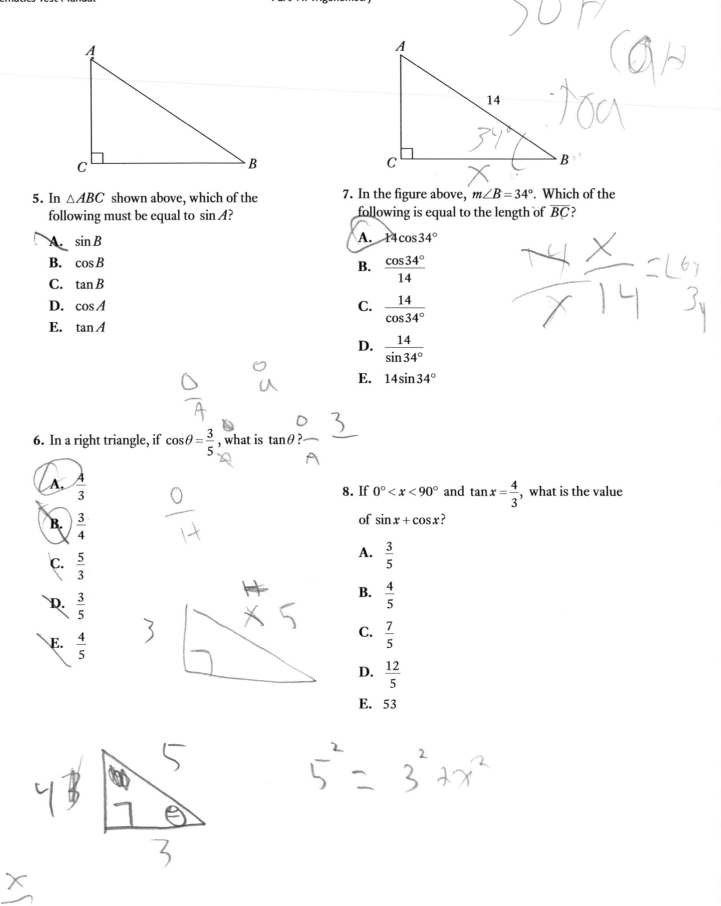

5. In $\triangle ABC$ shown above, which of the following must be equal to $\sin A$?

   A. $\sin B$

   B. $\cos B$

   C. $\tan B$

   D. $\cos A$

   E. $\tan A$

6. In a right triangle, if $\cos\theta = \dfrac{3}{5}$, what is $\tan\theta$?

   A. $\dfrac{4}{3}$

   B. $\dfrac{3}{4}$

   C. $\dfrac{5}{3}$

   D. $\dfrac{3}{5}$

   E. $\dfrac{4}{5}$

7. In the figure above, $m\angle B = 34°$. Which of the following is equal to the length of $\overline{BC}$?

   A. $14\cos 34°$

   B. $\dfrac{\cos 34°}{14}$

   C. $\dfrac{14}{\cos 34°}$

   D. $\dfrac{14}{\sin 34°}$

   E. $14\sin 34°$

8. If $0° < x < 90°$ and $\tan x = \dfrac{4}{3}$, what is the value of $\sin x + \cos x$?

   A. $\dfrac{3}{5}$

   B. $\dfrac{4}{5}$

   C. $\dfrac{7}{5}$

   D. $\dfrac{12}{5}$

   E. 53

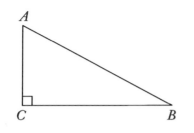

A

C B

9. For the triangle shown above, which of the following statements is true?

A. $\sin B = \dfrac{AC}{BC}$

B. $\sin B = \dfrac{BC}{AB}$

C. $\sin B = \dfrac{AB}{AC}$

D. $\sin B = \dfrac{AB}{BC}$

E. $\sin B = \dfrac{AC}{AB}$

11. You are standing 22 feet from the base of a flagpole, looking up at an angle of 34° in order to see the flag at the top. How high above your eye level, in feet, is the flag?

A. $22\sin 34°$

B. $\dfrac{22}{\sin 34°}$

C. $22\cos 34°$

D. $\dfrac{22}{\tan 34°}$

E. $22\tan 34°$

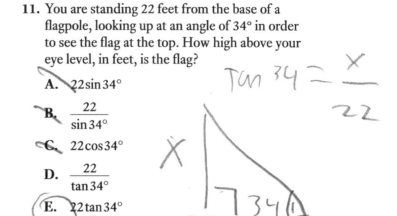

12. If $\tan\theta = 4$, what is $\dfrac{\cos\theta}{\sin\theta}$?

A. $\dfrac{1}{10}$

B. $\dfrac{1}{4}$

C. $\dfrac{1}{2}$

D. 2

E. 4

10. The height of a telephone pole is 45 feet, and it casts a shadow 13 feet in length. What is the angle of the sun above the horizon?

A. $\dfrac{13}{45}$

B. $\sin^{-1}\left(\dfrac{13}{45}\right)$

C. $\cos^{-1}\left(\dfrac{13}{45}\right)$

D. $\tan^{-1}\left(\dfrac{13}{45}\right)$

E. $\tan^{-1}\left(\dfrac{45}{13}\right)$

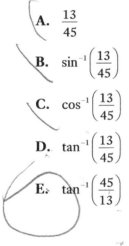

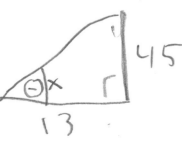

13. From a spot 50 feet from the base of a building, Kiran views the top of the building with an angle of elevation of 70°. How many feet above Kiran's eye level is the top of the building?

A. $\dfrac{50}{\tan 70°}$

B. $\dfrac{\tan 70°}{50}$

C. $50 \tan 70°$

D. $50 \sin 70°$

E. $\dfrac{50}{\sin 70°}$

15. Which of the following angles is NOT coterminal to 110°?

A. −250°

B. 250°

C. 470°

D. 830°

E. 3710°

14. The angles $\angle P$ and $\angle Q$ are co-terminal. If $\angle P$ has a measure of 800°, which of the following could be the measure of $\angle Q$?

A. 8°

B. 80°

C. 180°

D. 400°

E. 880°

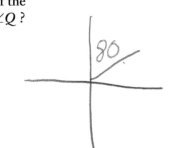

Trigonometry Problem Set 2

1. If $0 < \theta < \dfrac{\pi}{2}$ and $\cos\theta = \dfrac{1}{2}$, what is $\sin\theta$?

   A. 0

   B. $\dfrac{1}{2}$

   C. $\dfrac{\sqrt{2}}{2}$

   D. $\dfrac{\sqrt{3}}{2}$

   E. 1

2. If $6\cos^2\theta + 6\sin^2\theta = 3x$, what is x?

   A. −3

   B. −2

   C. 0

   D. 2

   E. 3

3. Which of the following is equal to $(3\sin^2 x + 3\cos^2 x - 5)^3$?

   A. −64

   B. −8

   C. 8

   D. 64

   E. 512

4. If θ is an acute angle and $\dfrac{\cos^2\theta}{\sin^2\theta} = \dfrac{1}{3}$, then $\tan\theta$?

   A. $\dfrac{1}{3}$

   B. $\dfrac{1}{\sqrt{3}}$

   C. 1

   D. $\sqrt{3}$

   E. 3

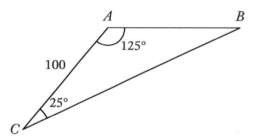

5. In $\triangle ABC$, shown above, angle measurements are as marked and the length given is in centimeters. Which of the following is an expression for the length, in centimeters, of AB?

   A. $\dfrac{100\sin 25°}{\sin 135°}$

   B. $\dfrac{100\sin 30°}{\sin 25°}$

   C. $\dfrac{100\sin 25°}{\sin 30°}$

   D. $\dfrac{100\sin 30°}{\sin 135°}$

   E. $\dfrac{100\sin 135°}{\sin 20°}$

6. If θ is an acute angle, then $\dfrac{\tan\theta\cos\theta}{\sin\theta} =$

A. $\dfrac{1}{\tan\theta}$

B. $\tan\theta$

C. 1

D. -1

E. $\sin\theta$

7. If $\sin x = -\dfrac{1}{3}$, what is $\cos 2x$?

(Note that $\sin^2 x = \dfrac{1-\cos 2x}{2}$)

A. $-\dfrac{8}{9}$

B. $-\dfrac{7}{9}$

C. $\dfrac{1}{9}$

D. $\dfrac{7}{9}$

E. $\dfrac{8}{9}$

8. What is the amplitude of the graph of $y = 3 + 4\sin(2x)$?

A. 2

B. 3

C. 4

D. 8

E. $\dfrac{\pi}{2}$

9. In triangle ABC, the measure of $\angle A$ is 66°, the measure of $\angle C$ is 51°, and the length of side AB is 12 inches. Which of the following is the correct expression for the length of side BC, in inches?

A. $\dfrac{\sin 66°}{12\sin 51°}$

B. $\dfrac{\sin 51°}{12\sin 66°}$

C. $\dfrac{12\sin 66°}{\sin 51°}$

D. $\dfrac{12\sin 51°}{\sin 66°}$

E. $\dfrac{\sin 51°\sin 66°}{12}$

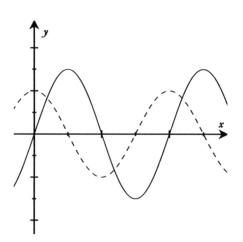

10. The equations of the two graphs shown above are $y = a\cos(bx)$ and $y = c\sin(dx)$. Which of the following statements are true about the constants a and c?

A. $a < c < 0$

B. $a < 0 < c$

C. $c < 0 < a$

D. $0 < a < c$

E. $0 < c < a$

11. What is the period of the function

$$y = 2\cos\frac{\pi}{6}x - 5?$$

  A. 2

  B. 6

  C. 12

  D. $\frac{\pi}{6}$

  E. 12π

14. The height, h, of a ferris wheel car, can be modeled by the function $h = 48 - 44\cos\frac{\pi}{20}t$, where t represents the time, in seconds, after the car reaches its lowest point. How many seconds long is one rotation of the ferris wheel?

  A. 20

  B. 40

  C. 44

  D. 46

  E. 48

12. Which of the following equations could be used to properly solve for the smallest angle, θ, in a triangle with sides of 12, 15, and 23?

  A. $12^2 = 15^2 + 23^2 - 2(15)(23)\cos\theta$

  B. $15^2 = 12^2 + 23^2 - 2(12)(23)\cos\theta$

  C. $23^2 = 12^2 + 15^2 - 2(12)(15)\cos\theta$

  D. $\dfrac{\sin\theta}{12} = \dfrac{\sin 15}{23}$

  E. $\dfrac{\sin\theta}{12} = \dfrac{\sin 23}{15}$

15. If $0 \le \theta < 2\pi$, what are the values of θ for which $\cos^2\theta - \frac{1}{2}\cos\theta = 0$?

  A. $\left\{0, \dfrac{\pi}{6}, \dfrac{5\pi}{6}, \pi\right\}$

  B. $\left\{\dfrac{\pi}{3}, \dfrac{\pi}{2}, \dfrac{2\pi}{3}, \dfrac{3\pi}{2}\right\}$

  C. $\left\{\dfrac{\pi}{3}, \dfrac{\pi}{2}, \dfrac{3\pi}{2}, \dfrac{5\pi}{3}\right\}$

  D. $\left\{\dfrac{\pi}{3}, \dfrac{2\pi}{3}\right\}$

  E. $\{0, \pi\}$

13. What is the range of the function

$$y = 5\sin 2x - 1?$$

  A. $-6 \le y \le 4$

  B. $-3 \le y \le 1$

  C. $-5 \le y \le 5$

  D. $0 \le y \le 5$

  E. $-6 \le y \le 6$

Part VII: Higher Level Topics

There are some miscellaneous topics that come up, on average, about once per ACT Math section. These need not be mastered if your goal is to score in the middle or upper 20s. However, if you are aiming for a top math score, you will want to ensure that you've covered the concepts on the following pages. They are arranged roughly in order from the most frequently tested to the most rare, and, in fact, the final set is simply a combination of the two rarest topics you could see:

- Matrices
- Asymptotes and End Behavior
- Imaginary and Complex Numbers
- Logarithms
- Vectors
- Conic Sections and Polar Graphs

Since there are six problem sets of ten questions each in this section, a top test-taker could use those 60 questions as a kind of an ultra-difficult ACT Math section, full of questions that you might only see in the 40s or 50s on an actual ACT. Still, making smart *calculator maneuvers*, *backsolving*, and *plugging in numbers* may be useful strategies for some of these questions.

Matrices

A matrix is an array of terms that is arranged in rows and columns. Matrices can sometimes be used to represent the elements or coefficients of a system of equations. A matrix is described as having dimensions $m \times n$, meaning it has m rows and n columns.

Example 1   This matrix is a 3×2 matrix (i.e. three rows and two columns): $\begin{bmatrix} 1 & 14 \\ -2 & 1 \\ 5 & 3 \end{bmatrix}$

Addition and Subtraction

You can only add or subtract matrices that have the same dimensions. In order to add matrix **B** to matrix **A**, simply add the corresponding elements.

Example 2 $\begin{bmatrix} 3 & a \\ -5 & 1 \end{bmatrix} + \begin{bmatrix} 1 & 0 \\ 3 & b \end{bmatrix} = \begin{bmatrix} 4 & a \\ -2 & b+1 \end{bmatrix}$

Multiplying by a Term

If a matrix is multiplied by a single term, that term multiplies with all elements of the matrix, and the resulting matrix will have the same dimensions as the original.

Example 3 $-3 \begin{bmatrix} 2 & a \\ 0 & 5 \end{bmatrix} = \begin{bmatrix} -6 & -3a \\ 0 & -15 \end{bmatrix}$

Matrix Multiplication $[m \times n][n \times p] = [m \times p]$

To multiply two matrices, the number of columns of the first matrix must be the same as the number of rows of the second matrix. The resulting matrix will have the same number of rows as the first matrix and the same number of columns as the second matrix. Note that the order in which matrices are multiplied matters.

Example 4   If matrix **A** is a 2×3 matrix, and matrix **B** is a 3×1 matrix, then **AB** will be a 2×1 matrix, and **BA** cannot be calculated.

The actual work of multiplying two matrices is rarely tested and involves adding the products of each row/column pairing, but it is better to just use your calculator (F3 or MATRIX menu on the TI-84).

Determinants

You may be asked to calculate the determinant (sometimes denoted by absolute value bars) of a 2×2 matrix, which can be done with the following formula, but you will not be asked to calculate determinants for larger matrices:

Example 5   If $\mathbf{A} = \begin{bmatrix} a & b \\ c & d \end{bmatrix}$ then $\det(\mathbf{A}) = \begin{vmatrix} a & b \\ c & d \end{vmatrix} = ad - bc.$

Matrices Problem Set

$$2x + 3y = 17$$
$$4x - 2y = -6$$

1. Which of the following matrices could be used to represent the system of equations shown above?

A. $\begin{bmatrix} 2 & 3 & | & 17 \\ 4 & -2 & | & -6 \end{bmatrix}$

B. $\begin{bmatrix} 2 & 3 & | & 17 \\ 4 & 2 & | & 6 \end{bmatrix}$

C. $\begin{bmatrix} 2 & 4 & | & 17 \\ 3 & -2 & | & -6 \end{bmatrix}$

D. $\begin{bmatrix} 2 & 3 & | & 4 \\ -2 & 17 & | & -6 \end{bmatrix}$

E. $\begin{bmatrix} 2 & 3 & | & 17 \\ 2 & -1 & | & -6 \end{bmatrix}$

$$[9 \ \ -2] - [4 \ \ 2] = [x \ \ y]$$

2. In the equation above, what is the value of xy?

A. 20

B. 1

C. 0

D. −1

E. −20

3. If $\mathbf{A} = \begin{bmatrix} 4 & -5 \\ -1 & 9 \end{bmatrix}$ and $\mathbf{B} = \begin{bmatrix} 2 & 7 \\ -4 & 0 \end{bmatrix}$, then which of the following equals $2\mathbf{A} - 3\mathbf{B}$?

A. $\begin{bmatrix} 2 & -31 \\ 10 & 18 \end{bmatrix}$

B. $\begin{bmatrix} 14 & 11 \\ -14 & 18 \end{bmatrix}$

C. $\begin{bmatrix} 2 & 31 \\ -10 & 18 \end{bmatrix}$

D. $\begin{bmatrix} 8 & -10 \\ -2 & 18 \\ -6 & 12 \\ -21 & 0 \end{bmatrix}$

E. $\begin{bmatrix} 8 & -10 & -6 & -21 \\ -2 & 18 & 12 & 0 \end{bmatrix}$

4. If $\begin{bmatrix} 3 & -5 \\ 2 & 0 \\ -1 & 7 \end{bmatrix} + \begin{bmatrix} 2 & 5 \\ a & -3 \\ 1 & b \end{bmatrix} = \begin{bmatrix} 5 & 0 \\ 6 & c \\ d & 5 \end{bmatrix}$, then what is the sum of a, b, c, and d?

−9

−1

1

3

9

5. When multiplying a matrix with dimensions $[4 \times 5]$ by a matrix with dimensions $[5 \times 2]$, what will be the dimensions of the product?

   A. $[4 \times 2]$

   B. $[5 \times 5]$

   C. $[9 \times 7]$

   D. $[20 \times 10]$

   E. The product does not exist.

6. What is the product $n \begin{bmatrix} i & t \\ i & n \end{bmatrix}$?

   A. -1

   B. 0

   C. $\begin{bmatrix} ni & nt \\ ni & n^2 \end{bmatrix}$

   D. $\begin{bmatrix} -ni & nt \\ -ni & 0 \end{bmatrix}$

   E. $[nitin]$

7. What is the result of the product:

   $[2 \quad -3 \quad 0] \times \begin{bmatrix} 1 & 1 \\ 0 & 2 \\ 5 & -4 \end{bmatrix}$?

   A. $[0 \quad -8]$

   B. $[2 \quad -4]$

   C. $\begin{bmatrix} 2 \\ -4 \end{bmatrix}$

   D. $\begin{bmatrix} 2 & 0 & 0 \\ 2 & -6 & 0 \end{bmatrix}$

   E. The product does not exist.

8. What is $\begin{bmatrix} -y \\ 0 \\ x \end{bmatrix} \times [x \quad y \quad 0]$?

   A. The matrices cannot be multiplied

   B. $[-xy]$

   C. $[0]$

   D. $\begin{bmatrix} -xy & -y^2 & 0 \\ 0 & 0 & 0 \\ x^2 & xy & 0 \end{bmatrix}$

   E. $\begin{bmatrix} -xy & 0 & x^2 \\ -y^2 & 0 & xy \\ 0 & 0 & 0 \end{bmatrix}$

9. What is the determinant of the matrix $\begin{bmatrix} 3 & -2 \\ 1 & 4 \end{bmatrix}$?

   A. -24

   B. -14

   C. 9

   D. 10

   E. 14

10. What is $\begin{vmatrix} f^2 & g \\ -g & f \end{vmatrix}$?

    A. $f^3 - g^2$

    B. $f^3 + g^2$

    C. f^3

    D. $f^2 + f - 2g$

    E. $f^2 + f + 2g$

Asymptotes and End Behavior

An asymptote is a line that a graph bends closer and closer to without crossing. **Vertical asymptotes** signify numbers that are not in the domain of a function. **Horizontal and slant asymptotes** (also known as oblique or diagonal asymptotes) approximate the end behavior of a function as x approaches positive and negative infinity. Usually, *if you just graph a function on your calculator*, the asymptotes will be clear.

Rational Functions

A rational function is a fraction of two polynomials, and it can have vertical asymptotes at x values that make the denominator equal 0, as well as a horizontal or slant asymptote, depending on its end behavior. Slant asymptotes occur when the degree of the numerator is one greater than that of the denominator.

Example 1 $f(x) = \dfrac{x-4}{(x+1)(x-2)}$ has vertical asymptotes with equations $x = -1$ and $x = 2$. It also has a

horizontal asymptote with the equation $y = 0$, the x-axis, because as x gets larger and larger (and as it gets smaller and smaller in the negative direction), $f(x)$ gets closer to 0.

Example 2   If we flip the previous function upside down, $f(x) = \dfrac{(x+1)(x-2)}{x-4}$ has a vertical asymptote

with the equation $x = 4$. It also has a slant asymptote with the equation $y = x + 3$, a linear function that $f(x)$ approximates at its extremes.

BE CAREFUL: If an x value makes both the top and bottom of a rational function equal 0, the graph will not have a vertical asymptote at that x. There will be a hole in the graph instead

Example 3   The function $f(x) = \dfrac{(x-3)(2x+1)}{(x+7)(x-3)}$ has a vertical asymptote of $x = -7$ but not $x = 3$ because

3 is a zero for both the top and bottom. There will be a hole in the graph at the point $\left(3, \dfrac{7}{10}\right)$.

There will also be a horizontal asymptote of $y = 2$ since very large and very small x values will yield values for $f(x)$ that approach 2.

Other Functions with Asymptotes

Exponential functions, logarithmic functions, trigonometric functions, and even some non-function relations like hyperbolas can have asymptotes.

Example 4   The function $y = \left(\dfrac{1}{2}\right)^x$ has a horizontal asymptote at $y = 0$ which is only relevant as x values

approach positive infinity. Explore this on your graphing calculator.

Asymptotes and End Behavior Problem Set

1. Which of the following is a vertical asymptote for the graph of $y = \dfrac{x^2 - 10x + 21}{x^2 + 3x}$?

   A. $y = 0$

   B. $y = -3$

   C. $x = -3$

   D. $x = 3$

   E. $y = 7$

3. What are equations of all vertical asymptotes for the graph of the function $y = \dfrac{2x - 6}{x^2 - 9}$?

   A. $x = 3$ and $x = -3$

   B. $x = 3$ only

   C. $x = -3$ only

   D. $x = 0$ only

   E. $x = 3$, $x = -3$, and $x = 0$

2. Which of the following functions has a vertical asymptote at $x = \dfrac{3}{7}$?

   A. $y = \dfrac{3x + 5}{7x}$

   B. $y = \dfrac{x - 3}{x - 7}$

   C. $y = \dfrac{x + 2}{3x - 7}$

   D. $y = \dfrac{x + 2}{7x - 3}$

   E. $y = \dfrac{7x - 3}{x + 2}$

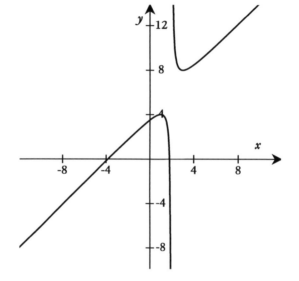

4. Above is the graph of the function $y = \dfrac{x^2 + 2x - 7}{x - 2}$ in the xy-coordinate plane. What is the equation of the slant (oblique or diagonal) asymptote of this function?

   A. $y = 2$

   B. $x = 2$

   C. $y = 2x$

   D. $y = x + 4$

   E. $y = 2x - \dfrac{7}{2}$

5. What is the horizontal asymptote for the function $y = \dfrac{4x^2 - 1}{2x^2}$?

   A. $x = \dfrac{1}{2}$

   B. $y = \dfrac{1}{2}$

   C. $y = -\dfrac{1}{2}$

   D. $x = 2$

   E. $y = 2$

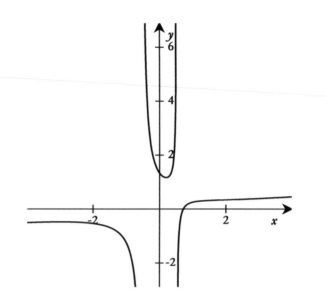

8. Above is a portion of the graph of the function $y = \dfrac{x^3 + 5x - 4}{11x^2 - 3}$. Which of the following asymptotes does this graph have?

   I. Vertical
   II. Horizontal
   III. Slant

   A. I only

   B. III only

   C. I and II only

   D. I and III only

   E. I, II and III

6. What is the equation of the only asymptote for the graph of the function $f(x) = 2(3)^{x+4} + 5$?

   A. $y = -4$

   B. $y = 2$

   C. $y = 3$

   D. $y = 4$

   E. $y = 5$

7. How many of the graphs of the six basic trigonometric functions ($y = \sin x, y = \cos x, y = \tan x, y = \sec x, y = \csc x,$ and $y = \cot x$), have vertical asymptotes?

   A. None

   B. Two

   C. Three

   D. Four

   E. Six

9. Which of the following describes the end behavior for $y = \dfrac{5x^2 + 18}{3x^2 - 9}$?

   A. The graph tends toward the line $y = \dfrac{5}{3}$ as x approaches $\pm\infty$.

   B. The graph tends toward the line $y = \dfrac{5}{3}x - 2$ as x approaches $\pm\infty$.

   C. The graph tends toward the line $y = -\sqrt{3}$ as x approaches $-\infty$, and toward $y = \sqrt{3}$ as x approaches ∞.

   D. The graph tends toward the line $y = -9$ as x approaches $-\infty$, and toward $y = 18$ as x approaches ∞.

   E. The graph tends toward the line $y = 2x + 9$ as x approaches $\pm\infty$.

10. Which of the following relations has a graph that does NOT have any vertical, horizontal or slant (diagonal) asymptotes?

   A. $y = \dfrac{x^2 - 9}{x^2}$

   B. $y = \dfrac{x^2 - 9x + 20}{2x + 15}$

   C. $y = \dfrac{x^3 - 9x^2 + 20x}{2x^2 + 15}$

   D. $4x^2 + 9y^2 = 36$

   E. $4x^2 - 9y^2 = 36$

Imaginary and Complex Numbers

The number i is the base of the imaginary number system. It is equal to $\sqrt{-1}$.

Example 1 $\sqrt{-16} = 4i$

Example 2 $\sqrt{-12} = 2i\sqrt{3}$

Complex numbers   have the form $a + bi$, where a and b are real numbers. Most operations on complex numbers can be done on the calculator using, for example, $\boxed{\text{2ND}} \rightarrow \boxed{\overset{i}{.}}$ on a TI-84.

Addition, Subtraction and Multiplication of Complex Numbers

Complex numbers can be added and subtracted by combining like terms, just like binomials, but when they are multiplied, i^2 should be converted to –1.

Example 3 $(2+i)(3-5i) = 6-10i+3i-5i^2 = 6-7i-(-5) = 11-7i$

Conjugates and Division

Each complex number $a + bi$ has a *complex conjugate*, $a - bi$. When conjugates are multiplied, the resulting product will be a pure real number (that is, with no imaginary part). Whenever anything is divided by a complex number, you should multiply both the numerator and denominator by the conjugate of the bottom to make the denominator real and rational.

Example 4 $\dfrac{4-i}{3+2i} = \dfrac{4-i}{3+2i} \cdot \dfrac{3-2i}{3-2i} = \dfrac{12-8i-3i+2i^2}{9-6i+6i-4i^2} = \dfrac{10-11i}{13}$ or $\dfrac{10}{13} - \dfrac{11i}{13}$

Powers of i

Every power of i is equivalent to either i, $i^2 = -1$, $i^3 = -i$, or $i^4 = 1$. If you find the remainder when the power is divided by 4, you can then raise i to the power of that remainder.

Example 5 $i^{87} = i^{84+3} = i^3 = -i$

Graphing Complex Numbers

Complex numbers can be graphed as either points or vectors in the complex coordinate plane, where the horizontal x-axis is the real axis and the vertical yi-axis is the imaginary axis. So, the complex number $5 - 3i$ would look very much like the point $(5,-3)$ or the vector $\langle 5,-3 \rangle$.

Imaginary and Complex Number Problem Set

1. What is the sum of $(3-5i)$ and $(-7-2i)$ if $i=\sqrt{-1}$?

   A. $-4+7i$

   B. $-4-3i$

   C. $-4-7i$

   D. $4-3i$

   E. $4+3i$

2. Which of the following results from the computation $(12-11i)-(8-6i)$ if $i=\sqrt{-1}$?

   A. $-4-17i$

   B. $4-17i$

   C. $4+5i$

   D. $-4+5i$

   E. $4-5i$

3. What is the product of $(6-3i)$ and $(2+5i)$ if $i=\sqrt{-1}$?

   A. $12-15i$

   B. $12-9i$

   C. $-3+24i$

   D. $27+24i$

   E. $27+36i$

4. What is the product of $(4-2i)$ and $(4+2i)$ if $i=\sqrt{-1}$?

   A. -12

   B. 12

   C. 20

   D. $16-4i$

   E. $12-4i$

5. What is the square of the complex number $(2-i)$ if $i=\sqrt{-1}$?

   A. $3-4i$

   B. $4-4i$

   C. $4-5i$

   D. 3

   E. 5

6. What is the value of i^{314} if $i=\sqrt{-1}$?

   A. -1

   B. $-i$

   C. i

   D. 1

   E. -314

7. Which of the following complex numbers is equivalent to $\dfrac{12}{2+3i}$ if $i = \sqrt{-1}$?

A. $6 + 4i$

B. $6 - 4i$

C. $-\dfrac{24}{5} + \dfrac{36i}{5}$

D. $\dfrac{24}{13} - \dfrac{36i}{13}$

E. $\dfrac{6}{13} - \dfrac{4i}{13}$

8. What is the value of $i^3 + i^2 + i$ if $i = \sqrt{-1}$?

A. -1

B. $-i$

C. i

D. 1

E. i^6

9. If the complex numbers $5 + 2i$ and $-2 + 4i$ and their sum are all graphed in the complex plane, which of the following is true?

A. All three are in the first quadrant

B. All three are in the second quadrant

C. Two are in the first quadrant

D. Two are in the second quadrant

E. All three are in different quadrants

10. What is the distance in the complex coordinate plane between the points $3 - 5i$ and $-7 + 19i$?

A. $-4 + 14i$

B. $10 + 24i$

C. $\sqrt{212}$

D. 26

E. 34

Logarithms

A **logarithm**, or log, is simply an exponent written in a different form. In exponential form, when a base, b, is raised to an exponent, c, you'll see the equation $a = b^c$. This same equation in logarithmic form is $\log_b a = c$. Some calculators, like the TI-84, have a logBase function, that allows you to enter numbers into $\log_\square(\square)$ to calculate a log.

Example 1   Since $3^2 = 9$, you can also write $\log_3 9 = 2$.

Common and Natural Logs

When a log is used and no base is written, the number 10 is the base. A button on your calculator that just says $\boxed{\text{LOG}}$ will operate in base 10. When the irrational number e (an important number in calculations involving exponential growth and decay that is approximately 2.718) is used as the base, you are taking what is called the "natural" log, or **ln**. Calculators have $\boxed{\text{LN}}$ buttons as well.

Example 2 $\log 1000 = 3$

Example 3 $\ln(e^5) = 5$

Properties of Logs

Power Rule:	$\log_b(a^x) = x\log_b(a)$
Product Rule:	$\log_b(xy) = \log_b x + \log_b y$
Quotient Rule:	$\log_b\left(\dfrac{x}{y}\right) = \log_b x - \log_b y$

Example 4 $\log\left(\dfrac{3x}{y}\right) = \log 3 + \log x - \log y$

Example 5 $\ln e^2 x^3 = 2\ln e + 3\ln x = 2 + 3\ln x$

Graphs of Log Functions

Since $y = \log_b x$ and $y = b^x$ are inverse functions, the graph of $y = \log_b x$ will look like the graph of $y = b^x$ reflected over the $y = x$ line. Instead of having a horizontal asymptote at the x-axis, an unshifted log graph will have a vertical asymptote at the y-axis. The domain of $y = \log_b x$ is $x > 0$.

Logarithms Problem Set

1. If $\log_x\left(\dfrac{1}{4}\right) = 2$, what is the value of x?

    A. -2

    B. $\dfrac{1}{16}$

    C. $\dfrac{1}{2}$

    D. 4

    E. 16

2. If $\log_3(\log_2 8) = y$, what is the value of y?

    A. -1

    B. 0

    C. $\dfrac{1}{2}$

    D. 1

    E. 27

3. What is $\log_2 2 + \ln e + \log 10$?

    A. $12 + e$

    B. $20e$

    C. 1

    D. 3

    E. $104 + e^e$

4. If $\log_k 2 = p$ and $\log_k 3 = q$, then $\log_k 12 = ?$

    A. $2p + q$

    B. $p + 2q$

    C. $p^2 + q$

    D. $6p + 4q$

    E. $2pq$

5. What is the value of t, in terms of a, in the equation $y = a \cdot b^t$ if $b = 2$ and $y = 60$?

    A. $\dfrac{a}{30}$

    B. $\dfrac{30}{a}$

    C. $\log_a 30$

    D. $\log_{2a} 60$

    E. $\log_2\left(\dfrac{60}{a}\right)$

6. If $\log x = 2\log m + 5\log n$, which of the following is equal to x?

    A. $(\log m^2)(\log n^5)$

    B. $m^2 + n^5$

    C. $10mn$

    D. $\log(10mn)$

    E. $m^2 n^5$

7. If $f(x) = \log_3 x$, and $x > 0$, then $f^{-1}(x) = ?$

    A. x^3

    B. 3^x

    C. $\dfrac{3}{x}$

    D. $\log_x 3$

    E. $\dfrac{x}{3}$

9. If $a \ln b^x = xa$, which of the following MUST be true?

    A. $b = 1$

    B. $\ln b = 1$

    C. $b = 0$

    D. $ab = 1$

    E. $x = 1$

8. What is the equation of an asymptote for the function $y = \log(x - 3) + 5$?

    A. $y = 5$

    B. $y = -5$

    C. $x = 3$

    D. $x = -3$

    E. $x = 2$

10. For positive numbers x and y, $\log x = a$, and $\log y = b$. Which of the following is equal to $\log \dfrac{x^3}{\sqrt{y}}$?

    A. $3 \log a - \dfrac{1}{2} \log b$

    B. $3a - \sqrt{b}$

    C. $3a - \dfrac{1}{2} b$

    D. $\log \dfrac{3a}{\sqrt{b}}$

    E. $\dfrac{3a}{2b}$

Vectors

A vector is a quantity with both magnitude (length) and direction. When represented physically, a vector is simply a one-sided arrow with specified length and direction. The notation for vectors can vary. Keep in mind that a vector can be represented by a bolded letter (**v**), a letter with a one-sided arrow above it ($\vec{v}$), a pair of endpoints with a one-sided arrow above it ($\overrightarrow{AB}$), or a letter with a one-sided half-arrow above it ($\vec{v}$).

Unit Vectors and Component Form

Unit vectors are vectors with a magnitude of one. Horizontal unit vectors are usually called **i** or $\hat{\mathbf{i}}$, and vertical unit vectors are usually called **j** or $\hat{\mathbf{j}}$. Vectors can be expressed in component form, for example $\langle 2, 5 \rangle$, or as a sum of unit vectors, for example $2\mathbf{i} + 5\mathbf{j}$.

The Magnitude of a Vector

The magnitude of a vector is expressed using absolute value bars and is found using the formula $|\vec{v}| = \sqrt{a^2 + b^2}$, where a and b are the vector components.

Example 1   If $\vec{v} = \langle 3, -5 \rangle$, the magnitude of $\vec{v}$ is $|\vec{v}| = \sqrt{3^2 + (-5)^2} = \sqrt{34}$

Addition, Subtraction and Multiplication

Addition and subtraction of vectors simply involves adding or subtracting the component parts. Multiplying a vector by a scalar (non-vector quantity that only has magnitude, like a number) requires multiplying each component of the vector by the scalar quantity.

Example 2 $\langle -4, 9 \rangle + \langle 2, -1 \rangle = \langle -2, 8 \rangle$

Example 3 $5\langle 1, 3 \rangle - 2\langle 6, 0 \rangle = \langle 5, 15 \rangle - \langle 12, 0 \rangle = \langle -7, 15 \rangle$

The Triangle Inequality for Vectors

Since vectors can be represented by arrows, vector addition and subtraction can look like the creation of either a triangle or a line. A version of the triangle inequality results that says that the magnitude of the sum of two vectors cannot exceed the sum of the magnitudes of the two vectors: $|\vec{v} + \vec{u}| \leq |\vec{v}| + |\vec{u}|$.

Vectors Problem Set

1. What is the magnitude of the vector $\langle 7, -24 \rangle$?

   A. -17

   B. $\sqrt{17}$

   C. $\sqrt{527}$

   D. 25

   E. 31

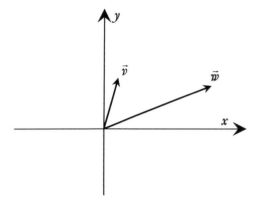

2. If $\mathbf{v} = \langle 3, 8 \rangle$ and $\mathbf{u} = \langle -2, 4 \rangle$, what is the component form of $2\mathbf{v} + (-4\mathbf{u})$?

   A. $\langle -2, 32 \rangle$

   B. $\langle -1, 10 \rangle$

   C. $\langle 14, 0 \rangle$

   D. $\langle -2, 0 \rangle$

   E. $\langle 14, 32 \rangle$

5. If vector $\vec{v}$ in the diagram above is $\langle 2, 7 \rangle$ and vector $\vec{w}$ is $\langle 15, 6 \rangle$, which of the following vectors or descriptions is equal to $\vec{v} + \vec{w}$?

   A. A vector connecting the heads of each arrow to form a triangle with $\vec{v}$ and $\vec{w}$

   B. A vector in the third quadrant

   C. The bisector of the angle created by $\vec{v}$ and $\vec{w}$

   D. $\langle 13, -1 \rangle$

   E. $\langle 17, 13 \rangle$

3. If $\vec{v} = \langle 9, -12 \rangle$, and $\vec{u} = -3\vec{v}$, what is scalar value $|\vec{u}|$?

   A. -45

   B. -9

   C. $\sqrt{189}$

   D. $\sqrt{567}$

   E. 45

6. If $\vec{a} = 3\mathbf{i} + 10\mathbf{j}$ and $\vec{b} = 4\mathbf{i} - 2\mathbf{j}$, and if $2\vec{a} + 5\vec{b} + \vec{c} = 0$, what is $\vec{c}$ equal to when written as a composition of unit vectors?

   A. $-26\mathbf{i} - 10\mathbf{j}$

   B. $-26\mathbf{i} + 10\mathbf{j}$

   C. $-9\mathbf{i} - 13\mathbf{j}$

   D. $9\mathbf{i} + 13\mathbf{j}$

   E. $26\mathbf{i} + 10\mathbf{j}$

4. If the magnitude of vector $\vec{v}$ is 11, and the magnitude of vector $\vec{w}$ is 17, which of the following <u>cannot</u> be the magnitude of a vector that represents $\vec{v} + \vec{w}$?

   A. 6

   B. 11

   C. 17

   D. 28

   E. 30

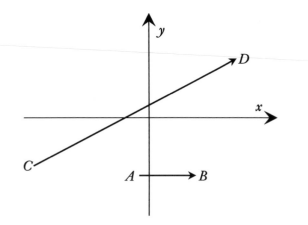

8. What is the magnitude of the vector form of the complex number $8 - 15i$?

    A. -7

    B. 7

    C. 17

    D. 23

    E. 120

7. In the diagram above, $A(-1,-6)$ and $B(5,-6)$ are endpoints of vector $\overrightarrow{AB}$, and $C(-12,-5)$ and $D(9,4)$ are endpoints of vector $\overrightarrow{CD}.$ Which composition of unit vectors represents the vector sum $\overrightarrow{AB} + \overrightarrow{CD}$?

    A. $\mathbf{i} - \mathbf{j}$

    B. $7\mathbf{i} + \mathbf{j}$

    C. $15\mathbf{i} + 9\mathbf{j}$

    D. $27\mathbf{i} + 9\mathbf{j}$

    E. $126\mathbf{i} + 0\mathbf{j}$

9. The vector $\vec{v} = \langle -3, -4 \rangle$ and another vector $\vec{u}$ are added together, and the magnitude of $\vec{u}$ is 12, which of the following could <u>not</u> be the magnitude of the resultant sum vector?

    A. 7

    B. 12

    C. 13

    D. 17

    E. 19

10. If $\vec{v} = \langle -2, 7 \rangle$ and $\vec{u} = 5\vec{v},$ the magnitude of $2\vec{u}$ is how many times the magnitude of $\vec{v}$?

    A. $\dfrac{5}{2}$

    B. 10

    C. 20

    D. 25

    E. 100

Conic Sections and Polar Graphs

When the trajectories of the lines that make up a cone are extended infinitely and the cone is sliced by a plane, the resulting cross-section can have one of four shapes: a circle, an ellipse, a hyperbola, or a parabola. These are called **conic sections**. The standard forms of parabolas and circles are often tested on the ACT, and both have been covered in earlier chapters. Ellipses and hyperbolas are rarely tested.

Ellipses

The equation of an ellipse is $\dfrac{(x-h)^2}{a^2} + \dfrac{(y-k)^2}{b^2} = 1$ where:

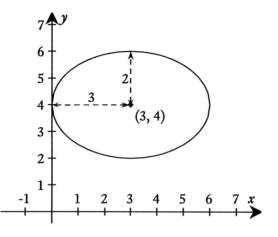

(h,k) = the center of the ellipse

a = semi-x-axis (horizontal radius)
b = semi-y-axis (vertical radius)

Example 1   The ellipse in the figure on the right is given by the equation:

$$\frac{(x-3)^2}{9} + \frac{(y-4)^2}{4} = 1$$

It is centered at (3, 4) and has semi-axes of $\sqrt{9} = 3$ and $\sqrt{4} = 2$ in the x and y directions, respectively.

Hyperbolas

A hyperbola's equation is similar to that of an ellipse, but there is a subtraction instead of an addition: $\dfrac{(x-h)^2}{a^2} - \dfrac{(y-k)^2}{b^2} = 1$ or $\dfrac{(y-k)^2}{b^2} - \dfrac{(x-h)^2}{a^2} = 1$. The graph of a hyperbola has two vertices and curves away from each of those vertices along diagonal asymptotes that cross each other at the center point (h,k).

Polar Graphs

The polar coordinate system assigns a coordinate pair to each point (r,θ), where r is the distance the point is away from the origin, or *pole*, and θ is the angle off the positive x-axis, or *polar axis*, that dictates where the point sits. Since the x and y coordinates of a rectangular coordinate pair and the r of a polar coordinate pair form a right triangle, you can use the Pythagorean Theorem and simple trigonometry to convert from polar to rectangular coordinates and back:

$$x = r\cos\theta \qquad\qquad r = \sqrt{x^2 + y^2}$$

$$y = r\sin\theta \qquad\qquad \theta = \tan^{-1}\left(\frac{y}{x}\right)$$

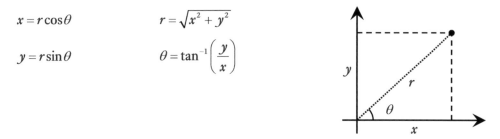

Conic Sections and Polar Graphs Problem Set

1. Which of the following is the center point of an ellipse with the equation
$$\frac{(x-7)^2}{16}+\frac{(y+2)^2}{25}=1?$$

   A. $(4,5)$

   B. $(-7,2)$

   C. $(7,2)$

   D. $(7,-2)$

   E. $(16,25)$

2. Which of the following can be graphed entirely in the first quadrant?

   A. $\dfrac{x^2}{4}+\dfrac{y^2}{1}=1$

   B. $\dfrac{(x+3)^2}{4}+\dfrac{(y+4)^2}{1}=1$

   C. $\dfrac{(x+3)^2}{4}-\dfrac{(y+4)^2}{1}=1$

   D. $\dfrac{(x-3)^2}{4}-\dfrac{(y-4)^2}{1}=1$

   E. $\dfrac{(x-3)^2}{4}+\dfrac{(y-4)^2}{1}=1$

3. About which of the following lines is the ellipse $\dfrac{(x-5)^2}{36}+\dfrac{(y-2)^2}{9}=1$ symmetric?

   A. $x=0$

   B. $x=2$

   C. $x=3$

   D. $x=5$

   E. $x=6$

4. The graph of $x^2-y^2-4x-2y+2=0$ is a hyperbola centered at what point?

   A. $(2,-1)$

   B. $(4,2)$

   C. $(-1,4)$

   D. $(-3,2)$

   E. $(-2,1)$

5. If a plane sliced a cone such that the plane was not parallel to the cone's base, which of the following could be the shape of the cross section created?

   A. A circle

   B. An ellipse

   C. A rectangle

   D. Two interlocking circles

   E. A parallelogram

6. Which of the following sets of polar coordinates indicates the same point as $(5, 60°)$?

    A. $(5, 120°)$

    B. $(5, -60°)$

    C. $(5, 300°)$

    D. $(5, 420°)$

    E. $(5, -120°)$

9. Which of the following are approximate polar coordinates of a point with rectangular coordinates $(3, 4)$?

    A. $(2, 53.13°)$

    B. $(2, 306.87°)$

    C. $(5, 36.87°)$

    D. $(5, 53.13°)$

    E. $(5, 306.87°)$

7. In the polar coordinate plane, what will the graph of $r\sin\theta = 4$ look like?

    A. A circle

    B. An ellipse

    C. A line

    D. A point

    E. A periodic wave

10. The equation $r = 9$ defines a graph in the polar coordinate plane. Which of the following equations defines the same graph in the rectangular coordinate plane?

    A. $x = 9$

    B. $y = 9$

    C. $x^2 + y^2 = 3$

    D. $x^2 + y^2 = 9$

    E. $x^2 + y^2 = 81$

8. A point has polar coordinates $(4, 150°)$. What are the rectangular coordinates of this point?

    A. $\left(-2, 2\sqrt{3}\right)$

    B. $\left(-2\sqrt{3}, 2\right)$

    C. $\left(2, 2\sqrt{3}\right)$

    D. $\left(2\sqrt{3}, 2\right)$

    E. $(-2, 2)$

Reading Test Manual

The Reading portion of the ACT is the third section and consists of four passages with 10 questions each. Students are given 35 minutes to complete this section, and most students find it difficult to finish answering all questions within this time. A passage and its questions will always be on facing pages, which makes it easier to look in the passage for correct answers. The questions test your knowledge of both the central themes of the passage and specific details from the passage.

Overview

There are four passages on the ACT Reading section. Each passage is followed by 10 questions that ask you about information presented in the passage. All the answers are based on the passage, so none of the questions require any outside knowledge.

The passages always appear in the following order:

Passage I: Literary Narrative

This passage is an excerpt from a story, such as a novel, short story, or memoir. Read the selection as a story. Pay close attention to plot, characters, mood, chronology, and relationships. Less recent ACTs label this passage "Prose Fiction."

Passage II: Social Science

This passage is about history, geography, political science, economics, or civics. Since these topics involve the interactions of people, note all names and relationships you see.

Passage III: Humanities

This passage consists of criticism or analysis of something related to art and culture, such as literature, dance, music, painting, drawing, or some other visual, performing or literary art.

Passage IV: Natural Science

This passage relates to Biology, Chemistry, Physics, or Earth/Environmental Science. Any difficult, technical language will be explained within the passage.

Paired Passages

One of the four passages of the Reading section may be split into two shorter paired passages, called Passage A and Passage B, on related topics. This pair will have 10 questions total, including some about the first passage in the pair, some about the second, and some about both together. The test will label which questions go with which passage.

Many students find it useful to break the pair up:

    (1) Read Passage A first

    (2) Answer all of Passage A's questions

    (3) Read Passage B

    (4) Answer all of Passages B's questions as well as the questions about both passages

Reading Speed

The ACT Reading section gives you very little time per passage. Depending upon your reading speed, you may or may not have the time to read through and answer questions on all the passages.

If you struggle to complete all four passages and the questions comfortably in the allotted time, you are likely to get a higher score by answering **a limited number of passages accurately** and filling in guesses for the remaining questions than working more quickly and making many errors that could have been avoided. Work at a brisk pace, but focus on accuracy before focusing on total completion.

Based upon your reading speed, you should target a specific number of passages. The following is a rough guide:

ACT Reading Score Aim	17-22	23-27	28+
Complete	2 Passages	3 Passages	4 Passages

Remember also that your reading speed will improve with practice. You will have a much easier time improving if you start by aiming for a score slightly above your baseline practice test score and working up from there than by trying to go for a perfect score from the start.

Speed Training for Reading

If you would like to read faster and more accurately, consider completing the following reading program over the course of three to five months:

(1) **Assess your baseline reading level**. Do you read recreationally almost every day? Do you rarely read novels or news articles other than when assigned to do so for school? Do you feel like it takes you longer than most people in your class to finish reading something? Is it challenging for you to read and understand an article from publications like *The New Yorker* or *The Economist*? Depending on your answers to these questions, you might want to start this reading program at level 1 or at level 2 (see below).

(2) **Read two pieces per day** (see recommended sources in the table below), and post the name of each of the pieces along with a short summary on a spreadsheet that your tutor or parent can check over now and then. It is okay to occasionally include a sports or style article, but these should make up a minority of the pieces you are reading for the program.

(3) **Honestly assess your progress each week**. If you started at Level 1 and, after following these steps for a few weeks, you feel very comfortable with the articles you have been reading, advance to Level 2. If you started at Level 2 and feel that most of the articles you are reading are too difficult to understand, go to Level 1.

	Level 1	Level 2
Recommended Sources	Articles from *The Washington Post*, *The New York Times*, *Foreign Affairs*, and *Scientific American*	Opinion Pieces from *The Washington Post* and *The New York Times* Articles and Opinion Pieces from *The New Yorker* and *The Economist*

Section Strategy

Though the passages on the ACT Reading section follow the specific content order mentioned earlier, they are not in order of difficulty. Each passage has a similar level of difficulty, though some content areas, like Literary Narrative and Natural Science, can prove more challenging for some students.

If you work through the passages that will be easier for you first, you will either bank time that can be used on passages that give you more difficulty or, if you run out of time, save your random guesses for the passage that you would be less likely to do well on anyway. Consider the strategies below:

- You do not have to work through the passages in order, and for most students, it is better **not to work through them in order**.
- For many students, Passage I (Literary Narrative) will be the most time-consuming and challenging, and it should therefore be done **last**.
- To maximize your efficiency, try to do the passages in the following order depending how many passages you are targeting in total.

Targeting 2 passages	Targeting 3 passages	Targeting 4 passages
First II Social Science Second III Humanities	First II Social Science Second III Humanities Third IV Natural Science	First II Social Science Second III Humanities Third IV Natural Science Fourth I Literary Narrative

Passage Strategy

Everybody reads at a different pace and with a different level of comprehension. Some students take notes when they read; others don't ever put their pencil to paper while reading.

Still, the ACT Reading section favors some strategies over others. For example, reading the questions before reading the passage is *not* advised and usually leads to *less* accuracy and *less* efficiency.

The following four steps comprise a strategy that works very well for most students:

(1) **Read through the entire passage before looking at the questions**. Read at a brisk pace. Keep in mind that this section is like an open-book test. You will be able to come back to the passage to clarify any detail you may miss on the first read.

   • <u>Underline</u> **the topic sentence or main idea of each paragraph.** Once you have found this, read the rest of the paragraph as fast as you can. For instance, say you find out from the first two lines that a paragraph details the life cycle of a particular type of insect. Underline this main idea and quickly read over all the specifics about the life cycle that follow.

   • **Circle proper nouns and numbers from the passage**, including the names of characters or experts, dates, and locations. It's helpful to circle each of these every time you see it in the passage. This will help you focus on the information and create an outline you can use to more quickly look up answers to the questions. The first time you do this, it will probably feel like it is really slowing you down. Don't worry—most students find that with practice, this technique actually helps improve both comprehension and reading speed.

(2) **Focus first on the easiest questions**. Remember, the questions don't go in order of difficulty or chronological order, so answer questions in an order that follows the path of least resistance.

   • The first question in each passage often refers to the passage as a whole. **This should be the last question you do**. You'll know more about the passage after answering the other questions.

   • **Focus on answering detail-specific questions first**, especially those with line numbers or proper nouns and numbers that you circled in the passage. Answering these will aid your understanding of the passage as a whole.

   • Questions that ask about **inference, tone, or the big picture concepts** in the passage should be done last. Because you don't want to get bogged down on any one question, these can also be candidates for educated guesses.

(3) **When working through almost any type of question, look up the answer in the passage**. Remember that this is a standardized test and that the answer to every question has to be in the passage. Students who answer the questions only from memory don't score as well as those who look up the answers, even when taking into account the time this takes. Just make sure *not* to overinvest in any one question. There are very few trick questions on the Reading section of the ACT; the correct answer is almost always the one that is most obvious from the passage.

(4) **Work strategically on your final passage.** If you know that you won't have time to both read the passage fully and work through the questions, focus first on questions that ask for the meaning of a word or phrase. These can often be answered without reading the passage—just look at the sentences around the word or phrase in question. Then look for questions that provide specific line numbers and do not ask you to make an inference. The answers to these are often in the few lines before or after the lines given in the question. Remember to bubble in an answer for every question, even those that you do not have time to work through.

Practice Passage for Marking Up

On the next page is an example of a passage that is marked up in a way that exhibits the kinds of markings discussed in step 1 of the Passage Strategy.

On the pages that follow, the same passage is paired with questions and left clean for you to mark up in a similar way. You don't need to make exactly the same markings, but you should come up with something similar in a system that works well for you. Then try to answer the questions to see the difference reading strategically can make.

Time your work to see how long the process takes you. Remember, with practice, your timing will become more efficient. Check your answers in the back of the book when you are done, and review any that you get wrong.

NATURAL SCIENCE: This passage is adapted from S. Galinez et al., "Stroke: Historical Review and Innovative Treatments." ©2014 by the National High School Journal of Science.

The medical knowledge of strokes has progressed significantly from ancient understandings of the brain and nervous system to modern technological advances in both treatment and
5 prevention. The first historical reference to the nervous system was found in ancient Egyptian records dating back to 3500 BCE, when Papyrus described the brain and the fluids that covered the brain.

10 Hippocrates, in 400 BCE, first described paralysis and convulsion or seizures that resulted after brain injuries, along with the observation that paralysis to the opposite side of the body resulted when a section from one half of the brain was in-
15 jured. In the 17th century, Thomas Willis conducted a detailed study of the brain and nervous system at Oxford University. Willis did experiments on cadavers and discovered that dye injected into one carotid artery would be expelled from the
20 opposing carotid artery. He classified the nerves of the brain and described the communication of the arteries at the base of the brain that we now call the Circle of Willis. He also recognized that lesions in a specific part of the brain led to weakness in an
25 associated part of the body.

In the 1800s carotid surgery became a more prevalent procedure and reports of successful closures of injuries to the carotid arteries were documented. The first documented case of successful
30 carotid artery surgery in the United States was performed by Dr. Amos Twitchell in New Hampshire on October 18, 1807. Another milestone came in 1927 when Egas Moniz of Portugal successfully performed cerebral arteriograms for the study of
35 cerebral tumors.

Despite these advances, there were actually very few effective treatments for an acute stroke. In the early 1900s most of the treatments for stroke patients were limited to rehabilitation after an acute
40 stroke, and most patients were usually left with permanent and severe deficits. In the 1950s it was recognized that disease in the carotid arteries could also cause transient ischemic attacks resulting in temporary weakness or blindness that resolved
45 within a few hours, and that these attacks could be warning signs for future strokes. Doppler ultrasound studies were first used to identify plaque and disease in the carotid arteries, and aggressive treat-

ment of high blood pressure also was found to be
50 very important.

In the 1960s carotid endarterectomy was greatly improved but this procedure was used mostly for stroke prevention and there was still no effective treatment after an acute stroke. The inven-
55 tion of the computed tomography scan (CT scan) greatly assisted in the diagnosis of stroke, and it became widely used in the United States to help distinguish between the different types of stroke. In the 1970s aspirin was found to be very effective in
60 stroke prevention. In the 1980s another breakthrough was the discovery that cigarette smoking was a definite risk factor for stroke; after this, smoking cessation programs became very important. A major breakthrough came in 1996
65 when the FDA approved stroke treatment using tissue plasminogen activator, a protein that is now widely used to break down blood clots. Soon rapid diagnosis became crucial for immediate treatment, whereas in the past rehabilitation was the most
70 common response and doctors often waited 12–24 hours before giving a diagnosis of acute stroke.

As advances continue in the future, strokes may become a temporary illness for which rapid and minimally invasive treatments allow for maxi-
75 mum recovery. Such treatments would be coupled with an emphasis on healthy lifestyles and prevention. For immediate improvement in blood flow to the area of the stroke, we suggest an ultrasound device that allows delivery of Vascular Endothelial
80 Growth Factor (VEGF) directly into the affected tissue with minimal risk to the patient. A specialized minute pellet provides a dual mechanism of releasing medication into the affected tissue: Fifty percent is processed onto a porous scaffold and
85 immediately released, and the remaining fifty percent is processed into specialized glycolide spheres with semipermeable membranes to provide additional sustained release of the medication into the affected tissue. The pellet thus provides both
90 immediate and sustained gradual delivery of VEGF to provide immediate and sustained neovascularization. We propose that VEGF administered directly into acute ischemic tissue will lead to dramatic advances in the treatment of stroke.

NATURAL SCIENCE: This passage is adapted from S. Galinez et al., "Stroke: Historical Review and Innovative Treatments." ©2014 by the National High School Journal of Science.

The medical knowledge of strokes has progressed significantly from ancient understandings of the brain and nervous system to modern technological advances in both treatment and
5 prevention. The first historical reference to the nervous system was found in ancient Egyptian records dating back to 3500 BCE, when Papyrus described the brain and the fluids that covered the brain.

10 Hippocrates, in 400 BCE, first described paralysis and convulsion or seizures that resulted after brain injuries, along with the observation that paralysis to the opposite side of the body resulted when a section from one half of the brain was in-
15 jured. In the 17th century, Thomas Willis conducted a detailed study of the brain and nervous system at Oxford University. Willis did experiments on cadavers and discovered that dye injected into one carotid artery would be expelled from the
20 opposing carotid artery. He classified the nerves of the brain and described the communication of the arteries at the base of the brain that we now call the Circle of Willis. He also recognized that lesions in a specific part of the brain led to weakness in an
25 associated part of the body.

In the 1800s carotid surgery became a more prevalent procedure and reports of successful closures of injuries to the carotid arteries were documented. The first documented case of successful
30 carotid artery surgery in the United States was performed by Dr. Amos Twitchell in New Hampshire on October 18, 1807. Another milestone came in 1927 when Egas Moniz of Portugal successfully performed cerebral arteriograms for the study of
35 cerebral tumors.

Despite these advances, there were actually very few effective treatments for an acute stroke. In the early 1900s most of the treatments for stroke patients were limited to rehabilitation after an acute
40 stroke, and most patients were usually left with permanent and severe deficits. In the 1950s it was recognized that disease in the carotid arteries could also cause transient ischemic attacks resulting in temporary weakness or blindness that resolved
45 within a few hours, and that these attacks could be warning signs for future strokes. Doppler ultrasound studies were first used to identify plaque and disease in the carotid arteries, and aggressive treat-

ment of high blood pressure also was found to be
50 very important.

In the 1960s carotid endarterectomy was greatly improved but this procedure was used mostly for stroke prevention and there was still no effective treatment after an acute stroke. The inven-
55 tion of the computed tomography scan (CT scan) greatly assisted in the diagnosis of stroke, and it became widely used in the United States to help distinguish between the different types of stroke. In the 1970s aspirin was found to be very effective in
60 stroke prevention. In the 1980s another breakthrough was the discovery that cigarette smoking was a definite risk factor for stroke; after this, smoking cessation programs became very important. A major breakthrough came in 1996
65 when the FDA approved stroke treatment using tissue plasminogen activator, a protein that is now widely used to break down blood clots. Soon rapid diagnosis became crucial for immediate treatment, whereas in the past rehabilitation was the most
70 common response and doctors often waited 12–24 hours before giving a diagnosis of acute stroke.

As advances continue in the future, strokes may become a temporary illness for which rapid and minimally invasive treatments allow for maxi-
75 mum recovery. Such treatments would be coupled with an emphasis on healthy lifestyles and prevention. For immediate improvement in blood flow to the area of the stroke, we suggest an ultrasound device that allows delivery of Vascular Endothelial
80 Growth Factor (VEGF) directly into the affected tissue with minimal risk to the patient. A specialized minute pellet provides a dual mechanism of releasing medication into the affected tissue: Fifty percent is processed onto a porous scaffold and
85 immediately released, and the remaining fifty percent is processed into specialized glycolide spheres with semipermeable membranes to provide additional sustained release of the medication into the affected tissue. The pellet thus provides both
90 immediate and sustained gradual delivery of VEGF to provide immediate and sustained neovascularization. We propose that VEGF administered directly into acute ischemic tissue will lead to dramatic advances in the treatment of stroke.

1. The main purpose of the passage is to:

   A. debunk Hippocrates' observations on the brain because they are outdated.
   B. argue that a stroke is now easily curable with a simple rehabilitation effort.
   C. convey the severity of acute stroke and the long-term effects it has on a person's life.
   D. describe a brief history of stroke research and modern technological advancements.

2. The tone of the passage is best described as:

   A. critical but constructive.
   B. rhetorical and wordy.
   C. measured and questioning.
   D. informative and optimistic.

3. Based on the second paragraph of the passage (lines 10–25), in relation to the work of Hippocrates, Willis' research:

   A. rejects some of Hippocrates' findings.
   B. confirms all of Hippocrates' claims.
   C. builds on Hippocrates' earlier findings.
   D. is unrelated to Hippocrates' work.

4. In line 82, *minute* most nearly means:

   A. condensed.
   B. very small.
   C. very brief.
   D. unimportant.

5. In line 93, *dramatic* most nearly means:

   A. unbelievable.
   B. theatrical.
   C. significant.
   D. distressing.

6. Which of the following was NOT described in the passage as an advancement in stroke prevention?

   A. high blood pressure treatment
   B. patient weight loss
   C. smoking cessation
   D. aspirin prescription

7. The final paragraph (lines 72–94) in the passage primarily serves to:

   A. propose a promising treatment that should be tried in the future.
   B. review the historical timeline of notable contributes to stroke research.
   C. warn the reader of likely roadblocks to future advancements in stroke research and prevention.
   D. criticize the current pace of advancement in stroke research.

8. According to the passage, a computed tomography scan is now commonly used to:

   A. identify plaque and disease in the brain.
   B. study cerebral tumors.
   C. distinguish between different types of strokes.
   D. describe the fluid that covers the brain.

9. It can be reasonably inferred from the information in lines 10–15 that:

   A. early researchers understood the connection between seizures and brain injuries well before 400 BCE.
   B. Papyrus was the first to describe the connection between seizures and brain injuries.
   C. Hippocrates was the first to recognize that lesions in the brain lead to weakness in other parts of the body.
   D. it was not until around 400 BCE that researchers made the connection between brain injuries and seizures.

10. Considering the passage as a whole, the reader can reasonably infer that:

    A. advancements in stroke research and treatment have stalled and patients in the future will not see much better treatment than we have today.
    B. stroke research continues to progress and patients in the future will likely have much better outcomes than patients have today.
    C. strokes are now considered a minor issue and current treatments allow for maximum recovery.
    D. the most promising stroke treatments were discovered decades ago and medical researchers now focus more on other neurological diseases and disorders.

Alternate Passage Strategy: Headlining

Students often associate margin annotations with close reading, but you'd be surprised how easily you can write a three- or four-word note about a paragraph after just a targeted skim read. Call it **HEADLINING**. A short headline, like you'd see on a tabloid newspaper, can be a useful guidepost when navigating the scavenger hunt that is the ACT Reading section. Here's how it works:

(1) **Read to get the topic of *each paragraph*.** Read the first line of each paragraph and then skim read the rest of the text by accelerating to reading just the nouns and verbs while hunting for the paragraph's chief focus. Most ACT Reading passages are made up of between 6 and 10 large paragraphs. Each of these has a separate focus, though together they build toward a common message.

(2) **After completing each paragraph, write a HEADLINE in the margin.** This should be no more than four words and should encapsulate that paragraph's focus. Do not try to summarize, and don't be nitpicky. Your headline should be obvious and come to you quickly.

(3) **Use your paragraph headlines as a road map.** Many of the questions ask about a specific element that can be found directly in one of the paragraphs. Answer these first. Whether the question tells you which paragraph to look at or doesn't, it will be helpful to have your headlines steering you to where the answer lies. Once you've answered those questions, the bigger picture questions will be easier because you will know more about the passage as a whole.

(4) **When you find an answer in the text, underline or star the line where you find it.** The correct choice will paraphrase that line, whereas the incorrect choices will often use words and phrases that are in other parts of the passage but don't correctly answer the question.

Imagine a passage that describes both the natural and the learned processes that cause lions to become expert hunters. You may produce, as you skim, headlines that say things like **life on the savannah, lions as predators, cub play, stalking and pouncing, pride social hierarchy**, and **first hunts**.

If a question asks about the animals that lions prey upon, you might consult the **lions as predators** or possibly the **first hunts** paragraph. On the other hand, if a question directs you to the fifth paragraph, you will be immediately reminded by your headline that that paragraph deals primarily with the social strata associated with lion prides.

The following are example headlines for the six paragraphs in the passage discussed earlier entitled *Stroke: Historical Review and Innovative Treatments.*

- Paragraph 1: **early stroke understanding**
- Paragraph 2: **brain/body interaction**
- Paragraph 3: **surgery for brain**
- Paragraph 4: **knowledge of stroke causes**
- Paragraph 5: **stroke treatment and prevention**
- Paragraph 6: **new stroke treatment technology**

Practice Passage for Headlining

On the next two pages, you'll find an example of a passage paired with questions. Use this passage to practice the Headlining strategy if you think that strategy might work well for you.

Time your work to see how long the process takes you. Remember, with practice, your timing will become more efficient. Check your answers in the back of the book when you are done, and review any that you get wrong.

NATURAL SCIENCE: This passage is adapted from Lydia Pyne, "Neanderthals in 3D: L'Homme de La Chapelle." ©2015 by The Public Domain Review.

On August 3, 1908, French prehistorian Jean Bouyssonie, his brother, Amédée Bouyssonie, and their colleague Louis Bardon found a Neanderthal skeleton in a system of caves near La Chapelle-aux-
5 Saints in south-central France. The discovery was exciting for the newly-emerging field of paleoanthropology because the Neanderthal was found in its original, undisturbed archaeological context—in situ—and excavations of the skeleton
10 revealed that it was more complete than anything else in the fossil record. La Chapelle quickly became an iconic fossil within scientific and popular circles and went on to inspire everything from dioramas at the Field Museum of Natural History
15 to science fiction's *A Guerredu Feu* (Quest for Fire).

After the skeleton was excavated, the Bouyssonies sent the remains to the eminent Marcellin Boule, the Director of the Laboratory of Palaeontology at the prestigious Musée d'Histoire
20 Naturelle in Paris.

Boule conducted a two-year detailed anatomical study of the fossil that culminated in a hefty monograph, *L'Homme Fossile de La Chapelle-aux-Saints*, published in 1911. *L'Homme* was the
25 first and most comprehensive publication of Neanderthal skeletal anatomy in scientific literature, establishing the La Chapelle skeleton as the most complete fossil reference for early paleo-studies. Boule's detailed anatomical description of
30 the skeleton provided a framework for any new Neanderthal fossils discovered, and the 1911 reconstructions of La Chapelle became the basis for all subsequent Neanderthal research. The book is filled with chapters of anatomical descriptions,
35 careful measurements, photographs of the skeleton in the ground prior to excavation, as well as sketches of geomorphic cross-sections from the cave. In addition to the tables of metrics and photographs of the La Chapelle fossil, Boule included
40 another type of medium that gave readers of *L'Homme* a way to interact with the fossil for themselves. At the back of the book, Boule included six stereoscopic plates of the Neanderthal skull.

By the time *L'Homme* was published, the
45 stereoscope would have been a familiar object, one of the many optical toys—along with kaleidoscopes, zoetropes and cameras—through which the nineteenth-century eye had peered in wonder. The stereoscope's particular trick was to give a
50 two-dimensional image an illusion of depth. Gazing through its viewfinder, the two slightly offset images of the stereoscopic plate, or stereogram, positioned in front would combine to create an illusion of three dimensions.

55 The device, however, was much more than just a toy or illustrative distraction—it developed into an important tool for laboratory and scientific work in the late nineteenth and early twentieth centuries. Just as telescopes and microscopes expan-
60 ded what is visible, the stereoscope expanded how researchers were able to see different specimens.

As fossils were themselves too rare and important to send between researchers, proxies—casts, measurements, sketches, photographs, and
65 highly detailed descriptions—were needed to provide accurate and sufficient information. Drawing from a tradition of stereoscopic anatomical atlases, the La Chapelle-aux-Saints Neanderthal plates gave the reader a first-person experience of interacting
70 with the fossil in three dimensions.

The stereo cards of the Neanderthal skull gave readers of the *L'Homme Fossile de La Chapelle-aux-Saints* the opportunity to see for themselves the complexity of the Neanderthal cranium. This ad-
75 ded dimensionality of the stereo cards helped bring the La Chapelle skeleton to the forefront of paleoanthropological research in the early twentieth century—the stereo plates deepened viewers' connections to the fossil. *L'Homme's* beautifully de-
80 tailed stereoscopic prints of each bone from the skeleton were the 1911 version of data sharing.

While it is easy to think of 3D rendering of fossils as a recent technological phenomenon, stereograms offer a glimpse at the explanatory power
85 of stereoscopic images and highlight the connections three-dimensional viewing made between viewer and object. Boule's inclusion of stereoscopic images of the La Chapelle Neanderthal helped solidify the fossil's iconic status in the early-twen-
90 tieth-century paleoanthropology.

1. The passage indicates that the discovery of the Neanderthal skeleton at La Chapelle-aux-Saints was exciting for paleontologists because:

   A. Neanderthal remains had not been discovered previously.
   B. the remains unearthed were the most complete of any that had yet been found.
   C. Neanderthal remains had never been found in France before.
   D. the remains matched those that had been described in a famous anatomical study of Neanderthals.

2. The passage makes clear that the stereoscopic plates in *L'Homme* were valuable to readers because:

   A. they gave flat images of the bones an illusion of depth.
   B. they provided cross–sectional pictures of the cave where the fossils were found.
   C. they provided detailed measurements of the skeleton in the ground.
   D. they provided anatomical descriptions of the complete skeleton.

3. As used in line 9, *in situ* most nearly means:

   A. in a seated position.
   B. into an underground location.
   C. in its original setting.
   D. in a place set aside for a purpose.

4. The primary purpose of the second paragraph (lines 16–20) is to shift the focus of the passage from the discovery of the fossil to:

   A. an explanation of the fossil's achievement of iconic status and its impact on modern science.
   B. an analysis of the influence of a scientist's contributions to a particular field of study.
   C. biographical information of an important scientist and a summary of his anatomical study.
   D. a detailed description of a scientific publication about the fossil which included an example of an important optical technology.

5. It can be inferred from the passage that the Bouysonnie brothers sent the La Chapelle skeletal remains to Marcellin Boule in order to:

   A. encourage him to make stereoscopic plates of the Neanderthal skull.
   B. allow him to distribute the fossils to other researchers.
   C. enable him to conduct a complete anatomical study.
   D. prove to Boule that the skeleton they found was iconic.

6. According to the passage, Marcellin Boule's *L'Homme* provided all of the following EXCEPT:

   A. photographs of the skeleton in situ.
   B. precise measurements of the skeleton remains.
   C. kaleidoscopic photos of the skull.
   D. anatomical descriptions of the skeleton.

7. In lines 79–81, the author includes a comparison between stereoscopic prints and modern data sharing in order to:

   A. provide the reader with a metaphor for envisioning what stereoscopic prints look like.
   B. give the reader a better understanding of the purpose and impact of Boule's inclusion of stereoscopic images in his book.
   C. describe in modern terms how Boule made the stereoscopic images that he included in his book.
   D. Emphasize the significant differences between a method of data sharing in 1911 and the modern technology used today.

8. As used in line 63, *proxies* most nearly means:

   A. bones.
   B. substitutes.
   C. fossils.
   D. diagrams.

9. It can be reasonably inferred that the reaction of Boule's colleagues to the stereograms in his book would most likely have been:

   A. bewildered confusion: the stereoscope was an unusual object and viewed as a distraction at the turn of the century.
   B. sincere appreciation: they provided a first-person experience of an important discovery.
   C. grudging acceptance: in 1911 stereograms weren't as useful for presenting images as photographs.
   D. surprised delight: stereoscopic images had never been used in a scientific publication before.

10. The passage indicates that, in the early 20th century, fossils were:

    A. infrequently, if ever, sent from one researcher to another.
    B. usually mailed back and forth among researchers.
    C. so numerous that virtually every researcher in the world had many samples.
    D. not of interest to researchers.

Practice Reading Section

Try to apply reading comprehension strategies that work well for you, and time how long this full section takes you.

Passage I

LITERARY NARRATIVE: This passage is adapted from the novel *The Iron Woman* by Margaret Deland (1911).

"Climb up in this tree, and play house!" Elizabeth Ferguson commanded. She herself had climbed to the lowest branch of an apple-tree in the Maitland orchard, and sat there, swinging her
5 white-stockinged legs so recklessly that the three children whom she had summoned to her side, backed away for safety. "If you don't," she said, looking down at them, "I'm afraid, perhaps, maybe, I'll get mad."

10 Her foreboding was tempered by a giggle and by the deepening dimple in her cheek, but all the same she sighed with a sort of impersonal regret at the prospect of any unpleasantness. "It would be too bad if I got mad, wouldn't it?" she said
15 thoughtfully. The others looked at one another in consternation. They knew so well what it meant to have Elizabeth "mad," that Nannie Maitland, the oldest of the little group, said at once, helplessly, "Well."

20 Nannie was always helpless with Elizabeth, just as she was helpless with her half-brother, Blair, though she was ten and Elizabeth and Blair were only eight; but how could a little girl like Nannie be anything but helpless before a brother whom she
25 adored, and a wonderful being like Elizabeth? Elizabeth, who always knew exactly what she wanted to do, and who instantly "got mad," if you wouldn't say you'd do it, too; got mad, and then repented, and hugged you, and actually cried (or got mad
30 again), if you refused to accept as a sign of your forgiveness her new pencil, decorated with strips of red and white paper just like a little barber's pole! No wonder Nannie, timid and good-natured, was helpless before such a sweet, furious little creature!
35 Blair had more backbone than his sister, but even he felt Elizabeth's heel upon his neck. David Richie, a silent, candid, very stubborn small boy, was, after a momentary struggle, as meek as the rest of them. Now, when she commanded them all to climb, it
40 was David who demurred, because, he said, he spoke first for Indians tomahawking you in the back parlor.

"Very well!" said the despot; "play your old Indians! I'll never speak to any of you again as long
45 as I live!"

"I've got on my new pants," David objected.

"Take 'em off!" said Elizabeth.

"That's not proper to do out-of-doors; and Miss White says not to say 'pants.'"

50 Elizabeth looked thoughtful. "Maybe it isn't proper," she admitted; "but David, honest, I took a hate to being tommy-hocked the last time we played it; so please, dear David! If you'll play house in the tree, I'll give you a piece of my taffy." She took a lit-
55 tle sticky package out of her pocket and licked her lips to indicate its contents; David yielded, shinning up the trunk of the tree, indifferent to the trousers, which had been on his mind ever since he had put them on his legs.

60 Blair followed him, but Nannie squatted on the ground content to merely look at the courageous three.

"Come on up," said Elizabeth. Nannie shook her little blond head. At which the others burst into
65 a shrill chorus: "'Fraid-cat! 'fraid-cat! 'fraid-cat!" Nannie smiled placidly; it never occurred to her to deny such an obviously truthful title. "Blair," she said, continuing a conversation interrupted by Elizabeth's determination to climb, "Blair, why do you
70 say things that make Mamma mad? What's the sense? If it makes her mad for you to say things are ugly, why do you?"

"'Cause," Blair said briefly. Even at eight Blair disliked both explanations and decisions, and his
75 slave and half-sister rarely pressed for either. With the exception of his mother, whose absorption in business had never given her time to get acquainted with him, most of the people about Blair were his slaves. Elizabeth's governess, Miss White—called
80 by Elizabeth, for reasons of her own, "Cherry-pie"—had completely surrendered to his brown eyes; the men in the Maitland Works toadied to him; David Richie blustered, perhaps, but always gave in to him; in his own home, Harris, who was a

85 cross between a butler and a maid-of-all-work,
adored him to the point of letting him make candy
on the kitchen stove—probably the greatest expression of affection possible to the kitchen; in fact,
little Elizabeth Ferguson was the only person in his
90 world who did not knuckle down to this pleasant
and lovable child. But then, Elizabeth never
knuckled down to anybody! Certainly not to kind
old Cherry-pie, whose timid upper lip quivered like
a rabbit's when she was obliged to repeat to her
95 darling some new rule of Robert Ferguson's for his
niece's upbringing; nor did she knuckle down to her
uncle; she even declared she was not at all afraid of
him! This was almost unbelievable to the others,
who scattered like robins if they heard his step. And
100 she had greater courage than this; she had, in fact,
audacity, for she said she was willing—this the
others told each other in awed tones—she said she
had "just as gladly" walk right up and speak to Mrs.
Maitland herself, and ask her for twenty cents so
105 she could treat the whole crowd to ice cream! That
is, she would just as gladly, if she should happen to
want to.

1. The passage is told from the point of view of:

   A. Elizabeth Ferguson.
   B. David Richie.
   C. Mrs. Maitland.
   D. an unnamed narrator.

2. In line 40, *demurred* most nearly means:

   A. expressed reluctance.
   B. enthusiastically agreed.
   C. walked away.
   D. smiled broadly.

3. The passage describes Elizabeth in all of the following ways, EXCEPT:

   A. mad.
   B. repentant.
   C. timid.
   D. confident.

4. Which of the following best characterizes Blair's relationship with most of the people around him?

   A. He was disliked by all of the children, but
      doted on by the adults.
   B. He was ignored by his mother, but loved by
      most others.
   C. He was mistreated by the other children and
      ignored by the adults.
   D. He was spoiled by Harris, but ignored by all
      others.

5. In line 43 of the passage, the author uses *despot* to
   illustrate:

   A. Elizabeth's kindness.
   B. Elizabeth's tyranny.
   C. David's rudeness.
   D. David's boldness.

6. In line 99, the author uses the phrase "scattered
   like robins" to illustrate how:

   A. the birds shifted when the children were play-
      ing nearby.
   B. the other children reacted when Elizabeth's
      uncle approached them.
   C. "Cherry-pie" responded when Elizabeth
      yelled at her.
   D. the rabbits startled when Blair walked by.

7. In the passage, Nannie is:

   A. Elizabeth's governess.
   B. Blair's older half-sister.
   C. David's younger sister.
   D. Robert's niece.

8. In the eighth paragraph (lines 50–59), the taffy
   could best be described as:

   A. a bribe to get David to climb the tree.
   B. a trick played on David to make his trousers
      messy.
   C. a secret between Elizabeth and the Maitland
      kids.
   D. a special treat that only Miss White dispensed.

9. Which of the following statements best characterizes Nannie's response to being challenged
   for being afraid?

   A. She treated the rest of the kids like her slaves.
   B. She bossed the other kids around by threat-
      ening to get mad.
   C. She reasoned that it was more prudent to avoid
      damaging her clothes.
   D. She accepted the label as evident and accurate.

10. It can reasonably be inferred from the passages that
    David Richie is:

    A. younger but much larger than Blair.
    B. older than 12.
    C. younger than 10.
    D. Elizabeth's older half-brother.

Passage II

SOCIAL SCIENCE: This passage is adapted from an essay.

Joseph Stalin's harsh dictatorship in Soviet Russia during the 1930s and 1940s was characterized by an attempt at totalitarian control over every aspect of his citizens' lives, including the
5 music they listened to. Stalin sought to ensure that all Soviet music functioned as propaganda for his regime. Like other authoritarian regimes, Stalin's government believed it should define truth and beauty. Composers who did not conform to Stalin's
10 standards were subject to public criticism, state persecution and even exile.

Dmitri Shostakovich, born in September, 1906, in St Petersburg, maintained a complex and difficult relationship with the Soviet government.
15 Although he achieved initial recognition for his work by Soviet chief of staff Mikhail Tukhachevsky, he subsequently offended the regime with both the style and content of his music. Shostakovich was influenced by non-traditional trends in music. His
20 music featured sharp contrasts, ambivalent tonality, and grotesque elements. In his memoir, *Testimony*, published in 1979 by Solomon Volkov, Shostakovich wrote, "I was a formalist, a representative of an antinational direction in music." Shostakovich's
25 modern, avant-garde style of music clashed with Soviet requirements for art which emphasized the "heroic, the bright and the beautiful."

After a performance of his provocative opera "Lady MacBeth of the Minsk District," Shos-
30 takovich faced harsh scrutiny from Stalin's government. The state newspaper, *Pravda*, denounced his opera for its "intentionally unharmonious muddled flow of sounds." Fellow composers supported *Pravda*'s attacks and assertions that Shostakovich
35 was a "petty bourgeois" composer. Shostakovich responded to the attacks with his Fifth Symphony, which he obsequiously dubbed "A Composer's Response to Just Criticism." Shostakovich recognized that in order to rehabilitate himself and thus survive
40 in Stalin's Russia, his new symphony needed to meet Soviet requirements for music: realism, simplicity, heroism and "accessibility to all." Music was supposed to glorify the state and the working people.

45 Shostakovich was well aware of the dangers of antagonizing the regime. During the late 1930s, his sister was exiled to France, his mother-in-law and brother-in-law were arrested, and his uncle, despite his communist affiliation, was arrested and held

50 until his death. His mentor Tukhachevsky was arrested, tortured, and executed during Stalin's purge of military leaders. It was within this environment that Shostakovich composed his Fifth Symphony. He took care to use a more traditional approach and
55 minimize abrasive dissonances. His Fifth Symphony displays a heroic tone, takes inspiration from Russian literature and folk songs, employs simple melodies and a conservative structure, and ends with a positive, upbeat fanfare.

60 The symphony succeeded in placating the regime, but historians and musicologists debate the true meaning of the symphony. The finale features a fanfare of brass and percussion, which could be heard in different ways. Is it a message of triumph
65 and pride in a populist regime? Or does that final fanfare contain "a mask of jollity that conceals tears beneath?" in the words of one critic. One musicologist writes that the last movement of the Fifth Symphony is a "gradual acceleration of forces, an
70 increasing sense of hysteria and loss of control until things break down and the fanfare becomes almost nightmarish in sound." Is this nightmarish sound Shostakovich's true view of the Stalinist regime?

It is possible that Shostakovich's negative feel-
75 ings towards the regime actually propelled him to create an accurate portrayal of all that the regime epitomized in his music. Often, the most powerfully satirical social protest manifests as an accurate portrayal of the flaws in society. In its adherence to
80 Soviet Marxist themes, Shostakovich's Fifth Symphony finale may be an attempt to paint a raw satirical portrait of Stalin's regime. Some have pointed out that to survive under Stalin's regime, Russian artists had to be masters of dissembling.
85 Shostakovich is alleged to have stated privately that his Fifth Symphony finale was a satirical picture of the dictator dressed up in exuberant adoration. But listeners can read into the symphony whatever meaning they may find there.

11. The main purpose of this passage is to:

   A. describe a composer's most famous musical piece and the process by which he created it.
   B. explore the relationship between Communist ideology and music.
   C. describe the work of musicians who epitomized 20th century Soviet Realism.
   D. provide an overview of one composer's response to political oppression.

12. Based on the passage, prior to his Fifth Symphony, Shostakovich:

   A. was heavily inspired by Russian folk music.
   B. employed unconventional elements in his music.
   C. used his music to glorify the working people.
   D. preferred traditional melodies.

13. The author characterizes the immediate effect of the *Pravda* article on Shostakovich as:

   A. influential; Shostakovich conformed to the musical expectations of the Stalin regime in his next work.
   B. imperceptible; Shostakovich's music changed only subtly from his previous works.
   C. life-changing; Shostakovich abandoned all musical elements he had previously employed.
   D. marginal; Shostakovich was more influenced by the criticism by his peers.

14. According to the passage, Shostakovich's Fifth symphony featured all of the following elements EXCEPT:

   A. uncomplicated melodies.
   B. an optimistic finale.
   C. recognizable literary elements.
   D. sharp contrasts in tone.

15. According to the passage, music critics:

   A. agree that Shostakovich's Fifth symphony was a firm denunciation of Stalinist Russia.
   B. suggest that the Fifth Symphony could be interpreted in different ways, as intended by the composer.
   C. concur that Shostakovich never recovered from the betrayal by his fellow composers.
   D. disagree on whether the Fifth symphony is Shostakovich's most revolutionary work.

16. As used in line 37 of the passage, *obsequiously* most nearly describes what kind of response from Shostakovich?

   A. Antagonistic
   B. Submissive
   C. Angry
   D. Grateful

17. All of the following family members of Shostakovich were described in the passage as being harmed in some way EXCEPT:

   A. his sister.
   B. his brother.
   C. his mother-in-law.
   D. his uncle.

18. As used in line 60 of the passage, *placating* most nearly means:

   A. enraging.
   B. saddening.
   C. satisfying.
   D. disappointing.

19. In line 84 of the passage, the author portrays Russian artists as "masters of dissembling" to describe those who:

   A. spoke their minds, without fear of punishment.
   B. disguised their true beliefs in works that appeared to please the government.
   C. were only successful when defying the government.
   D. publicly tried to deconstruct the whole of the Stalin's regime.

20. In the passage, Shostakovich's relationship with the Soviet government was characterized as:

   A. always contentious.
   B. complicated and difficult.
   C. generally positive.
   D. positive in his early career, but later combative.

Passage III

HUMANITIES: This passage is adapted from an essay.

Christopher Marlowe may be literature's best-known second-place finisher. Though doomed to stand in the shadow of his contemporary, William Shakespeare, Marlowe wrote plays that are still
5 widely read and performed today.

Marlowe, a clever and controversial writer with a university education, is typically viewed as the playwright who adapted medieval dramatic forms and made them popular for an educated ur-
10 ban audience in sixteenth century London, while Shakespeare is seen as almost single-handedly creating modern drama in writing for that audience. However, Marlowe's true significance as an innovator and an influence upon Shakespeare is under-
15 appreciated. Critics commonly concede that Marlowe preceded Shakespeare in writing serious tragedy for the English stage, but Marlowe also wrote a history play, the form usually considered to be one of Shakespeare's great innovations, and its effect on
20 Shakespeare's later history plays is clear.

Shakespeare, then considered an undereducated upstart, wrote the first three parts of *Henry VI*, his first series of historical plays, in the late 1580s, while Marlowe's *Edward II* was likely staged
25 for the first time in 1593. Despite some interesting characters and powerful lines, Shakespeare's three *Henry VI* plays lack dramatic unity and present history as a loosely connected series of events, essentially episodes drawn from historical chron-
30 icles without a coherent structure. It wasn't until Marlowe, who was then regarded as the premier playwright for the London stage, made his first foray into English history that the history play became its own form of cohesive art—it is this
35 Marlovian sample that Shakespeare would later draw upon in creating his best-known historical plays.

In telling the story of Edward II, a weak-willed failure of a monarch, Marlowe combined traditional
40 elements from both a morality play and a classical tragedy. In the play, history was not a collection of events but a narrative corresponding to recognizable types, a true work of art. Like a character in a morality play, Marlowe's Edward is overcome by
45 a corrupting influence, that of Gaveston, a self-indulgent flatterer who has stolen the heart of the king. Although the fall of the central character is the essential plot of any morality play, the protagonist is supposed to be surrounded by good

50 angels who work to turn him back to the correct path. Edward, however, has no "good angels" to help him become a better ruler—the king's counselors, who should act in that role, murder Gaveston only to increase their own power. The
55 nobles never truly attempt to "redeem" the king: they merely maneuver themselves into positions of greater power and even use the king's own excesses to serve their own purposes. Thus, Marlowe uses a form that traditionally enacts divinely established
60 moral order to show that history does not reflect this order.

Later in the play, Marlowe largely discards the morality form in favor of that of tragedy. Edward, initially an unreflective character who cannot con-
65 trol his impulses and is easily manipulated through his desires, becomes a more introspective character as he loses his kingly authority. His speeches gain a tragic power as he grapples with betrayals and losses. After Edward's wife, brother, and several
70 nobles turn against him, Edward is brutally murdered. Marlowe, never afraid to present the most unsettling scenes on stage in any of his plays, puts this brutal murder before the audience, and Edward's dying scream, which his murderers fear will
75 wake the entire town, has awakened horror in audiences for over four hundred years. Thus, in the eyes of the audience, the king is transformed from a pathetic character to one who arouses pity and fear —qualities that Aristotle claimed tragedy required.
80 Further, by constructing English history into a tragic shape, Marlowe engages his audience in considering the brutality and injustice of the politics of power.

Shakespeare's later history plays show evi-
85 dence that he learned a great deal from Marlowe's great play: aspects of classical tragedy and English morality are clear in many of Shakespeare's best historical dramas of the mid-to-late 1590s. *Richard II*, the start of Shakespeare's second
90 historical tetralogy, is almost a rewrite of Marlowe's *Edward II*, with Richard II enacting the same switch from failed moral hero to tragic figure, and the entire Prince Hal/Falstaff plot from *Henry IV, Parts 1 and 2* is essentially a long experiment in how ap-
95 propriate the morality form is as an expression of historical action.

Marlowe cannot compete with Shakespeare: he died too young, never having reached the level of subtlety and sophistication Shakespeare attained in
100 his career. However, Marlowe should not be considered a second-place finisher to Shakespeare. It is more accurate to characterize him as the first to

arrive at the finish line, whereas Shakespeare reached that line and found that he had merely 105 begun to race.

21. According to the passage, Christopher Marlowe's influence on Shakespeare was:

A. marginal; Shakespeare wrote the *Henry VI* plays before Marlow had written any history plays.

B. significant; Shakespeare incorporated aspects of classical tragedy and morality into his plays inspired by Marlowe's history play.

C. imperceptible; Shakespeare is unlikely to have known of Marlowe's history plays.

D. dictatorial; Shakespeare radically changed his style of writing to copy Marlowe's *Edward II*.

22. The author suggests that Christopher Marlowe's work:

A. deserves greater acknowledgement for its innovative elements.

B. lacks the technical ability required to be considered great literature.

C. is derivative of Shakespeare's work.

D. warrants second-class status to that of Shakespeare.

23. The author would most likely agree with which of the following statements?

A. Marlowe did not have sufficient opportunity to develop his full potential as a playwright.

B. Marlowe focused too little on writing history plays.

C. Shakespeare failed to develop significantly as a writer.

D. The history play was unknown as a genre before Marlowe wrote *Edward II*.

24. The passage suggests that Shakespeare used all of the following aspects from *Edward II* EXCEPT:

A. placing horrific scenes directly on stage.

B. focusing on a king who fails and is overthrown.

C. combining aspects of tragic and moral plays.

D. comparing historical action to the plot structure of a morality play.

25. The main purpose of the fourth paragraph (lines 38–61) is to:

A. establish the superiority of *Edward II* to the history plays of Shakespeare.

B. reveal the weaknesses of King Edward II.

C. show how Marlowe used and changed the morality play form in *Edward II*.

D. show how *Edward II* reflects the divinely established moral order.

26. In line 64, the word *unreflective* is intended to suggest that Edward is:

A. not an ideal king.

B. unable to fulfill others' expectations.

C. not thoughtful about his own experiences.

D. incapable of producing a reflection in a mirror because he is a ghost.

27. The author refers to Shakespeare as an "undereducated upstart" in lines 21–22 primarily to:

A. show that Marlowe is better than Shakespeare.

B. indicate that Shakespeare was not held in as high regard as Marlowe at the time.

C. suggest that Shakespeare could never have written plays like those of Marlowe.

D. explain why Shakespeare's early history plays are inferior to his later plays.

28. The author suggests that *Edward II* is NOT like a traditional morality play in that:

A. the protagonist becomes corrupted.

B. it reveals the excesses of its main character

C. it is more violent.

D. there are no "good angels" to redeem the central character.

29. According to the passage, which of the following took place *earliest*?

A. Shakespeare wrote the *Henry IV, Parts 1 and 2*.

B. Marlowe wrote *Edward II*.

C. Shakespeare wrote three parts of *Henry VI*.

D. Shakespeare wrote *Richard II*.

30. The author uses the analogy of a running race in the final paragraph to:

A. demonstrate the ways that Shakespeare and Marlowe actively competed with one another in their lifetimes.

B. suggest that Shakespeare was able to continue on after arriving where Marlowe had finished.

C. indicate that Shakespeare and Marlowe assisted each other in their writing careers.

D. suggest that Shakespeare had to outrun Marlowe in order to be considered a success.

Passage IV

NATURAL SCIENCE: This passage is adapted from Jingwen Zhang "Twenty-first Century Genetics: Power and Responsibility." ©2013 National High School Journal of Science.

Of the relatively recent, notable advancements in the fields of medicine and biotechnology, many are connected to the study of genetics and genomics. Following Watson and Crick's discovery
[5] of the DNA double helix, research on DNA and its implications in genetics and life escalated through the 1980s and 1990s to the epic, groundbreaking work of the Human Genome Project in 2003. Today, ten years later, genetic information plays a
[10] significant part in public health and medicine. Along with the unveiling of genetics as an integral factor in the 21st-century world comes the realization of responsibilities and future complications that cloud its newfound role.

[15] The expanding field of molecular biology has already translated notable scientific progress from the lab bench to the clinics. For example, thorough exploration and experimentation with the ApoE and BRCA1/BRCA2 genes—associated with Alz-
[20] heimer's disease and breast cancer, respectively—have allowed specialists to identify high-risk patients before the onset of any symptoms. Before the days of targeting the known genes, breast cancer was usually only detected by physical examinations
[25] and mammograms, and Alzheimer's went unnoticed until memory loss actually began. Individuals now have the option to take a proactive, rather than reactive, stance in their medical future. Genetics is used to assess football players' (and
[30] other high-impact sports athletes') risks of getting Alzheimer's, and to determine the appropriateness and effectiveness of certain medical procedures such as mastectomies. Unfortunately, the absence of the above mutations is not evidence that an
[35] individual is not at risk for breast cancer or Alzheimer's disease, since those mutations are found only in a small subset of patients diagnosed clinically. Both diseases are simply too complex and can arise via multiple mechanisms.

[40] Biotechnological advancements have also kept pace with the recently expanding role of genetics in everyday life. With improvements in rapid whole-genome sequencing, companies such as *23 and Me* allow the public to see some of what might come in
[45] their future based on their unique genes. Non-invasive whole genome sequencing for fetuses, a way to use maternal plasma to explore the fetal genetic information, was successfully developed in 2012 and has been seen as a large step toward improving
[50] neonatal and pediatric treatments with a genetic approach.

With these drastic medical advances made in part due to the advent of genetic studies, it becomes very easy to overstate the importance of ge-
[55] netics in changing the course of personalized medicine and in determining an individual's future. The world may seem to believe that genes are all-important: information regarding genetics can be found in almost every hospital, news headlines fre-
[60] quently report how diseases are connected to our genes, public figures like actress Angelina Jolie—who, after learning she had the breast cancer-associated version of the BRCA1 gene, had a preventive double mastectomy—advocate for preven-
[65] tative measures largely based on genetic tests.

These events are certainly not bad in themselves; the problem arises when the public is led to believe that DNA is destiny, when the truth is that singular genetic makeup is only one of many factors
[70] contributing to disease development. In addition, although genetic information, hailed as the "language" or "blueprint" of life, can seem very scientifically straightforward with little room for error or doubt, genetics itself is in fact far from an
[75] exact science. Much of the human genome has not been studied in depth yet, as it had previously been thought to be "junk" DNA; it has only recently been found to be vital to the expression of exons, the coding regions. Scientists have also discovered
[80] that variants in certain genes do not result in the predicted phenotype or condition for every individual, which further complicates the use of genetic information as guides to personal health forecasts. Furthermore, diseases can arise via multiple
[85] mechanisms: for example the BRCA1 and BRCA2 genes are found to be mutated only in approximately 10% of patients diagnosed with breast cancer.

Advancements in genetics can be extremely
[90] helpful in developing future medical treatments, but putting too much stock into them certainly can be harmful. Environmental factors—maternal smoking and drinking, folic acid intake, diet and exercise, etc.—play a significant and often deciding
[95] role as well, yet their importance is not accentuated appropriately. Using genomic information, personalized medicine may allow patients to take more control over their own treatments, but if non-genetic factors are not viewed crucial as well, pa-
[100] tients may lose some of the power they have over their health.

31. The main purpose of the first paragraph is to:

    A. praise Watson and Crick for their discovery of DNA double helix.
    B. provide a brief chronology of the advancements and applications of genetic research.
    C. provide an explanation of how genetics is used to predict the development of specific diseases.
    D. describe in detail the new role of genetics in the 21st century world.

32. The author of the passage would most likely agree with which of the following statements?

    A. People should not feel a responsibility for their own health.
    B. The most important advancements in medicine have taken place in the 21st century.
    C. The human genome has already been thoroughly studied by specialists.
    D. In studying the causes of diseases, it is important to consider the role of both genes and environmental factors.

33. According to the passage, one consequence of applying advances in genetics to medicine is:

    A. the recognition by scientists that much of our DNA is insignificant "junk."
    B. an erroneous belief that a person's DNA will predict whether he or she will develop a disease.
    C. a recognition by doctors that environmental factors are less important than genes in triggering disease.
    D. an identification of the connections between genes associated with Alzheimer's and breast cancer.

34. The author discusses the BRCA1 and BRCA2 genes to support his argument that:

    A. mammograms are not useful in the detection of breast cancer.
    B. the development of breast cancer cannot be fully accounted for by genetic factors.
    C. these genes may cause both breast cancer and Alzheimer's disease.
    D. the majority of patients with breast cancer are found to have mutated versions of these genes.

35. The author uses the phrase "DNA is destiny" in line 68 to indicate that:

    A. individuals have distinct genetic sequences.
    B. genetics should be regarded as an exact science.
    C. many people believe that genetics are the sole predictor of disease.
    D. genetic information plays a significant role in medicine.

36. According to the passage, which of the following is true of Alzheimer's disease?

    A. It can always be detected before symptoms present.
    B. It is generally diagnosed based on genetic mutations in the APOE gene.
    C. It can arise via multiple mechanisms.
    D. It affects football players more frequently that other members of the population.

37. According to the passage, what complicates the use of genetic information in devising personal health forecasts?

    A. Mutations in genes do not result in predicted conditions for every individual.
    B. "Junk" DNA interferes with the ability to develop an accurate health forecast.
    C. The expression of exons can be unpredictable.
    D. Genetic mutations are often discovered too late to be of use to an individual.

38. The following are all examples of environmental factors that might affect the development of disease EXCEPT:

    A. folic Acid intake.
    B. maternal smoking.
    C. exercise.
    D. chromosomal defects.

39. The author is most likely to agree that genetics:

    A. is an exact science with little room for further study.
    B. can unambiguously predict a person's health.
    C. continues to benefit from new discoveries that can inform medicine.
    D. should play no role in doctors' diagnoses.

40. The attitude of the author towards media coverage of genetics and disease is likely to be one of:

    A. indifference; media reports on health issues have little influence on individuals.
    B. caution; individuals may be encouraged to take preventative measures based on genetic tests and discount other factors.
    C. amusement; journalists are unlikely to understand the ramifications of gene sequencing.
    D. alarm; individuals may be needlessly panicked by reports of celebrities who have opted for double mastectomies.

When Time is Running Out

Many students arrive at their final passage, whether they are targeting three or four, with less time remaining than they'd prefer to have. If this happens to you, your standard passage strategy may need to be abandoned or altered, and you'll need to triage, or set urgency priorities, in order to maximize your limited amount of time. Make sure you have a watch with you at the test so you can monitor your time smartly. Here are a few time-crunch scenarios, along with triage suggestions for each:

Scenario 1: Seven Minutes Remain

Even if you regularly finish the whole Reading section, taking 8-9 minutes per passage, you may find yourself just a little bit behind the clock and in need of a strategy to speed things up at the end.

(1) When reading the passage, skip about a quarter of the text—either the third quarter or the last quarter.

(2) After reading, go directly to questions you know you can answer quickly, like questions with line numbers or ones that reference material you remember well.

(3) Save any question that is abstract or seems to be about something you don't recall reading about until the end. You may still be able to do these by skimming the quarter you skipped.

Scenario 2: Five Minutes Remain

At a certain point, it won't make sense to spend any initial time reading the passage because you'll run out of time before being able to take a legitimate shot at any questions.

(1) Hunt for line-number questions. Read the lines they refer to as well as the lines around them, and see if you can use that context to make an informed choice.

(2) For each line-number question you answer, try to expand your reading to an entire paragraph. If other questions clearly refer to that paragraph, answer those next.

(3) Once you've answered about half the questions, you may be able to take at least educated guesses on the broader, whole-passage questions that remain.

(4) Any specific-detail questions you haven't yet answered will likely pertain to the paragraphs you haven't touched yet, so skim those for answers if any time remains.

Scenario 3: Under Three Minutes Remain

It is always uncomfortable when you realize that you have only two or three minutes left and an entire passage to cover. However, you may still be able to salvage three or four questions, and you could still get another question or two correct by guessing randomly on those that remain.

(1) Hunt for line-number questions first, starting with any word-in-context questions. Skim the lines around them to try to give yourself as much context as you can as quickly as you can.

(2) See if there are multiple questions asking about a common narrow topic. Hunt for the paragraph those questions might be referencing, skim it, and answer the questions as well as you can.

(3) Don't forget to bubble in any questions you have not answered during the remaining seconds of the section. Pick something simple, like the first choice, to bubble in for all of these, and be careful not to fill in multiple bubbles for any question.

Science Test Manual

The ACT Science section is the fourth and final section of the multiple-choice part of the ACT. The Science section has 40 questions, which are asked over the course of either six or seven passages, and students are given 35 minutes to finish. Passages generally have questions going from easy to hard, so that the hardest questions are typically the last ones in each passage. This section is difficult for most students to complete in the allotted time.

Overview

The Science section of the ACT is organized into passages, each presenting a series of experiments, a lab procedure with results, or a set of conflicting hypotheses. On all but one released ACT test since 2015, there have been exactly six passages in the Science section, though in the past, Science sections with seven passages were the norm. Expect to see six passages, which paces to **just under six minutes per passage**, but be prepared for the possibility of seven passages.

The content of the passages in the ACT Science section is challenging for many students, though **it is built to appear more confusing and technical than it actually is**. Usually all but one of the passages will be accompanied by data in the form of charts, graphs, and tables. The data are sometimes represented using intentionally unique or unfamiliar formats.

While some of these passages are based on topics from core science classes like Biology, Chemistry, and Physics, many deal with topics outside the scope of most high school science courses. Keep in mind that **this section is *not* a test of your accumulated science knowledge**—it is a measure of how quickly and thoroughly you can sift through the given information.

Of the 40 questions, which generally go from easy to hard in each passage, there will usually be two or three that require specific science knowledge. One or two more might just require a little common sense. The rest can be answered entirely by using the given data or text.

With practice, and a little bit of strategy, you can become confident and comfortable working through the Science section passages and finding the information necessary to answer the questions in a timely manner.

Strategy

Since the ACT Science section is essentially an open book test, with the majority of the questions based on your ability to analyze data, it can often be terribly inefficient to read all of the information provided or to try to gain a deep understanding of the material. Because many of the answers are directly visible in the data presented to you, it is often possible to solve all the questions of a Science passage without having really understood all that much about the scientific concepts upon which the passage is based.

There are two types of passages on the ACT Science Section:

- Data passages
- Conflicting hypotheses passages

In the following pages, we will discuss how to work with each type.

A Note on Guessing

It is very important to strategically guess on the ACT Science section. If you spend too much time trying to figure out any given question, you will likely not have time to complete the whole section. You also shouldn't assume that you will have time at the end of a Science section to come back to questions that you may have skipped.

If you've thought about a question for a minute or so and are not able to decide on an answer, take your best guess and bubble in an answer. Remember also that the last question in a passage is usually the hardest. You don't want to overcommit your time to some very hard questions at the end of early passages and then not have any time left to answer the easier questions at the beginning of the last passage or two.

Data Passages

Data passages provide a combination of tables, graphs, figures, and text. The descriptions of experiments and procedures are dry and technical. Reading them thoroughly to try to fully understand them can be an expensive use of your time and is more likely to confuse than enlighten you.

Instead, treat the data based passages of the Science section like *a scavenger hunt*: find the most items you can in the time allotted. The most valuable tool you can have in any scavenger hunt is a map. The data in the tables and graphs and the information in the text are like locations on your map, but you have to locate the waypoints you're asked for and make the connections necessary to navigate that map in the direction of correct answers. This is best accomplished with a *three-stage marking strategy*:

(1) **CIRCLE TITLES, HEADINGS AND KEYS**
Circle every mention of a numbered **Table**, **Figure**, **Trial**, or **Experiment**. Then circle every **column heading** and **axis label** that you see, along with each element of any **key** or **formula**. While circling these, be sure to *say them in your head*, even if they are just abbreviations or unfamiliar terms. This will burn them into your short-term working memory and begin to organize them into a map of information in your brain.

If multiple tables or graphs reference the same heading or label, connect them with lines, thus expanding your map into a web of related data.

This first stage should take less than half a minute since you are not spending any time reading the descriptions of the experiments.

(2) **UNDERLINE KEY WORDS IN THE QUESTIONS**
While reading each question, underline any **Figure**, **Table**, or other data category that is named with your right hand (if you're a righty) while simultaneously pointing to where it is in the passage with your left hand. These motions will take a mere second since your mental map will be triggered.

(3) **BOX, CONNECT, UNDERLINE OR SLASH**
This third stage can vary from question to question.

- **SECONDARY DATA MARKING** If a line or column of data from a table is referenced in a question, box that line or column in the table. If a coordinate is referenced, draw lines from the appropriate axis to the relevant point. Extend trend lines as needed.

- **SKIMMING THE TEXT** If the question references information that is clearly not among the data, skim the relevant portion of the text for a key word or phrase from the question. When you find it, underline the sentence it's in and match that information with the correct choice.

- **SLASHING THE ANSWER CHOICES** Often when the answer choices are wordy, you can learn more from them than from the question. If one, two or three of the choices contain objectively false information, slash the parts of those choices that make them false. Sometimes the false information in one choice will lead you to either a better understanding of the question or a clue to which remaining choice is correct.

Keep in mind that the questions in each passage go from easy to hard, so treat each question with the appropriate level of respect. Learn about the passage from the easy questions to assist you on the harder ones. If a question refers to something you didn't see in the data, assess whether it is asking for outside science knowledge.

Each data based passage should take between 4 and 6 minutes to complete. If you're not finding an answer, especially if you're on the hardest question of a passage, take an educated guess and move on to the next passage. Scavenger hunts don't require that you find every object in order; they simply reward the people who have found the most objects in a set amount of time.

Data Passage Strategy in Action

Look at the passage on the following page to see the kinds of markings that can be made in the few moments before moving on to the questions. Look for what should be circled and which connections can be made.

Then take a look at what information should be underlined in each of the questions that follow, and return to the relevant information in the passage to answer the questions correctly. Remember, it is not essential to read any of the information in the paragraphs unless a question forces you to.

After you've tried to answer the questions, turn the page to see the correct answers and explanations of how one might use the third phase of marking to arrive at those answers.

Example Passage

When a beam of light passing through air hits another medium such as water or glass, the angle at which it travels changes. This phenomenon is known as *refraction*. As shown in Figure 1, the angle that a light ray meets the *normal* (line perpendicular to the surface of the refracting medium) is called the *angle of incidence*.

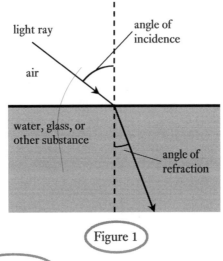

Figure 1

Experiment 1

A light beam was projected with an angle of incidence of 30° to the normal on four different materials. The angle of refraction was measured and recorded in Table 1.

Table 1	
Material	Angle of Refraction
W	27.0°
X	22.4°
Y	19.5°
Z	12.1°

Experiment 2

A light beam was projected with an angle of incidence of 30° to the normal on four different materials whose *index of refraction*, or *n*, is known. The angle of refraction was measured for each material and recorded in Table 2.

Table 2	
n	Angle of Refraction
1.2	24.6°
1.6	18.2°
2.0	14.5°
2.7	10.7°

Experiment 3

A light beam was projected at various incident angles to the normal on a single material whose index of refraction is unknown. The angles of incidence and refraction were measured and recorded in Table 3.

Table 3	
Angle of Incidence	Angle of Refraction
15°	10.7°
30°	20.9°
45°	30.3°
60°	38.2°

1. When light with an <u>angle of incidence</u> of <u>30°</u> hits Material Z, what is its <u>angle of refraction</u>?

   A. 12.1°
   B. 19.5°
   C. 22.4°
   D. 30°

2. Acrylic glass has an index of refraction $n = 1.5$. If a light beam were to hit acrylic glass with an <u>angle of incidence</u> of <u>30°</u>, its <u>angle of refraction</u> would be closest to which of the following?

   A. 16.2°
   B. 19.5°
   C. 25.5°
   D. 29.5°

3. Based on the results of <u>Experiments 2 and 3</u>, which combination of refractive index n and <u>angle of incidence</u> would produce the smallest <u>angle of refraction</u>?

	Angle of Incidence	n
A.	25°	2.5
B.	20°	1.5
C.	15°	1.5
D.	10°	2.5

4. Another experiment was performed in which a light beam was aimed at <u>Material X</u> with an <u>angle of incidence</u> of <u>30°</u>. According to <u>Table 1</u> and <u>Table 2</u>, which of the following is closest to the index of refraction n for <u>Material X</u>?

   A. 0.8
   B. 1.1
   C. 1.3
   D. 2.4

5. If a beam of light passed through the material used in <u>Experiment 3</u> with an <u>angle of incidence</u> of <u>45°</u>, and then the refracted beam passed through another sheet of the same material which was parallel to the first, the <u>angle of refraction</u> after the second time through the material would most likely have been:

   A. less than 15°.
   B. between 15° and 25°.
   C. between 25° and 35°.
   D. over 35°.

6. If a light beam met the refracting material used in <u>Experiment 3</u> such that the beam and the *surface* of the material made a <u>75°</u> angle, which of the following would most likely be the <u>angle of refraction</u>?

   A. 10.7°
   B. 45.9°
   C. 48.9°
   D. 51.2°

Answers and Explanations for the Example Passage

Here you will find the answers to the passage that was partially marked up on the previous pages.

1. A

Though the question does not mention Table 1, when you underline "Material Z" in the question, your free hand should point right to Table 1 since that is where you circled the word *Material*. Then just look across to the angle of refraction for Z in the table, and you will find that 12.1° is the correct answer. This question is very easy, which should feel right since it is the first question of the passage.

2. B

The only table that mentioned *n* was Table 2, and though there was no *n* equal to 1.5 in that table, you can draw a line between the *n* values 1.2 and 1.6 to find where the angle of refraction should lie for an *n* value of 1.5:

n	Angle of Refraction
1.2	24.6°
1.6	18.2°
2.0	14.5°
2.7	10.7°

Since the angles of refraction are decreasing while the *n* values are increasing, the answer needs to be between 24.6° and 18.2°, and only 19.5° fits that description.

3. D

As soon as you underline "Experiments 2 and 3" in the question, your free hand should be pointing at both Table 2 and Table 3, which are connected because they both deal with the angle of refraction. Then notice from Table 2 that the angle of refraction gets smaller as *n* gets larger. Also notice from Table 3 that the angle of refraction gets smaller as the angle of incidence gets smaller. Taken together that means that we are looking for a small angle of incidence and a large *n* value.

4. C

Since you are instructed to examine Table 1 and the question is dealing with Material X, box that information in Table 1. Then, using the angle of refraction for Material X from Table 1, go to Table 2 to ascertain which *n* value you might be dealing with:

Material	Angle of Refraction
W	27.0°
X	22.4°
Y	19.5°

n	Angle of Refraction
1.2	24.6°
1.6	18.2°
2.0	14.5°
2.7	10.7°

The *n* value should be between 1.2 and 1.6, so 1.3 is the only choice that fits.

5. B

By now, your free hand should be naturally pointing to Table 3's 45° angle of incidence by the time you've finished reading the first clause in the question. That shows an angle of refraction of 30.3° after the first pass through the material. Then recognize that this 30.3° angle will be the angle of incidence for the second pass through the material. Since that is close to 30°, the second angle of refraction should be close to 20.9°, and that fits very well into choice **B**.

6. A

As the last question of this passage, expect it to be a little tricky. Notice that the fact that the beam is meeting the *surface* of the material is emphasized. This is a clue that you should try to look at the given information. There you should find and underline "the angle that a light ray meets the *normal* (line perpendicular to the surface of the refracting medium) is called the *angle of incidence*." Therefore the angle of incidence for the beam in the question would be 15° since $90 - 75 = 15$. Table 3 will then give you the angle of refraction of 10.7°.

Conflicting Hypotheses Passages

Typically, one science passage will be a reading passage, where multiple opinions, hypotheses, or student viewpoints are presented. These passages will usually take slightly longer than the data passages, as they do require more focused reading to answer the questions.

Keep in mind that in this type of passage **the questions *don't* generally go from easy to hard**, and they don't follow in the order of the viewpoints, so there is no need to try to answer these questions in order. In fact, jumping around is part of the key to doing these passages cleverly.

Follow the steps below for the most efficient approach to conflicting hypotheses passages:

(1) Glance at the passage and **note its organization**. Does it reference just Scientist 1 and Scientist 2? Maybe it has Student 1, Student 2, Student 3, and Student 4. Are there any tables, graphs, figures, or equations included along with the paragraphs?

(2) Quickly look through the questions and **mark next to each which viewpoint(s) it refers to**. For example, if a question, or its choices, refers to Student 2 and Student 3 only, jot down **2, 3** next to it in the margin.

(3) **Read the background information and the viewpoints one at a time!** Don't just jump in and read the passage from start to finish. Read the introductory paragraphs first to get helpful background information. Then see if you can answer any questions that are specifically about only that information.

Continue in this manner, reading only one viewpoint at a time before seeing which questions you can answer based on that viewpoint. Remember, you are not reading with the intent of becoming an expert in the field they're discussing. You're just trying to get the gist.

(4) **Answer questions in a strategic order!** Answer all questions that are entirely about a viewpoint you've just read. These will have wrong choices that will immediately seem ridiculous because they reference material you've yet to read.

NOTE: Many questions will have choices that combine the viewpoints. You can still partially answer these by eliminating any answer choices that contradict what the viewpoint you've just read promotes.

ACT Science Terms and Concepts

Every ACT Science section has 2 or 3 questions that require some outside scientific knowledge. Though you can never be certain what will be tested, several terms and concepts have appeared many times on past ACTs, so it is a good bet you might see them tested again. Here is a selection of some of the most often tested terms and concepts.

General Science

Lab Equipment

Balance   a device for measuring mass

Beaker   short, wide glassware used to hold or measure liquid

Graduated cylinder   tall, narrow glassware with markings, used to measure the volume of a liquid

Calorimeter   a device in which a chemical reaction is performed so that the temperature change can accurately be measured

Litmus paper   strips that turn color based on the pH of a solution (red = acid; blue = base)

Water bath, **sand bath**, or **ice bath**   used to evenly heat or cool a solution by putting a container into the bath to spread the temperature change more evenly

Math Calculations and Terms

Percent error   method used to calculate how close experimental results are to the expected results

$$\text{percent error} = \frac{|\text{expected value} - \text{measured value}|}{\text{expected value}} \times 100$$

Direct and **inverse relationships**   directly related, or proportional, measurements will increase together (as x increases, y increases), where inversely related measurements will have opposite outcomes (as x increases, y decreases)

Metric measurements   different units of measurement vary by a factor of 10

kilo one thousand	1 kilogram = 1000 grams	1 kilometer = 1000 meters
centi one one-hundredth	100 centiliters = 1 liter	100 centimeters = 1 meters
milli one one-thousandth	1000 milligrams = 1 gram	1000 milliliters = 1 liter

Experimental Terms

Control group   the group that receives no treatment or "normal" treatment; the basis for comparison

Experimental group   the group that is given the variable (drug, treatment...) that is being tested

Independent vs. **dependent variable**   the dependent variable should be evident by the fact that it is affected, either positively or negatively, by changes in the independent variable, which may be itself changing at a constant rate

Biology

Genetics

Genes   individual units of hereditary information, encoded in a specific sequence of DNA

Genotype   the genetic makeup of an organism

Phenotype   the actual physical traits of an organism, which are determined by its genotype

Alleles   the different traits that one can have from alternate genetic combinations
For example, brown eyes (B allele) are dominant over blue eyes (b allele), which are recessive

Homozygous   having a pair of matching alleles

Heterozygous   having a pair of unmatched alleles

DNA   the primary genetic material, found in the nucleus in the form of a double helix

RNA   intermediate genetic material, created from DNA by the process of transcription and found in and outside the nucleus in the form of a single helix

Mitosis   the process of cell division, wherein a cell replicates its genetic material and splits into two genetically identical daughter cells

Punnett square   a method for determining percent probabilities of different alleles for genetic crosses (mating). Usually it is a two by two square, with the traits of each parent on two of the sides. The inside squares represent the possible combinations that can be passed along to children. The example to the right is a cross between two parents who both carry the dominant (A) and recessive (a) gene for a trait. If blonde hair is dominant and red hair is recessive, then in this case there is a 75% chance that the child will have blonde hair.

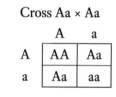

Cross Aa × Aa

	A	a
A	AA	Aa
a	Aa	aa

Energetics

Glucose   the basic source of energy for all animals; structures composed of chains of glucose make up structural parts of plant cells. Glucose is a sugar, or saccharide, and has the chemical formula $C_6H_{12}O_6$.

ATP   a high-energy molecule providing cellular energy for many processes

Cellular respiration   the process by which cells break down glucose to obtain chemical energy in the form of ATP

Aerobic   in the presence of oxygen

Anaerobic   no oxygen

Photosynthesis   the process by which green plants utilize chemical energy from the sun to create carbohydrates and oxygen from carbon dioxide and water

Classification

Genus and **species**   the two most specific categories of classification, the name by which most animals and plants are known

Endothermic   warm-blooded organisms that can regulate their body temperature

Ectothermic   cold-blooded organisms that are dependent on external sources to heat their bodies

Chemistry

Phase Changes

Freezing   changing from liquid to solid (the freezing point of water is 0°C)

Melting   changing from solid to liquid

Condensation   changing from gas to liquid

Vaporization   changing from liquid to gas (the boiling point of water is 100°C)

Sublimation   changing from solid to gas

Deposition   changing from gas to solid

Miscellaneous Chemistry

Reactants and **products**   reactants are the starting materials, which are written on the left of a chemical equation, while products are what is created, and they are written on the right.

   In the example $A + B \rightarrow C + D$, **reactants** A and B combine to form **products** C and D.

pH scale   measures the acidity of a solution from 0–14

   7 is neutral (pure water)

   any solution with a pH below 7 is acidic

   any solution with a pH above 7 is basic

Solvent   a liquid that a solute can be dissolved into

Solute   the component that dissolves into a solvent in a solution

Density   mass divided by volume, commonly in **g/mL** (the density of water is 1 g/mL)

Viscosity   a measure of a liquid's resistance to flow (syrup is more viscous than water)

Porous or **permeable**   having small spaces or holes though which liquid or air can pass

Physics

Subatomic Particles

Proton   a particle in the nucleus of an atom having a positive charge of +1 and a mass of 1

Neutron   a particle in the nucleus of an atom having no charge and a mass of 1

Electron   a particle outside of the nucleus of an atom, in the electron cloud, having a negative charge of −1 and negligible mass

Charged particles   opposite charges will attract each other, while like charges will repel each other

Energy

Potential energy   stored energy, due, for example, to an object's height or the tightness of a wound spring, that could result in motion

Kinetic energy   the energy of an object in motion

Heat   a form of energy associated with the movement of atoms and molecules in a material

Miscellaneous Physics

Mass   the quantity of matter in a body

Velocity   the magnitude (speed) and direction of motion, usually measured in **meters per second**

Acceleration   the rate of change of velocity over time, usually measured in **meters per second per second** or **m/s^2**

Force   the mass multiplied by the acceleration of an object, commonly measured in **newtons**

Drag force   a type of resistance, which is always in the opposite direction of the relative motion of an object

Work   a force multiplied by the distance over which that force is exerted

Momentum   the mass times the velocity of an object

Sample Science Passages

Try to use the strategies discussed on the previous pages to work your way through the four passages that follow. Then check your answers in the back of this book.

Passage I

A group of students wanted to know if stream health was affected by acid rain or runoff contents. Acid rain is typically a result of coal burning power plants releasing hydrogen sulfide into the atmosphere, where it combines with water and is deposited back to earth in rainfall. The pH of stream or ground water is a good measure of how much acid rain falls in a given area. Nitrates and Phosphates are commonly used in fertilizers and building applications, and are found in many streams and lakes near farms and other human development.

Experiment 1

The students researched stream water quality by collecting and analyzing samples. They collected samples at 6 sites along a stream at known elevations descending a mountain. They measured the pH and water temperature at the collection site.

Table 1
(collected on site)

Site	Elevation (ft)	pH	Water Temp(°C)
1	4310	5.9	44
2	4260	6.0	44
3	3710	6.0	46
4	3380	6.1	47
5	3240	6.3	48
6	2700	6.4	50

Experiment 2

At 6 other sites along the stream, the students measured the amounts of nitrates (NO_3^-), phosphates (PO_4^{-3}), and sulfates (SO_4^{-2}) in parts per million.

Table 2
(results from lab analysis)

Site	NO_3^- (ppm)	PO_4^{-3} (ppm)	SO_4^{-2} (ppm)
7	.0012	.035	5.76
8	.0032	.030	5.60
9	.0060	.025	5.21
10	.0011	.007	1.24
11	.0213	.182	4.21
12	.0204	.180	3.95

1. Which of the following sites had the lowest concentration of phosphates in the samples?

   A. Site 8
   B. Site 9
   C. Site 11
   D. Site 12

2. Which sample site had the most acidic water?

   A. Site 1
   B. Site 4
   C. Site 5
   D. Site 6

3. According to Experiment 1, as elevation increased:

   A. pH of the water increased and water temperature increased.
   B. pH of the water increased and water temperature decreased.
   C. pH of the water decreased and water temperature increased.
   D. pH of the water decreased and water temperature decreased.

4. One of the students is concerned that the liquid chromatography apparatus that measures the nitrate amounts is inaccurate. How would they best determine if the machine is accurate or not?

   A. Test samples of known concentrations of NO_3^-
   B. Test all the samples again and compare those values to the first values
   C. Compare the nitrate results to the phosphate results and determine if they change at the same rate
   D. Compare the nitrate results to the results from the same experiment the previous year

5. One of the students is inexperienced, and accidentally left some distilled water in the collection bottle for one of the sites, which diluted that particular sample. According to Table 2, which site was most likely the one with water in the collection bottle?

   A. Site 8
   B. Site 9
   C. Site 10
   D. Site 12

6. A student hypothesized before Experiment 2 that the site with the highest Sulfate concentration would also have the highest Nitrate concentration. Do the data in Table 2 support this student's hypothesis?

   A. Yes, because Site 8 had the highest Nitrate concentration.
   B. Yes, because Site 11 had the highest Nitrate concentration.
   C. No, because Site 8 had the highest Nitrate concentration.
   D. No, because Site 11 had the highest Nitrate concentration.

Passage II

It is difficult to determine exactly what foods or nutrients are best for certain activities, such as recovering after a strenuous workout. Below, two nutritional experts debate drinking milk versus drinking a protein shake after exercise.

Expert 1

Drinking milk after working out speeds up recovery time and helps repair damaged muscle tissue.

Certain nutrients enhance muscle growth and reduce recovery time, and milk contains many of these nutrients, such as calcium, potassium, and protein. Milk also has *bioactive compounds*—substances with nutritional value, some of which we do not yet understand.

Most protein shakes are simply derived from milk; for example, whey protein is often isolated from the whey manufactured from cow's milk. However, the bioactive compounds may be lost in the process.

Expert 2

Protein shakes are researched and formulated to contain the substances that best promote muscle restoration and growth according to our current understanding of nutrition.

While milk has many useful nutrients, the right mix of these nutrients is also important. A protein shake has more protein, fewer calories, less fat, and less cholesterol than an equivalent volume of milk, and thus it better promotes muscle development.

Protein shakes can also be processed to achieve further benefits. In *isolate* whey protein, the processing removes lactose carbohydrate, a substance many adults cannot digest. *Hydrolysate* whey protein contains partially hydrolyzed protein that is more easily absorbed.

1. Expert 2 would agree with which statement? Drinking a protein shake after a workout is better for building muscle than drinking milk because:

   A. milk has bioactive compounds.
   B. milk is derived from protein shakes.
   C. the protein shake contains more calcium than milk.
   D. the protein shake contains a mix of proteins and nutrients optimized for rebuilding muscle.

2. By referring to calcium and potassium, Expert 1 implies that:

   A. calcium is a type of protein.
   B. potassium is a bioactive compound.
   C. calcium and potassium help muscles recover and grow.
   D. calcium and potassium are not found in protein shakes.

3. Both experts claim that:

   A. milk contains more protein than protein shakes.
   B. milk has nutrients useful for muscle growth and restoration.
   C. milk and protein shakes contain bioactive compounds.
   D. protein shakes are derived from milk.

4. Which of the following observations, if true, contradicts Expert 2?

   A. Athletes who drank 1 cup of milk after working out gained, on average, 50 g of muscle mass.
   B. Athletes who performed the same workout and consumed the same amount of protein but more calories built more muscle than those who consumed fewer calories.
   C. Athletes who performed the same workout and consumed the same amount of protein but less fat built more muscle than those who consumed more fat.
   D. Athletes who drank protein shakes after working out gained, on average, 55 g of muscle mass.

5. According to the information in the passage, milk contains which of the following that *isolate* whey protein does not?

   A. Lactose carbohydrate
   B. Calcium and potassium
   C. Partially hydrolyzed protein
   D. Fat and cholesterol

6. Suppose it were discovered that milk contains a previously unknown bioactive compound that helps to rebuild muscle. Would it be possible to conclude that drinking milk is better than drinking a protein shake for rebuilding muscle?

   A. Yes, because the bioactive compound is more useful than protein and other nutrients for rebuilding muscle.
   B. Yes, because protein shakes contain no bioactive compounds.
   C. No, because protein shakes may also have that same bioactive compound.
   D. No, because protein shakes have more fat than milk.

7. Expert 2 would most likely agree with which of the following statements?

   A. Milk is beneficial for muscle recovery, but protein shakes are better because they have lactose carbohydrate.
   B. Milk is beneficial for muscle recovery, but protein shakes are better because of their mix of nutrients.
   C. Protein shakes are beneficial for muscle recovery, but milk is better because of its bioactive compounds.
   D. Protein shakes are beneficial for muscle recovery, but milk is better because it has more cholesterol.

Passage III

The structure of an atom is such that there is a positively charged nucleus of protons and neutrons surrounded by a negatively charged electron cloud. Electrons are arranged around atoms based on distinct energy levels, and atoms "like" to have 8 electrons in their outermost, or *valence*, energy level, as that is the most stable electron configuration.

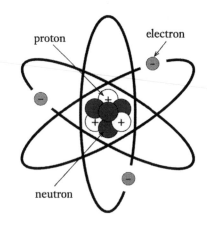

Table 1					
Element	Atomic #	Electronegativity	First Ionization Energy (kJ)	Atomic Radius (pm)	Ionic Radius (pm)
Group 1 Metals					
Li	3	1.0	520	152	90
Na	11	0.9	496	186	116
K	19	0.8	419	227	152
Rb	37	0.8	403	248	166
Cs	55	0.7	377	265	181
Group 7 Halogens					
F	9	4.0	1681	72	119
Cl	17	3.0	1251	100	167
Br	35	2.8	1140	114	182
I	53	2.5	1008	133	206

Table 1 presents information about elements in Group 1 and Group 7 of the periodic table.

Group 1 is the alkaline earth metal elements, and Group 7 is the halogen elements (non-metals).

Atomic number is the number of protons in an atom, and also the number of electrons in that element when it is neutral (uncharged). *Electronegativity* is a measure of an atom's ability to attract electrons to itself. *First ionization energy* is the energy required to remove the outermost electron from an atom, creating a +1 ion (charged atom). *Atomic radius* is a rough measure from the center of the nucleus to the outer edge of the electron cloud, and *ionic radius* is that same measurement for the + or – ion formed by that atom.

1. When forming an ion, which of the group 7 Halogens has the smallest radius?

   A. Li
   B. Cs
   C. F
   D. I

2. Scientists frequently focus on trends among elements in the periodic table. For the Group 1 metal elements in Table 1, which of the following two properties have inverse relationships with an element's Atomic Number?

   A. Electronegativity and Ionization Energy
   B. Electronegativity and Ionic Radius
   C. Atomic Radius and Ionization Energy
   D. Ionic Radius and Ionization Energy

3. Regular table salt is sodium chloride, NaCl, and is the combination of an Na^+ ion and a Cl^- ion. Based on the data, how much energy is required to create the Na^+ ion that bonds with chlorine to make NaCl?

   A. 0.9 kJ
   B. 116 kJ
   C. 496 kJ
   D. 1251 kJ

4. If Table 1 included the group 7 Halogen element astatine (At), with atomic number 85, what would the electronegativity value of At most likely be?

   A. 5.0
   B. 3.4
   C. 2.2
   D. 0.3

5. Bromine (Br) likes to gain an electron, forming an ion with a –1 charge. How many electrons does this Bromine ion have?

   A. 34
   B. 35
   C. 36
   D. 1140

6. Ionic bonds form between ions of different elements. The greater the difference in electronegativity between the two elements, the greater the ionic character of the bond. Which of the following bonds would have the LEAST ionic character?

   A. Na–Cl
   B. Li–I
   C. K–I
   D. Cs–F

Passage IV

A photogate is a C-shaped device with two prongs that sends a tiny beam of light from one prong to a light-sensor on the other prong. Any object passing through a photogate will break the beam of light; thus, a photogate can detect the time at which an object passes between its prongs.

Experiment 1

A small mass was attached to a spring. The spring was then stretched to 2 cm, and later 5 cm, in length before being released, resulting in the mass moving back and forth as shown in Figure 1.

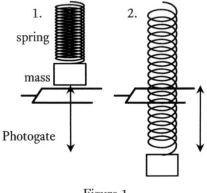

Figure 1

A photogate was placed at the *equilibrium point* (the point in the middle of the mass's movement). Each time the mass passed through the photogate, the time was recorded. The results of both trials are shown in Table 1 and Table 2.

Table 1		
Times when the mass passed through the photogate after the spring was originally stretched 2 cm		
Pass	Time (s)	Difference (s)
1	2.13	—
2	4.81	2.68
3	7.51	2.70
4	10.21	2.70
5	12.92	2.71

Table 2		
Times when the mass passed through the photogate after the spring was originally stretched 5 cm		
Pass	Time (s)	Difference (s)
1	1.24	—
2	3.93	2.69
3	6.62	2.68
4	9.32	2.70
5	12.01	2.69
6	14.73	2.72

Experiment 2

Three objects with different masses were attached to the same spring at different times. For each object, the spring was stretched the same distance while the photogate was placed at the equilibrium point, and the time was noted for three straight passes through the photogate. The average time between passes for each object through the photogate was then calculated, and all the information was recorded in Table 3.

Table 3				
Object	Time 1 (s)	Time 2 (s)	Time 3 (s)	Avg time difference (s)
A	1.33	6.73	12.14	5.41
B	0.53	3.24	5.97	2.72
C	0.61	1.96	3.31	1.40

1. The *period* of an oscillation can be calculated by finding twice the amount of time it takes for a mass to move from its equilibrium point back to its equilibrium point. In Experiment 2, which of the following is closest to the period of the spring for object C?

   A. 1.4 sec
   B. 2.8 sec
   C. 3.3 sec
   D. 6.6 sec

2. Based on the data from Table 1 and Table 2, what effect does stretching the spring to a different length have on the amount of time between passes through the photogate?

   A. Stretching the spring farther makes the time between passes longer because the time differences for the 5 cm stretch were longer than those for the 2 cm stretch.
   B. Stretching the spring farther makes the time between passes shorter because the time differences for the 5 cm stretch were shorter than those for the 2 cm stretch.
   C. Stretching the spring farther has no effect on the time between passes because the time differences were about the same for both stretches of the spring.
   D. The effect cannot be determined because whenever the string was stretched, it moved to its equilibrium point and stayed still.

3. If Experiment 2 were run again so that the objects were allowed to oscillate for at least 10 seconds, which of the objects would pass through the photogate the GREATEST number of times in 10 seconds?

   A. Object A
   B. Object B
   C. Object C
   D. Each object would pass through the photogate the same number of times.

4. According to Table 2, which of the following best describes the relationship between how many passes an object makes through the photogate and how long it takes to return to its equilibrium point?

   A. As the number of passes an object makes through the photogate increases, the time it takes to return to its equilibrium point decreases.
   B. As the number of passes an object makes through the photogate increases, the time it takes to return to its equilibrium point increases.
   C. As the number of passes an object makes through the photogate increases, the time it takes to return to its equilibrium point first increases and then decreases.
   D. As the number of passes an object makes through the photogate increases, the time it takes to return to its equilibrium point stays the same.

5. Increasing the mass of an object attached to a spring increases the amount of time it takes to oscillate up and down. Which of the objects from Table 3 must have the LEAST mass?

   A. Object A
   B. Object B
   C. Object C
   D. Each object has the same mass.

6. If the same spring was used in both Experiments 1 and 2, which object from Experiment 2 could have also been used in Experiment 1.

   A. Object A
   B. Object B
   C. Object C
   D. It cannot be determined.

Essay Manual

The ACT writing section asks you to read three perspectives on a certain topic and then write an essay in which you argue your own perspective on the topic and relate it to at least one of the perspectives given. You have 40 minutes to plan and write the essay.

Sample Essay Prompt

Controversy and Commencement

In recent years, students and faculty on many college campuses have urged their administrators to disinvite scheduled commencement speakers who hold political viewpoints with which the students disagree. For example, students have requested that speakers be disinvited because of their stances on the use of torture during times of war, their positions for or against abortion rights, and their opinions on legalizing gay marriage. Students argue that inviting speakers with certain viewpoints signals that a college is condoning those viewpoints. Opponents argue that while students can respond to speech they disagree with, colleges should nevertheless invite speakers of all political persuasions to schools to foster debate. Should students push colleges to "disinvite" scheduled speakers who hold controversial viewpoints?

Read and carefully consider these perspectives. Each suggests a particular way of thinking about the issue of controversial commencement speakers.

Perspective One	Perspective Two	Perspective Three
Students have a duty to speak out against notable figures who they believe hold positions that are offensive or immoral. Commencement speakers should embody exemplary citizenship. If that is in question, students are justified in requesting that a speaker be disinvited from delivering a speech.	Cancelling scheduled speakers is a form of censorship. It is important to hear from notable people whose views differ from one's own. Colleges must encourage a free exchange of ideas even if that is uncomfortable for some students.	College administrators should do a better job of including student and faculty representatives in decisions about whom to invite to speak on college campuses. Making the invitation process more democratic would avoid altercations and embarrassment when a college is forced to retract its invitation to a scheduled speaker due to student protest.

Essay Task

Write a unified, coherent essay discussing whether students should ever advocate disinviting scheduled commencement speakers. In your essay, be sure to:

- clearly state your own perspective on the issue and analyze the relationship between your perspective and at least one other perspective
- develop and support your ideas with reasoning and examples
- organize your ideas clearly and logically
- communicate your ideas effectively in standard written English

Your perspective may be in full agreement with any of those given, in partial agreement, or completely different.

General Tips

- Use 5–7 minutes to plan: read the prompt, brainstorm ideas, generate examples, and develop an outline.
- Have a default outline (see suggested outline below).
- Use good examples from history, current events, and personal experience.

Strategy

1. **Read the prompt and underline the question that is being asked.**

   The prompt will provide some background information on an issue before ending in a question or two. If you're confused about what you're supposed to address in your essay, the "Essay Task" will repeat the question or topic that needs to be addressed in your essay.

2. **Read the three perspectives.**

   Generally, one perspective will support a position, another perspective will oppose it, and the third will be somewhere in the middle. Underline key words that indicate what the main point of each perspective is. Think about the strengths and weaknesses of the perspectives provided and jot down your ideas.

3. **Develop your own perspective.**

   It's probably easiest to choose one of the perspectives provided to guide you as you develop your own.

4. **Choose a perspective you could use as a counterpoint to your own.**

   You will present this perspective in your essay but then rebut it.

5. **Brainstorm some examples to support your perspective and the counterpoint perspective.**

   Coming up with specific examples will lead to a stronger essay than using general statements.

6. **Develop your outline.**

   Suggested Outline:

   - *Introduction*: Introduce the paper with several general sentences that put the topic in context and illustrate the debate at hand. Finish with your thesis statement, which is your perspective and why you believe it is the strongest. (2–3 sentences)
   - *Body Paragraph One*: Support your perspective with specific examples and reasoning. Illustrate how these examples bolster your argument.
   - *Body Paragraph Two*: Support your perspective with specific examples and reasoning. Illustrate how these examples bolster your argument.
   - *Body Paragraph Three*: Present the opposing perspective. Provide examples or reasoning that supports this perspective. Discuss why this perspective is flawed or weaker than your own.
   - *Conclusion*: Conclude by restating *your* argument (2–3 sentences).

   Note: The suggested outline above is for a five-paragraph essay. If you struggle to write quickly, you can stick to writing a four-paragraph essay with one paragraph supporting your perspective instead of two.

7. **Proofread**

   Save 2–3 minutes at the end of your essay to proofread.

Scoring

ACT graders will give your essay a score from 1–6 on each of the following four domains:

- Ideas and Analysis
- Development and Support
- Organization
- Language Use

Two ACT graders will read your essay. The maximum total score you can receive from one grader is 24. The maximum total score you can receive from the two graders is 48. The ACT will divide your total score by 4 to give you a score from 2–12.

To get a top scoring essay

- Write a clear, precise thesis.
- Address multiple perspectives on the given issue.
- Use good examples and clear reasoning.
- Provide context for the issue being addressed.
- Use clear transitions between paragraphs.
- Vary your sentence structure and vocabulary.

Percentile Ranges for Essay Scores

Essay Score	Percentile
2	1
3	3
4	9
5	18
6	40
7	60
8	84
9	93
10	98
11	99
12	99+

Answer Keys

English Test Manual Answer Key

Grammar and Punctuation

Commas

1

1. As Jonathan walked down the street **,** he thought about how long it had been since he'd last been to this part of town.
2. Although I hadn't seen him in years **,** I recognized him instantly.
3. (NO CHANGE)

2

1. I like to sing loudly to myself **(NO COMMA)** as I take my shower.
2. (NO CHANGE)

3

1. Garrett wanted to throw Leila a surprise party **,** but he knew that it would be impossible to keep a secret from her.
2. I need to finish my Common Application by this weekend **,** so I need to start working on my supplements.
3. He knew he remembered the song **,** yet he couldn't recall what its name was.

4

1. Mary, who loved her little lamb **,** was sometimes a little careless about his whereabouts.
2. Mary's lamb **,** a little lamb, had white fleece.

5

1. When Brianna was younger, she would tell people her favorite colors were red **,** orange **,** yellow **,** green **,** blue **,** and purple.
2. My friends, Tommy **,** Bob **,** Chris, and Matt, are meeting me at the party.

6

1. Though Kevin wanted a red **(NO COMMA)** two-door **(NO COMMA)** sports **(NO COMMA)** car for his 16th birthday, his parents had said that was out of the question.
2. He recuperated from his injuries by resting in a small **(NO COMMA)** English **(NO COMMA)** country village away from the busy, crowded city.

7

1. Despite the hot **,** dry **,** strong wind, we decided to hike up the mountain anyway.
2. Her employer wrote a reference saying that Lisa is a smart, fun, interesting **(NO COMMA)** girl.

8

1. (NO CHANGE)
2. The opinion for the majority was given by the Chief Justice **,** John Roberts.

Editing Exercises for Commas

1. Although he was not previously known to be a great speaker **,** Jonathan impressed the audience with his witty stories.

2. Jonah ran a mile in six minutes **,** and directly afterwards he swam a mile in ten minutes.

3. Washington, who has phenomenal memory **,** won top prize in the Name-the-President contest.

4. Bilbao is a fascinating town **,** but we were too tired to enjoy it.

5. I need a new bookshelf **,** one **(NO COMMA)** that holds more.

6. I recently listened to an opera composed by eighteenth century philosopher **(NO COMMA)** Jean-Jacques Rousseau.

7. Ian **,** my high school's top basketball player **,** was recruited by several schools.

8. Daily aerobic exercise helps in blood circulation **,** heart-health, and blood pressure control.

9. After quitting gymnastics, Kathryn decided **(NO COMMA)** to run cross-country **,** a sport that doesn't require too much experience.

10. Virginia Woolf's greatest novel **,** in my opinion **,** was not *To the Lighthouse* but *Mrs. Dalloway.*

11. One of the reasons I love summer **(NO COMMA)** is the weather.

12. One way to help yourself get to bed earlier **(NO COMMA)** is to do your homework during your free period.

13. The only person in recorded history to be directly hit by a meteorite, Ann Hodges, was very **(NO COMMA)** lucky or very **(NO COMMA)** unlucky **,** depending **(NO COMMA)** on your point of view.

14. Arti's hastiness to finish **,** her Math teacher argued **,** indirectly caused most of her careless errors.

15. This summer **,** the last one before college **,** is bittersweet for most students and their families.

Semicolons

[1]

1. When Leslie was young, she could not stand her little sister **;** now that they are older, they are the best of friends.

2. *Beauty and the Beast* is my favorite Disney movie **;** however, *The Lion King* is a close second.

Colons

[1]

1. In order to bake my grandmother's favorite cookies tonight, I need to buy the following **:** flour, baking soda, eggs, and chocolate chips.

2. Barack Obama's campaign centered around three words **:** "Yes we can."

[2]

1. Mike has not yet made plans for his day off **:** he is either going hiking or taking his son to the zoo.

2. Summer is my favorite time of year **:** the weather is nice, the days are long, and school is out.

Dashes

1

1. The organization of one's pens in a pencil case is—contrary to what you might think — extremely important.

2. Hector could never have guessed—having never even suspected his friend of treachery — that he would be stabbed with a cocktail fork.

2

1. George has many pets — a dog, a cat, two birds, and about a dozen fish.

2. I prefer pancakes to French toast — I think that the latter is often too sweet.

Editing Exercises for Commas, Semi Colons, Colons, and Dashes

For these exercises, there may be more than one correct answer. The answers provided are one way of correcting the sentences.

1. (NO CHANGE)

2. Dalby is gifted at Math **;** however, he has a hard time learning vocabulary.

3. In their desire to win the contract, the firms bid the price too low **;** thereby **,** they made the project unviable.

4. Roger won the match **;** hence, he gets the trophy **;** it matters little that his opponent was injured.

5. After a long and dreary summer spent waiting at the bottom of the pile, Mr. Ripe N. Melon had the thought, or perhaps the flash of intuition **,** that he would never get consumed.

6. Because I grew up watching my brothers play basketball **,** I decided to try out for the high school team.

7. Just because I understood the game did not mean I could play **;** I spent most of the season on the bench.

8. The team with the most NCAA Basketball championships — the UCLA Bruins—was coached by John Wooden for 10 out of the 11 titles they won.

9. Krista moved home after graduation **,** ready for something new **,** but after a year at home **,** she moved to Louisiana to pursue her MBA.

10. Katie plans to stay in Chicago because she loves so much about the city **:** the beach, the architecture, the parks, and the people.

11. Advertising is a big reason why teens drink so much soda **;** lack of oversight is another reason.

12. Washington, D.C., the nation's capital, is well known for its monuments **;** however, some critics bemoan the lack of originality in its architecture.

13. (NO CHANGE)

14. Most of us can cook well **;** the problem is we don't have the time.

15. The décor of her office is, in general, too Spartan for my taste **;** however, I like the fresh flowers in the vases.

Mixed Punctuation Problem Set

1. D	6. D	11. D
2. A	7. A	12. B
3. C	8. C	13. D
4. D	9. D	14. B
5. C	10. A	15. A

Pronouns

1. they
2. she

2

1. the cat
2. Jacob

3

1. whom
2. who
3. who; whom

4

1. who
2. which

5

1. me
2. she, me

Exercises for Pronouns

1.	it	6.	her	11.	whom
2.	me	7.	I	12.	them
3.	who	8.	he; them	13.	me
4.	who	9.	Who	14.	who
5.	us	10.	Whom	15.	that

Apostrophes

Possessives

1

1. In many schools, it is the teacher**'s** responsibility to track attendance.
2. The students celebrated the School Board**'s** decision to build a new gym on campus.
3. When I cleaned up after the party, I found James**'** coat and Susan**'s** shoes.
4. Dani borrows Bess**'** car when she needs to run errands outside of the city.

2

1. At the track championship, it was all of the schools**'** responsibility to provide volunteers to time the races.
2. After the party, almost all of the girls**'** dresses were covered in cake.
3. The attendees of the 1851 Women**'s** Convention in Akron, Ohio, were privileged to hear Sojourner Truth**'s** famous "And Ain't I a Woman?" speech.
4. Even though Stephen is only 15, he is so tall that he needs to shop in the men**'s** department.

Contractions

1. My friend who**se** car I borrowed was somewhat angry when I returned it with one side mirror missing.
2. It**'**s been a long time, but I know a change is going to come.
3. Whatever **its** source, the noise outside greatly disturbed **your** dog.

Editing Exercises for Apostrophe

1. Its heart had stopped beating, but the amphibian's tail still quivered with life.

2. The bring-out-the vote effort rejuvenated the community and increased **its** involvement in social welfare.

3. Its appetite sated, the leopard wandered off leaving the remains of **its** kill to the hyenas.

4. "It's mid-day," mother exclaimed, "and you're still in bed!"

5. Harold argued that although Maud was old, she was still beautiful to him: "it's in the eyes of the beholder that beauty lies," he said.

6. It was snowing yesterday, but it's seventy-five degrees today; it's unnerving to have the weather change so suddenly.

7. You're going to have trouble being taken seriously if you don't perfect yo**ur** use of apostrophes.

8. These books' cover**s** were torn before they arrived here.

9. On Los Angeles' Rodeo Drive, most sho**ps** are too expensive for me to even look at.

10. Stephen's recently finished film is going to be shown at Sundance this year; he hopes **its** content will challenge his audience's thinking.

11. Although I have seen many professional photographers' representations of Half Dome, I have seen none that show the peak from my mother's favorite vantage point.

12. (NO CHANGE)

13. My dog's collar is blue, but both my cousin Joan's dogs' collar**s** are green; when our Chihuahuas play together we can only tell them apart by **their** collars.

14. (NO CHANGE)

15. Right there is the man who**se** cats have been causing me so much trouble!

Verb Usage Rules

Subject-Verb Agreement

1. Nouns separated from the verb
   1. makes
   2. is; is
   3. breathes

2. Collective Nouns
   1. was
   2. smells
   3. was the winner

Verb Tenses

1. Past, present and future
   1. went
   2. will review

2. Perfect Tenses
   3. had cooled
   4. have jumped

3. Irregular verbs
   1. had; drunk
   2. will have; sung
   3. has; come

Exercises for Verb Usage

1. writes		9. make	
2. is		10. was	
3. has		11. is	
4. was		12. include	
5. has		13. stampedes	
6. swum		14. are	
7. sang; sung		15. do	
8. were			

Verb Usage, Pronouns, and Apostrophes Problem Set

1. C		6. A	
2. B		7. B	
3. D		8. D	
4. C		9. A	
5. D		10. B	

Adjectives and Adverbs

Editing Exercises for Adjectives and Adverbs

1. Math can be **really** hard for some people; for others it can be **really easy**.
2. I read the **humorous** comic strip to my nephew.
3. Natalie runs **quickly** but talks **slowly**.
4. He who reads **carefully** scores **well**.
5. Ron swats at the **fast** fly, but he cannot get it.

Misplaced Modifiers

Editing Exercises for Misplaced Modifiers
(Correct answers may vary)

1. My cousin sold a house **with no hard wood floors** to a nice family.
2. Our favorite people on Halloween are the ones that give out brownies **wrapped in cellophane** to the children.
3. Waking up later than planned, **John missed his flight**.
4. After reading the book *Pride and Prejudice*, **I found the movie version dull and lifeless.**
5. **While I was outside her bedroom window,** I heard that my roommate intended to throw a surprise party for me.
6. Waiting for her brother's game to end, **Leslie grew impatient**.

Parallel Structure

Editing Exercises for Parallel Structure
(Correct answers may vary)

1. Chris loves writing stories, poems and ~~composing~~ songs.
2. Rick is either playing the fool or **telling jokes**.
3. Amanda has trouble with study skills, memory techniques, and **time management**.
4. The recommendations put forth by the committee include making annual standardized tests mandatory after the fourth grade and **randomly sampling** internal assessments for evidence of grade inflation.
5. Merab has neither played the trombone nor ~~has she played~~ the tuba.
6. Ashley will **write, proofread, and e-mail the essay** before tomorrow.

Modifiers, Parallel Structure, and Word Choice Problem Set

1. B
2. C
3. D
4. C
5. D
6. D
7. D
8. B
9. D
10. A

Rhetorial Skills

Rhetorical Skills Problem Set

1. B
2. D
3. C
4. B
5. C
6. B
7. C
8. C
9. D
10. D

Mathematics Test Manual Answer Key

Strategies

Backsolving

Problem Set

1.	C	8.	E	15.	B
2.	D	9.	B	16.	C
3.	E	10.	B	17.	D
4.	B	11.	D	18.	E
5.	B	12.	B	19.	C
6.	E	13.	C	20.	A
7.	D	14.	D		

Plugging in Numbers

Problem Set 1

1.	E	6.	B	11.	D
2.	E	7.	A	12.	E
3.	D	8.	D	13.	C
4.	D	9.	D	14.	A
5.	C	10.	B	15.	C

Problem Set 2

1.	C	6.	B	11.	C
2.	A	7.	E	12.	B
3.	B	8.	B	13.	B
4.	A	9.	C	14.	B
5.	B	10.	C	15.	C

Calculator

Problem Set

1.	B	6.	C	11.	E
2.	C	7.	D	12.	C
3.	B	8.	E	13.	C
4.	A	9.	C	14.	C
5.	A	10.	C	15.	C

Measuring

Problem Set

1.	C
2.	D
3.	C
4.	C

Geometry and Graphing

Geometry Nuts and Bolts

Angle Relationships

Vertical angles	congruent	
Adjacent angles	supplementary	
Supplementary to A	B, C, F, G	
Congruent with A	D, E, H	
Sum of interior angles of triangle		$180°$
Sum of interior angles of quadrilateral		$360°$
Sum of interior angles of pentagon		$540°$
Sum of interior angles of a polygon with n sides		$(n-2) \times 180°$
Measure of each interior angle for a regular polygon with n sides		$\dfrac{n-2}{n} \times 180°$

Formulas to remember

Triangle	Area $A = \frac{1}{2}bh$
Rectangle	Area $A = \ell w$ Perimeter $P = 2\ell + 2w$
Square	Area $A = s^2$ Perimeter $P = 4s$
Parallelogram	Area $A = bh$
Rectangular solid	Volume $V = abc = \ell wh$ Surface Area $A = 2ab + 2bc + 2ac$ Diagonal: $d^2 = a^2 + b^2 + c^2$
Trapezoid	Area $A = \frac{1}{2}h(b_1 + b_2)$
Circle	Circumference $C = 2\pi r = d\pi$ Area $A = \pi r^2$
Right Circular Cylinder	Volume $V = \pi r^2 h$

Triangles

Pythagorean Theorem	$a^2 + b^2 = c^2$
Pythagorean Triples	3–4–5, 5–12–13, 8–15–17, 7–24–25
Isosceles Triangle	2 equal sides
Equilateral Triangle	3 equal sides
Similar Triangles	Congruent angles Sides in proportion
45–45–90 Triangle	$1:1:\sqrt{2}$
30–60–90 Triangle	$1:\sqrt{3}:2$
Longest side < sum of the other sides	
Longest side in triangle opposite largest angle Shortest side in triangle opposite smallest angle	

Circles

Arc length	$\ell = \dfrac{\theta}{360} 2\pi r$
Sector area	$A = \dfrac{\theta}{360}\pi r^2$
Inscribed angle	$= \dfrac{1}{2}$ arc $= \dfrac{1}{2}$ central angle
Central angle	$=$ arc

Geometry Problem Sets

Geometry Problem Set 1

1.	B	8.	A	15.	C
2.	C	9.	D	16.	E
3.	C	10.	E	17.	A
4.	C	11.	D	18.	E
5.	B	12.	C	19.	C
6.	A	13.	E	20.	B
7.	B	14.	B		

Geometry Problem Set 2

1.	C	8.	C	15.	D
2.	C	9.	E	16.	B
3.	E	10.	B	17.	C
4.	D	11.	D	18.	C
5.	C	12.	B	19.	B
6.	C	13.	B	20.	B
7.	A	14.	C		

Coordinate Geometry Nuts and Bolts

Slope-intercept form of line is $y = mx + b$	
$m = $ slope	$b = y$-intercept
To find y-intercept of line, set $x = 0$	
To find x-intercept of line, set $y = 0$	

Slope, Midpoint, and Distance

Slope $= \dfrac{\text{rise}}{\text{run}} = \dfrac{y_2 - y_1}{x_2 - x_1}$
Slope of horizontal line $= 0$
Slope of vertical line $=$ undefined
Parallel lines have equal slopes
Perpendicular lines have negative reciprocal slopes
Midpoint $= ($average x, average $y)$ $= \left(\dfrac{x_1 + x_2}{2}, \dfrac{y_1 + y_2}{2} \right)$
Distance $d^2 = \text{run}^2 + \text{rise}^2$ $d = \sqrt{(x_2 - x_1)^2 + (y_2 - y_1)^2}$

Circles and Parabolas

Circle	$(x-h)^2 + (y-k)^2 = r^2$
Parabola in vertex form	$y = a(x-h)^2 + k$

Transformations

Across x-axis	$r_{x\text{-axis}}(x, y) \rightarrow (x, -y)$
Across x-axis	$r_{y\text{-axis}}(x, y) \rightarrow (-x, y)$
Across origin	$r_{\text{origin}}(x, y) \rightarrow (-x, -y)$

Coordinage Geometry and Graphing Problem Sets

Problem Set 1

1. C	6. B	11. E
2. C	7. B	12. C
3. E	8. E	13. A
4. B	9. A	14. B
5. D	10. D	15. C

Problem Set 2

1. C	6. B
2. D	7. B
3. C	8. E
4. C	9. C
5. B	10. A

Numbers and Operations

Number Terms

Problem Set

1. B	6. C	11. D
2. D	7. C	12. D
3. E	8. A	13. D
4. E	9. C	14. B
5. C	10. D	15. C

Sequences

Problem Set

1. C	6. D
2. D	7. B
3. E	8. C
4. C	9. B
5. A	10. E

Ratios and Proportions

Problem Set

1. D	8. B	15. B
2. D	9. C	16. D
3. C	10. D	17. D
4. B	11. E	18. D
5. B	12. A	19. D
6. C	13. B	20. B
7. E	14. C	

Percent

Problem Set

1. D	8. B	15. C
2. C	9. B	16. A
3. A	10. B	17. B
4. C	11. D	18. C
5. D	12. A	19. D
6. E	13. D	20. B
7. C	14. A	

Algebra and Functions

Algebraic Expressions

Problem Set

1. E	6. B	11. B
2. C	7. E	12. A
3. C	8. D	13. C
4. C	9. E	14. A
5. B	10. C	15. B

Linear Equations and Inequalities

Problem Set

1. C	6. D	11. B
2. B	7. B	12. C
3. A	8. B	13. E
4. B	9. C	14. B
5. D	10. A	15. D

Algebraic Word Problems

Problem Set

1. D	6. C	11. A
2. C	7. C	12. E
3. D	8. E	13. B
4. C	9. B	14. E
5. D	10. C	15. D

Functions

Try It!

1. 5
2. 12
3. 2.4
4. $a^2 + 2$
5. $(2a)^2 + 2$
6. $(3a - 1)^2 + 2$

Problem Set

1. C	8. C	15. E
2. C	9. C	16. B
3. D	10. B	17. D
4. D	11. A	18. C
5. C	12. D	19. E
6. E	13. D	20. E
7. A	14. D	

Exponents

Try It!

1. 9	5. 1/3	9. 36
2. 2	6. 12	10. 9
3. 6	7. 8	11. 36
4. 1/16	8. 2	12. 6

Problem Set

1. B	6. B	11. A
2. D	7. E	12. C
3. E	8. C	13. A
4. A	9. C	14. A
5. C	10. D	15. B

Absolute Value

Try It!

1. 17	2. 4

Problem Set

1. C	6. B
2. E	7. A
3. A	8. E
4. E	9. D
5. A	10. B

Distributing and Factoring

Problem Set

1. D	6. B	11. D
2. A	7. E	12. E
3. C	8. C	13. C
4. C	9. D	14. E
5. D	10. E	15. C

Statistics and Probability

Statistics

Statistics Problem Set 1

1. D	6. D	11. C
2. D	7. A	12. B
3. B	8. B	13. C
4. A	9. C	14. A
5. C	10. B	15. E

Distributions and Measurements of Spread

Statistics Problem Set 2

1. E	6. C	11. A
2. E	7. C	12. B
3. D	8. A	13. B
4. B	9. C	14. C
5. C	10. D	15. B

Probability

Problem Set

1. B	6. E
2. A	7. D
3. D	8. C
4. D	9. E
5. E	10. D

Arrangements

Problem Set

1. D	6. C	11. B
2. C	7. C	12. E
3. D	8. C	13. C
4. B	9. D	14. C
5. D	10. C	15. D

Trigonometry

Problem Set 1

1.	B	6.	A	11.	E
2.	B	7.	A	12.	B
3.	D	8.	C	13.	C
4.	D	9.	E	14.	B
5.	B	10.	E	15.	B

Problem Set 2

1.	D	6.	C	11.	C
2.	D	7.	D	12.	A
3.	B	8.	C	13.	A
4.	D	9.	C	14.	B
5.	C	10.	D	15.	C

Higher Level Topics

Matrices

Problem Set

1.	A	6.	C
2.	E	7.	B
3.	A	8.	D
4.	B	9.	E
5.	A	10.	B

Asymptotes and End Behavior

Problem Set

1.	C	6.	E
2.	D	7.	D
3.	C	8.	D
4.	D	9.	A
5.	E	10.	D

Imaginary and Complex Numbers

Problem Set

1.	C	6.	A
2.	E	7.	D
3.	D	8.	A
4.	C	9.	C
5.	A	10.	D

Logarithms

Problem Set

1.	C	6.	E
2.	D	7.	B
3.	D	8.	C
4.	A	9.	B
5.	E	10.	C

Vectors

Problem Set

1.	D	6.	A
2.	C	7.	D
3.	E	8.	C
4.	E	9.	E
5.	E	10.	B

Conic Sections and Polar Graphs

Problem Set

1.	D	6.	D
2.	E	7.	C
3.	D	8.	B
4.	A	9.	D
5.	B	10.	E

Reading Test Manual Answer Key

Practice Passage for Marking Up

Stroke: Historical Review and Innovative Treatments

1.	D	6.	B
2.	D	7.	A
3.	C	8.	C
4.	B	9.	D
5.	C	10.	B

Practice Passage for Skimming and Headlining

Neanderthals in 3D: L'Homme de La Chapelle

1.	B	6.	C
2.	A	7.	B
3.	C	8.	B
4.	D	9.	B
5.	C	10.	A

Practice Reading Section

Passage I: Literary Narrative

1.	D	6.	B
2.	A	7.	B
3.	C	8.	A
4.	B	9.	D
5.	B	10.	C

Passage II: Social Science

11.	D	16.	B
12.	B	17.	B
13.	A	18.	C
14.	D	19.	B
15.	B	20.	B

Passage III: Humanities

21.	B	26.	C
22.	A	27.	B
23.	A	28.	D
24.	A	29.	C
25.	C	30.	B

Passage IV: Natural Science

31.	B	36.	C
32.	D	37.	A
33.	B	38.	D
34.	B	39.	C
35.	C	40.	B

Science Test Manual Answer Key

Passage I
1. B
2. A
3. D
4. A
5. C
6. D

Passage II
1. D
2. C
3. B
4. B
5. A
6. C
7. B

Passage III
1. C
2. A
3. C
4. C
5. C
6. B

Passage IV
1. B
2. C
3. C
4. D
5. C
6. B

Notes Regarding Score Improvements Reported on the Back Cover

[1] ACT score improvements are calculated by subtracting the baseline score from the super-scored ACT score. Most tutoring students come to us in the summer before 11th grade. We thus use either an actual baseline ACT or the 10th grade PSAT (converted to an ACT score) as the baseline test. Students who came to us after taking the 11th grade PSAT improved almost as much, and their improvements are available on our website, marksprep.com.

[2] Full score improvements are available on marksprep.com. Calculations include data from students who saw us for six or more tutoring sessions and include approximately 99 percent of students who have worked with us. The data have been verified by parents of the students seen.

[3] On average, students see us for 10–11 tutoring sessions before a first administration of an SAT or ACT and 5–6 tutoring sessions before a second administration, for a total of 15–17 50-minute tutoring sessions.

[4] The years in the graph refer to the graduating class year of the students, not the year in which we tutored them.

Made in the
USA
Middletown, DE